FROM STOREFRONT
TO MONUMENT

A VOLUME IN THE SERIES

Public History in Historical Perspective

EDITED BY

Marla R. Miller

FROM STOREFRONT TO MONUMENT

TRACING THE
PUBLIC HISTORY
OF THE
BLACK MUSEUM
MOVEMENT

Andrea A. Burns

University of Massachusetts Press
Amherst and Boston

ISBN 978-1-62534-035-1 (paper);
ISBN 978-1-62534-034-4 (hardcover)

Designed by Sally Nichols
Set in Centaur MT and Adobe Castellar
Printed and bound by IBT/Hamilton Inc.

Library of Congress Cataloging-in-Publication Data

Burns, Andrea A., 1976–
From storefront to monument : tracing the public history
of the Black museum movement / Andrea A. Burns.
pages cm. — (Public history in historical perspective)
Includes bibliographical references and index.
ISBN 978-1-62534-035-1 (pbk. : alk. paper) — ISBN 978-1-62534-034-4
(hardcover : alk. paper) 1. African Americans—Museums—History. 2. Historical
museums—United States—History. 3. Public history—United States—History.
4. African Americans—History. I. Title.
E185.53.A1B87 2013
973'.0496073—dc23
2013028729

British Library Cataloguing-in-Publication Data
A catalogue record for this book is available from the British Library.

Publication of this book and other titles in the series
Public History in Historical Perspective is supported by the
Office of the Dean, College of Humanities and Fine Arts,
University of Massachusetts Amherst.

For Amelia Rose, my shining daughter
And in memory of my father, Grant,
who would have loved her so

CONTENTS

ACKNOWLEDGMENTS

The tentative idea for this book began with an impromptu conversation I had with Keith Mayes while standing in line for coffee (of course) at the University of Minnesota. As a graduate student, I was deeply interested in how people created, and interacted with, physical representations of their past, but I never thought that the result of our conversation would bring me here. For his scholarly guidance and support, I extend my sincere appreciation. I also thank Sara Evans, Elaine Tyler May, Kevin Murphy, and Yuichiro Onishi for their valuable comments.

This book, of course, would never have been possible without the dedicated assistance of numerous librarians, museum staff, and archivists. I would especially like to thank the staff and archivists of the Smithsonian Institution Archives, the Urban Archives at Temple University, the DuSable Museum of African American History, the African American Museum of Philadelphia, the Anacostia Community Museum (especially Shauna Collier), and the Charles H. Wright Museum of African American History in Detroit (especially the late Margaret Thomas Ward, and Alexis Braun Marks). I am also grateful to Rick Moss, chief curator and director of the African American Museum and Library at Oakland. Rick took the time to sit down with me and provide an instrumental interview; in doing so, he significantly shaped the conclusion of this book.

I would also like to thank my colleagues in the Department of History at Appalachian State University. The faculty and staff here have provided me with much needed logistical assistance and travel funding as I completed my research and presented at conferences. The students in ASU's public history program have offered another form of support, as they have consistently challenged me to think in new ways about museums, memory, and representation. In doing so, they have compelled me to revisit and reinterpret my previous assumptions about the source material.

It has been a privilege to work with the staff of the University of Massachusetts Press. Clark Dougan and Marla Miller have provided ready critical feedback and support as the manuscript slowly transformed into a book. Carol Betsch and Mary Bellino have shepherded the editing process; their careful attention has resulted in, I hope, a much improved narrative. I would also like to thank the anonymous readers of this manuscript for their invaluable critiques. Any errors in this manuscript are, of course, entirely my own.

Without the support, laughter, and conversations I have shared with my colleagues and friends in the history departments at the University of Minnesota and Appalachian State University, I truly could not have become a public historian, nor finished this book. My dear friend Ellen F. Arnold has pushed me to meet deadlines, finish troublesome paragraphs, and not give up—even as she has become a groundbreaking scholar in her own right. Mike Ryan and Salwa ben Zahra remain, despite the time and distance that separate us, most trusted friends. Sunny Townes Stewart, who created the index, and Bruce Stewart have become my closest friends and colleagues south of the Mason-Dixon Line.

My family—all of whom are self-confessed lovers of history—has consistently stood behind me and urged me to continue. This book is a result of their steady support, love, and assistance. My mother, Stephanie, helped edit and conduct research, as did my brother, Steven. My father, Grant, edited the very earliest version of my dissertation before his untimely passing in 2006. He will always be with me, in spirit and in my work.

On August 30, 2011, my blue-eyed daughter Amelia was born. My husband, Trent Margrif, was there to hear her first cries, and to hold both of us as we entered a new phase in our lives. His humor, patience, and love, his tolerance for cat shenanigans, and his own dedication to preserving the past make our family complete. I could not imagine my life without either of them.

A portion of chapter 3 appeared as "When 'Civil Rights Are Not Enough': The Creation and Work of the International Afro-American Museum of Detroit," in *Remembering Africa and Its Diasporas: Memory, Public History and Representations of the Past*, ed. Audra A. Diptee and David V. Trotman (Trenton, N.J.: Africa World Press, 2012), 197–215.

FROM STOREFRONT
TO MONUMENT

Introduction

MUSEUMS ON THE FRONT LINES

Confronting the "Conspiracy of Silence"

In November 1969, at the end of what had been a tumultuous decade across the United States, museum professionals and community activists gathered at the Bedford Lincoln Neighborhood Museum in Brooklyn, New York. Conference organizers intended to solicit discussion about how traditional museums could remain relevant in the context of recent social and political upheavals as well as explore the groundswell of interest regarding how, and whether, mainstream museums should open small branches in neighborhoods historically neglected by these institutions. Although the seminar's leaders originally expected just twenty to thirty participants from the New York City area, they were startled when the seminar drew over two hundred people from nineteen states.[1]

Emily Harvey, director of an eighteen-member New York City museum group known as the Museums Collaborative, or MUSE, compiled the conference proceedings. As she chronicled the multiple and conflicting ideas about the role and place of museums that emerged during the seminar dialogue, Harvey noted that, at times, unexpected voices of a "militant minority" threatened to overturn the scheduled agenda, eclipsing those who supported the concept of decentralized, "neighborhood" museums. Indeed, the seemingly innovative concept of decentralization was "overshadowed by the realization, brought home at times with brutal force, that such discussions are premature until more basic issues that concern minority groups have been dealt with."[2]

I

Harvey also observed with some dismay that "there were almost no rebuttals to scathing accusations that were sometimes accurate, at other times unjust and ill-informed. If museums have something to defend, why weren't they defending it?"[3]

Who was this "militant minority," and why did they levy such "scathing accusations" against museums—institutions often perceived as standing above the fray of political and social debate? The words of African American poet June Jordan, who attended the conference, offer a revealing glimpse of these unexpected dissidents:

> Take me into the museum and show me myself, show me my people, show me soul America. If you cannot show me myself, if you cannot teach my people what they need to know—and they need to know the truth, and they need to know that nothing is more important than human life—then why shouldn't I attack the temples of America and blow them up? This is one America, and after black cities have been manipulated and after something like a nigger room has been reserved in the basement of the Metropolitan Museum for us, the people who have the power and the people who count the pennies and the people who hold the keys better start thinking it all over again.[4]

If, as Jordan argued, cultural institutions like the Metropolitan Museum of Art did not and would not tell the stories of African Americans, then such places were denying the very lives and histories of African Americans themselves. Merely setting aside a room or a portion of an exhibit hall for artifacts related to black history would not suffice if the institution continued to blindly (or intentionally) neglect this community. Those in power had constructed these sites of "imagined belonging." In doing so, they rendered African American history and culture invisible, thereby deleting African Americans from the historical narrative.[5] If Jordan could neither see herself nor "soul America" in the powerful spaces set aside for national memory and identity, what should prevent her from attacking—in words and action—these ultimately meaningless temples to Euro-American hegemony?

Colin "Topper" Carew, African American director of the New Thing Art and Architecture Center in Washington, D.C., added his voice to the debate, accusing white museum professionals of being uninterested in real change and attending the seminar only for its political expediency: "You white people are here to get your rhetoric so you can go out and help your own hustle. . . . if this is a session, and there are those of you here who know it is, where all of you in museums are trying to find out how to get hip to run your own exhibitions for minority groups, forget it, because you can't and I won't help you. The only people you want are the ones who tell you what you want to hear; and those days are gone."[6] Carew and Jordan directed their anger at those who might be overly comfortable with the goals and pace of their museums, despite the charged and changing dynamics of race in America in the late 1960s. Indeed, many black activists believed that it was simply too late for these institutions to instigate real change in good faith—as Carew declared, "those days are gone." Carew and Jordan joined a host of other African American participants at the seminar in holding museums, long considered part and parcel of the white "establishment," accountable for their centuries-long practice of misrepresenting and denying black history and culture. In their view, white museum professionals continued to maintain and reinforce stereotypical depictions of black history even as they offered shallow gestures towards inclusivity.

Jordan's and Carew's heated commentaries drew from the often combative discourse of the Black Power Movement, which by 1969 had become a full-fledged undertaking in cities across the United States. Yet although they derided the offensively slow pace of change in the museum field, there were in fact a small but growing number of newly created African American neighborhood museums, such as the DuSable Museum of African American History in Chicago (founded in 1961), the International Afro-American Museum of Detroit (1965), and the Anacostia Neighborhood Museum in Washington, D.C. (1967), that had already begun to challenge this stagnancy. This study explores that phenomenon. Before most mainstream museums acknowledged that African American history and culture must be addressed in their exhibits and programs, leaders of the "black museum movement"—some of whom were represented at the seminar—were contesting and reinterpreting traditional depictions of African and African American history and culture.[7]

Cultural sites like the Metropolitan Museum of Art and the Smithsonian Institution represented grand paeans to European culture, with neoclassic architecture and extensive collections of objects categorized as either "high culture" or "primitive." African American neighborhood museums, on the other hand, took root in urban neighborhoods across the country after World War II and were created and staffed primarily by black community leaders rather than museum professionals. Born out of numerous meetings held by local activists and community leaders, these institutions were more likely to be situated in a former store or apartment building than in an imposing structure. Their collections, usually drew from neighborhood contributions and donations from other cultural organizations. Most crucially, the content of their collections offered a distinct rebuttal to the narrative of invisibility practiced by mainstream museums with regard to the presence and historical agency of African Americans.

During their early years, African American neighborhood museums typically had shortened hours, limited financial resources, and featured only temporary exhibits. Still, we should question the supposed "humbleness" of their origins and operations. In her analysis of New York City's El Museo del Barrio, founded as a neighborhood museum of Puerto Rican culture in 1969, Arlene Davila contends that the museum's "original mission as an institution . . . run by and for working-class people of El Barrio and that would provide alternative avenues of validation for local artists, was never a humble mission. On the contrary, it was an empowering and cosmopolitan vision."[8] Like El Museo del Barrio, the museums created by African American leaders presented institutional missions, exhibits, and educational programs that countered the skewed impressions of black history and culture that audiences absorbed when visiting traditional museums. If mainstream museums perpetuated white America's power over the historical narrative, then African American neighborhood museums must disrupt this exclusive, and excluding, account.

Reading Black Power within the History of the Black Museum Movement

Museums, of course, have never functioned simply as repositories for dusty artifacts. Rather, they and their collections are a product of social relations, both past and present. The creators of African American neighborhood museums understood this, believing that their institutions communicated a radical new agenda about power, memory, and identity. The African American museums that emerged during the 1960s and 1970s challenged and re-created new national memories and identities that incorporated the ideas, events, objects, and places tied to black history. Many African American museum leaders also maintained that their institutions should serve as conduits for the needs of the black community—a characteristic noted by the African American Museums Association (founded in 1978), which observed that "a distinguishing trait of Black museums is the intimate relationship which they enjoy with their communities."[9] In this case, "community" may be identified both in terms of the physical—that is, the predominantly African American neighborhoods that typically surrounded these early museums—and the global community that comprises the African Diaspora.[10]

Museums devoted to African and African American history represent alternative or "free" spaces carved out of a cultural landscape that has consistently marginalized minorities. Free spaces offer a location where marginalized groups can acquire greater self-respect, strengthen their sense of dignity and independence, and work toward a heightened sense of communal and civic identity.[11] Located in the nexus between private life and the public sphere, churches, clubs, self-help groups, and other voluntary organizations all represent some examples of these democratic free spaces. African American churches, in particular, have long acted as places for self-expression and community organization during periods in which those who feared black resistance forcibly prohibited or outlawed these activities.[12] Black neighborhood museums like the DuSable Museum of African American History in Chicago, the International Afro-American Museum in Detroit, the Anacostia Neighborhood Museum in Washington, D.C., and the African American Museum of Philadelphia (founded in 1976) all function as examples of free space. While battling often adverse conditions, the leaders of these institutions elevated the recognition of black history and culture, provided space for community gatherings and attempted to develop a strong sense of identity and self-affirmation among African American audiences.

It was no coincidence that many who initiated African American neighborhood museums also played an active role in the groundswell of the modern Civil Rights Movement. Yet it was more than just integration and equal treatment under the law that fueled the leaders of the black museum movement. Rather, black museum leaders interpreted African American culture and history as standing separate from, but grimly intertwined with, Euro-American culture. They encouraged a uniquely "black" identity and consciousness through exhibits and educational programs, and emphasized the vital need for interaction between the museum and the local African American community. While African American museum leaders drew from the tradition of racial uplift exemplified by W. E. B. Du Bois's "Talented Tenth," they also grounded their institutions in the ideology of cultural black nationalism being promoted by the Black Power Movement.[13]

Stokely Carmichael's and Charles Hamilton's arguments in *Black Power: The*

Politics of Liberation in America (1967) articulated the direct relationship black museum leaders saw between the Black Power Movement and the reclamation of black history: "African American history means a long history beginning on the continent of Africa, a history not taught in the standard textbooks of this country. It is absolutely essential that black people know this history, that they know their roots, that they develop an awareness of their cultural heritage."[14] James Del Rio, an African American from Detroit who was elected to Michigan's House of Representatives in 1965, called for the repossession of black heritage far more bluntly. In his 1963 publication, "The Conspiracy," Rio asked, "Is the conspiracy of silence among Historians to forget African History, which includes Greeks, Turks, Egyptians, Ethiopians, Jews, Japanese, and Chinese people and their integration intentional?"[15]

In order for African Americans to fight this "conspiracy of silence," black power advocates like Del Rio, Malcolm X, and June Jordan demanded that the institutions and values of old be interrogated. And if these organizations were found to be unresponsive, African Americans must create new ones—political, cultural, religious, and economic—to replace them.[16] Black museum leaders believed that their institutions could, if not supplant mainstream museums, at the very least offer African Americans—particularly those who lived in deteriorating urban neighborhoods beset by municipal and federal neglect—a meaningful alternative to mainstream America's insistence on black history's invisibility and misrepresentation.

Linking the black museum movement with the Black Power Movement necessitates a more expansive definition of black power, however. Coined by Stokely Carmichael in 1966, the term "black power" in contemporary popular culture frequently recalls a series of iconic images (Afros, dashikis, the raised fists of Black Panthers) and the charisma of black militants like Huey Newton and Carmichael himself. These narratives typically reduce the movement's core beliefs to the constant necessity for racial struggle and black separatism from white America. Indeed, the Black Power Movement "most often serves as a twisted folklore, a cautionary tale featuring gun-toting militants who practiced politics without portfolio, vowed to die in the name of revolution, and who dragged down more promising movements for social justice."[17] Broadening the chronology and definition of black power, on the other hand, allows us to better understand the black museum movement that began in the early 1960s.[18] Black museum leaders consciously cultivated an assertive identity and cultural pride through exhibits, educational programs, and outreach to audiences "on the ground." Successful black museum makers understood that whites could be important to the black museum movement, though they were not central to its vision, mission, or execution. As a result, black museum leaders both confronted and negotiated with white politicians and mainstream cultural institutions even as they posited alternatives to the traditional model of museum as Eurocentric mausoleum.

The national Black Power Movement began to disintegrate during the mid-1970s; internal friction regarding the movement's ideological direction, coupled with municipal and federal harassment of its leaders, hastened its retreat from the national stage.[19] Nevertheless, black power persisted in various forms on a local level, with its cultural impact resonating well beyond the narrow time line typically ascribed to the movement's duration.[20] The continued popularity of Kwanzaa, an Afro-centered holiday created by Maulana (Ron) Karenga in 1966, attests to the lasting cultural, and local, legacy of Black Power.[21] In a sense, while Kwanzaa may be seen as the "cultural offspring" of the Black Power Movement, the black museum movement may be cast as both the movement's ancestor *and* its offspring, or beneficiary. Along with more readily known markers of cultural black power such the Black Arts Movement, clothing and hairstyles derived from African fashions, and holiday celebrations rooted in African traditions, the black museum movement contained the message of black cultural liberation and perpetuated the ideological goals of the Black Power Movement.

The Historical Roots of Black Public History

The presence of African American public history sites on the cultural landscape is clearly not a twentieth-century phenomenon, since African Americans have practiced what might be defined as "public history" since at least the early nineteenth century. The first era of black public history is generally said to fall between the late 1820s and the early 1900s, when African American elites in cities such as Philadelphia, New York, Boston, and Washington, D.C., started to establish churches, benevolent associations, and improvement and literary societies.[22] In Washington, D.C., black bibliophiles began contributing to Howard University's Moorland-Spingarn Library shortly after the African American university was chartered in 1873. The library became world-renowned after the Reverend Jesse Moorland's donation of three thousand books and pamphlets in 1914.[23] Other prominent organizations launched during this era include the Bethel Literary and Historical Association, founded in Washington, D.C., in

1881; Philadelphia's American Negro Historical Society (1897); and the Negro Society for Historical Research, cofounded by Arthur Schomburg and John E. Bruce in 1911.[24] African Americans also produced exhibits and created museums during this period. For example, African American curators at the Hampton University Museum, founded in 1868 as part of the Hampton Normal Agricultural Institute in Virginia (Booker T. Washington's alma mater), collected art and artifacts from cultures around the globe, with an early focus on African, Pacific Islander, and African American fine art. Still in operation, it is considered the oldest African American museum in the United States.[25]

At the 1895 Cotton States International Exposition in Atlanta, Georgia, Washington served as the spokesman for black-produced displays on African American culture and history. Exposition organizers, however, kept these exhibits segregated from the other displays.[26] By their very existence, it seems, black-produced exhibits such as those at the Exposition challenged the dominant cultural representations of African Americans and criticized the absence of African and African American historical and cultural artifacts from mainstream museums. Still, like the early African American literary and benevolent associations, these exhibits were primarily intended to serve as an avenue for the intellectual and spiritual improvement of middle-class African Americans.[27]

During the early 1900s, W. E. B. Du Bois and Carter G. Woodson began to promote the rich history of black folk culture rather than focusing exclusively upon the achievements and potential of the black elite.[28] Because Du Bois and Woodson were excluded from mainstream (i.e., white) scholarly organizations and associations, they necessarily had to construct "viable, productive autonomous academic institutions, scholarly approaches, and practical strategies for black mental and psychological liberation."[29] Du Bois's groundbreaking *Souls of Black Folk* (1903) and establishment of the NAACP, as well as Woodson's creation of the Association for the Study of Negro Life and History in 1915 and his initiation of Negro History Week in 1926, criticized the intentional "whitewashing" of collective memory regarding slavery and its legacy while celebrating African American accomplishments, history, and culture.[30]

Black public historians like Woodson still drew from the nineteenth-century intellectual tradition known as vindicationism, which historian Thomas J. Davis has defined as akin to the "we, too, were here" syndrome—an approach that "reveals itself in static, undifferentiated, impersonal exhibitions that sweep across time with the aim of showing that black people, like whites, were also here."[31] Although many academics today deem vindicationism to be intellectually stale, it should not be dismissed as an unimportant or unnecessary approach. Black museum leaders who employed this "we, too, were here" tactic in their exhibits demonstrated to audiences, both black and white, that African and African American history were worthy of respectful public representation and dialogue, and that historical discourse about black inferiority was dangerously incorrect. As black museums evolved throughout the twentieth century, their exhibits and outreach programs often (but not always, and not consistently) began to reflect a more complex methodology motivated less by the need to "vindicate the race" and more by the imperative to address and confront the ongoing economic, social, legal, and political issues facing the African American community.

The 1960s witnessed a surge of museums specifically themed around African American history and culture. From 1961 to 1967 alone, Chicago's DuSable Museum of African American History, Detroit's International Afro-American Museum, and the Anacostia Neighborhood Museum opened to the public. The Anacostia Neighborhood Museum developed as part of a unique partnership between the Smithsonian Institution and local African American community organizations based in the southeastern quadrant of Washington, D.C., known as Anacostia. Margaret and Charles Burroughs and Charles Wright established the DuSable Museum and the International Afro-American Museum of Detroit, respectively.[32]

The number of African American museums steadily increased over the next several decades, which may have also reflected, in part, the growing public and scholarly interest in slavery. Books like Alex Haley's *Roots* (1976), Dorothy Spruill Redford's *Somerset Homecoming: Recovering a Lost Heritage* (1989), and, more recently, James Oliver Horton and Lois Horton's *Slavery and Public History: The Tough Stuff of American Memory* (2008) contributed to this trend. By 1988, the African American Museums Association could publish a survey based on the responses of fifty-two African American museums located in twenty-three states and Canada. Eighty-nine percent of these museums were located in cities, and 82.6 percent were based in the East (and of those, 58 percent were located in the Northeast).[33] In a significantly smaller survey conducted in 1989, Azade Ardali found that, out of twenty-nine black and Hispanic art museums, the African American ones were mostly concentrated in the Northeast (38 percent). All five of the African American museums in the South that Ardali surveyed were attached to historically black colleges, such as Hampton University.[34]

By the early twenty-first century, well over two hundred African American museums could be found scattered across the United States and Canada. In 2003, to prepare for the creation of a national African American museum in Washington, D.C., the National Museum of African American History and Culture Plan for Action Presidential Commission distributed surveys to 237 African American museums in thirty-seven states, as well as Canada. Based on the responses from seventy-two museums (just under 30 percent of the total number of museum surveyed), African American stand-alone museums, university museums, and libraries were found to be heavily represented in both the South and the West.[35] While smaller in number, the presence of museums focused on black history and culture in Canada reflects the range of the diasporic experience, as African Americans both voluntarily and involuntarily migrated to Canada throughout the eighteenth and nineteenth centuries in response to conditions in the United States. More recently, significant numbers of migrants from the Caribbean and Africa have settled in Canada. Incorporating the stories and voices of these migrants presents a challenge for Canadian public history sites, but also offers a path for future comparative research with black public history sites in the United States.[36]

Approaching the Black Museum Movement

The geographic breadth and the varying economic, sociocultural, and political dynamics that shaped the black museum movement as it developed in disparate cities and towns across North America make it challenging to fully assess their collective histories and impact. Still, all of the museums featured in this study share several thematic characteristics that exerted a profound impact upon the development of these institutions and their work. First, all were based in major metropolises undergoing various degrees of postindustrial transformation after World War II. Factors such as "white flight," urban renewal and gentrification, housing shortages, skirmishes between the police and the black community, and unemployment all converged to exacerbate racial and class tensions. Second, as the black population in each of these cities steadily increased, more and more African Americans began holding local, state, and federal offices.[37] Indeed, fewer than two decades after these museums opened, voters in each of these cities would elect an African American mayor: Coleman A. Young (Detroit, 1974); Walter Washington (Washington, D.C., 1975); Harold Washington (Chicago, 1975); and Wilson Goode (Philadelphia, 1983). Though each of these cities claimed different traditions of black activism, an examination of how and why their respective African American museums emerged reflects the cities' shared history of increasing black political power during the late twentieth century.

Chapter I surveys the origin stories of three prominent African American neighborhood museums founded between 1961 and 1967: the DuSable Museum of African American History in Chicago; the International Afro-American Museum in Detroit; and the Anacostia Neighborhood Museum in Washington, D.C. While single individuals, such as Margaret Burroughs in Chicago or Charles Wright in Detroit, may have spearheaded the creation of these museums, the institutions emerged as a culmination of the spaces carved out by generations of local black community organizations. Because of this, the stories of these museums must be considered in the context of the neighborhoods and cities in which they originated. African Americans shaped these urban landscapes through their migrations, their labor (both slave and free), and their cultural and political evolutions. By examining how and why each of these museums began, it is possible to identify the historical contingencies that framed the process by which black neighborhood museums came into existence: civil rights, but especially the Black Power Movement; the African American search for a viable and meaningful public history; urban renewal and the transformation of central cities; and the black desire for institutional development.

Chapter 2 examines the genesis of the African American Museum of Philadelphia (AAMP), which opened in 1976. The AAMP is unique among the museums in this study, in that it was formed as a direct response to a specific event: the celebration of the American Bicentennial in 1976.[38] The national celebration of the Bicentennial was supposed to signal the end of a long period of social and political unrest in the United States.[39] Yet activists in Philadelphia and across the country believed that the Bicentennial programs planned by municipal leaders would not fairly or accurately represent the history and culture of African Americans and other minority groups. Consequently, in Philadelphia, black activists pressured municipal officials to create an African American museum, funded largely by the city, which would open in time for the celebrations. The museum's opening and success were by no means guaranteed, however, as numerous controversies—most notably, the site where the building was to be located—threatened to derail the project. Given its distinctive origin story and chronological distance from the other museums in the study, two separate chapters are devoted to this museum's emergence and work.

Chapter 3 transitions from the origin stories of African American neighborhood museums by exploring how three of these institutions functioned within their communities. The educational outreach programs initiated by Chicago's DuSable Museum, the International Afro-American Museum's innovative mobile unit, and the production of groundbreaking exhibits such as the Anacostia Neighborhood Museum's The Rat: Man's Invited Affliction (1968) publicly challenged the profoundly embedded sense of cultural and racial entitlement granted to those who ran traditional museums. Yet while some mainstream museums, such as the Metropolitan Museum of Art and the Smithsonian Institution, began to reexamine their collections and exhibits in response to the attention-garnering work of African American museums, this process was by no means swift or consensual.

Chapter 4 focuses on the African American Museum of Philadelphia and its uncertain reception after opening in the summer of 1976. Like its predecessors, the new museum challenged the politics of representation through African and African American-centered exhibits and outreach programs. Other African American museums across the country also seized upon the Bicentennial as a way to counter publicly the official narratives of American history promoted by city, state, and federal officials. For the AAMP, however, forging a positive relationship with Philadelphia's black community was a task made far more complicated because of the controversial circumstances in which the museum had been created, its complex administrative structure, and the compromised physical location of the museum itself. Internal financial and leadership struggles, played out in bold headlines, threatened to undermine the museum's achievements in the years after its opening.

Even taking into account its unique origins, chapter 5 underscores that the African American Museum of Philadelphia's difficulty in establishing itself as a viable institution was by no means an isolated problem within the black museum community. Factors such as unstable leadership and declining finances threatened to close black museums across the country during the 1980s and 1990s, while critics—some who worked in these very museums—charged that certain black museum leaders had lost touch with the needs of the African American community, as evidenced by their "elitist" fundraising and relocation or expansion campaigns. The black museum movement's shift from a nascent social movement largely driven by volunteers to its increased professionalization (and subsequent bureaucratization) played an important role in the frictions that developed both within and between African American museums and museum advocates during this period.[40]

Some of the struggles black museums faced during the 1980s and 1990s may be also traced to the "mainstreaming" of black history.[41] Prompted in part by the trend toward "new social history," or "history from the bottom up" that surged in scholarly popularity during the 1960s, traditional museums and other public history sites increasingly wrestled with whether, and how, to mainstream African American history into their exhibits and programs. The response of organizations like the DuSable Museum and the Anacostia Neighborhood Museum to the perceived infringement of mainstream public history sites upon the domain normally claimed by black museums reflected a battle over the ownership of "cultural territory." Furthermore, the unfolding conflict again raised the question left unanswered during that tense meeting of museum and community advocates during the 1969 seminar at the Bedford Lincoln Neighborhood Museum—could, and should, African American history be told by "white" institutions once historically dedicated to misrepresenting these narratives?

The trials of the International Afro-American Museum, renamed the Charles H. Wright Museum of African American History (MAAH) in 1997, encompassed many of these problems.[42] The MAAH garnered a significant amount of financial support from Coleman A. Young, Detroit's first African American mayor. Yet despite the MAAH's apparent political and financial successes, marked by the grand opening of a 120,000-square-foot building in 1997, the museum experienced financial upheaval, declining attendance, and a critical and popular rejection of its exhibitions.

The concluding chapters assess the black museum movement as it moved into the early twenty-first century. The first phase of the modern black museum movement consisted of the establishment of African American neighborhood museums during the 1960s and 1970s. The expansion of these neighborhood museums, as well as the creation of museums and historic sites devoted to the recent African American past, comprised the second (and ongoing) phase of the movement. With the opening of the National Museum of African American History and Culture (NMAAHC) on Washington, D.C.'s National Mall, the third phase of the black museum movement debuted in a highly public fashion.

The path to the national museum's unveiling was far from smooth, however. In addition to the usual problems that occur in earmarking federal funds for a cultural institution (and an African American one, at that), some black museum leaders objected to the very concept of a national museum. It was not just that this new institution might threaten some smaller African American museums, which shared neither the NMAAHC's financial resources nor its capacity for growth. The founder of Detroit's International Afro-American Museum, Charles Wright (1918–2002), campaigned throughout the 1960s to prevent the federal government from having any part in creating a national museum, arguing that its involvement would guarantee that black history and black voices would continue to be misrepresented and diminished. Other museum leaders, including Anacostia Neighborhood Museum director John Kinard, took up Wright's opposition in the 1980s. Determining the bases of their objections may prove instructive, as the national museum's advocates operate from within one of the most symbolic public sites in America, even as they solicit intensely personal stories and artifacts from African Americans who historically have been excluded from this very space.

As African American neighborhood museums continue to evolve, with many choosing to expand from their original identities as community centers to large-scale institutions intent on bringing black history to national and international audiences, it is inevitable that their ties to the ongoing national and local legacy of the Black Power Movement will persevere, change, and, at times, falter. Understanding the origins of this evolution helps us contextualize and historicize black public history, from its modest but courageous beginnings to its present-day manifestation as a bold and highly visible movement. Throughout this process, it is clear that the complex institutional histories of African American museums and other public history sites will become as vital for historians to preserve, document, and analyze as the artifacts that the public sees and interprets on a daily basis.

CHAPTER I

WHEN "CIVIL RIGHTS ARE NOT ENOUGH"

Building the Black Museum Movement

In a 2007 interview with *The Public Historian*, African American scholar John Hope Franklin deemed the DuSable Museum of African American History in Chicago to be "one of the pioneer African American museums in the country."[1] It is in the DuSable, which opened its doors in 1961 as the Ebony Museum of History and Art, that we may begin to identify the distinctive qualities that characterized many of the other African American museums established during the mid-late 1960s: the presentation of full-scale exhibits whose themes centered upon African and African American history and culture; the pursuit of a collections policy meant to challenge and remedy the absence of African American history and culture from mainstream institutions; and an emphasis on educational outreach to local black communities. Above all, these museums strove to instill the conviction that black art and history could communicate a message of identity and self-worth.[2] In all of these respects, the DuSable functioned as an African American "neighborhood" museum.

In 1972, the director of the Anacostia Neighborhood Museum in Washington, D.C., John Kinard, defined the neighborhood museum as an entity that "encompasses the life of the people of the neighborhood—people who are vitally concerned about who they are, where they came from, what they have accomplished, their values and their most pressing needs."[3] Kinard argued that the neighborhood museum's mission had to reject the traditional image of a museum as an elite cultural institution dedicated solely to collecting and displaying valuable artifacts. Rather, a museum's employees and volunteers ought to come from the very neighborhood in which the museum was located. Likewise, exhibits and collections should draw their inspiration from the present-day concerns and forgotten histories of the neighborhood, and the black community as a whole.

The successful emergence and institutionalization of African American neighborhood museums like the Anacostia Neighborhood Museum and the DuSable depended in varying degrees upon the groundwork laid by the preexisting "black places" of a city or a neighborhood.[4] Just as African American churches provided a source of leadership and spiritual camaraderie for the growth of the Civil Rights Movement during the 1950s, so a neighborhood's black organizations and places —churches, black history and literary associations, and more informal gathering spaces—inspired and often funneled volunteers into newly emerging black museums. For example, Philadelphia's wealth of black literary, historical, and social organizations, created in part by the migration of African Americans to the city during the early nineteenth century, preceded the institutional spaces forged by the city's civil rights and black power campaigns during the 1960s and 1970s and the creation of the African American Museum of Philadelphia in 1976.[5] Likewise, it was only through the strenuous activism of black community organizations in Anacostia, such as the Greater Anacostia People's Organization, that the Anacostia community ensured that their neighborhood would serve as the site of the Anacostia Neighborhood Museum.

In Detroit, numerous "black places" paved the way for the creation of the International Afro-American Museum (IAM), among them the black-owned Broadside Press, established in 1965; the black-owned radio station WCHB; and the Freedom Now Party, which emerged in 1963 as the "first all black political party in the country."[6] Many of Detroit's black churches served as ground central for social and religious activism and in turn forged a connection with the museum. Indeed, the link between the African American church and the museum was strong enough that several churches volunteered to host IAM's mobile museum during the late 1960s.

In Chicago in 1915, Carter G. Woodson began the Association for the Study of Negro Life and History (ASNLH). The ASNLH led a movement to establish local and federal recognition of "Negro History Week" in 1926.[7] Subsequent African American organizations built upon the work of the ASNLH (which later relocated to Washington, D.C.) by adopting the ideological and organizational premise of Negro History Week—that is, the public recognition of the history and the achievements of African Americans. As such, long before a group of concerned persons gathered at their home in 1960 to discuss the possible founding of an African American museum, Chicago's numerous black history clubs and associations shaped the activism of the DuSable's founders, Margaret and Charles Burroughs.

Born in Louisiana in 1915, DuSable Museum founder Margaret Burroughs moved to Chicago in 1922 with her parents, and graduated from Chicago Normal College (later known as Chicago State University) in 1937. By the early 1930s, she had become known as an accomplished artist, and received a master's degree from the School of the Art Institute of Chicago; her work would later be purchased and displayed by the Chicago Art Institute, as well as at other cultural organizations throughout the United States and abroad. Burroughs, together with her first husband, Bernard Goss, played an integral role in developing connections among Chicago's radical activists during the Great Depression. For example, Burroughs, who often wrote for the *Chicago Defender*, participated in interracial forums with artists and writers in Washington Park, located in the predominantly black area of Chicago known as the "South Side."[8] She also helped form the South Side Community Art Center, the largest Federal Art Project supported by the Works Progress Administration (WPA). Established in 1941 in a brownstone mansion located on Michigan Avenue, volunteers transformed the site into a space dedicated to the creative work of black artists.[9] In confluence with the work of African American activists like the poet Gwendolyn Brooks and the actor and singer Paul Robeson, the center translated Communist Party dogma into a "model and inspiration for cultural insurrection created and led by African Americans."[10]

During the early 1940s, Burroughs served as a secretary for the newly formed National Negro Museum and Historical Foundation in Chicago (NNMHF).[11] Headed by black labor activist Ishmael P. Flory, the foundation featured black history exhibits at a former packinghouse workers' hall on 49th Street and Wabash Avenue. The group's promotion of black history was so successful that Chicago mayor Martin H. Kennelly proclaimed the city's first "Negro History Week" in the late 1940s.[12] In the 1950s, a group known as the African American Heritage Association (AAHA) evolved out of the NNMHF, which had ceased to function. The AAHA engaged in immediate local activities to increase awareness of black history, such as helping DuSable Senior High School students raise funds for a sculpture of the school's namesake, Jean Baptiste Point DuSable (a black Haitian believed to be the first permanent settler of Chicago). The AAHA's members, who included Margaret and her second husband, artist Charles Burroughs, also pressured local organizations and the Illinois State government to continue their recognition of Negro History Week through financial and other material contributions, such as the distribution of hundreds of black history pamphlets to churches, schools, and other organizations.[13]

During the 1950s, McCarthyism threatened to dissolve the Chicago branch of the ASNLH and other local black organizations, including the South Side Community Art Center, for appearing to engage in activities or affiliations deemed to be "subversive." Burroughs recalled the internal divisions that developed between her local branch of the ASNLH and the national organization when a representative for the national ASNLH pressed its Chicago chapter to turn over their membership lists; the reason given, according to Burroughs, was to enable them to "screen our group to eliminate the 'subversives.'" Upon their refusal, the national ASNLH revoked the Chicago branch's charter.[14]

Yet despite the fragmentation experienced by some local African American organizations, accelerated by the federal government's prosecution of prominent black civil rights activists such as W. E. B. Du Bois and Paul Robeson, the Burroughses continued to pressure local and state officials to recognize black history. In a 1961 letter to Illinois governor Otto Kerner, for example, Margaret Burroughs argued that the legislature's planned observation of the one hundredth anniversary of the Emancipation Proclamation in 1963 should also include African Americans; indeed, the Centennial must belong to "all of the people of Illinois and not [be] engineered by any one small, unrepresentative, sectarian group organized for opportunistic purposes."[15] The commemoration of historically significant national anniversaries, such as the Centennial of the Emancipation Proclamation or the Bicentennial in 1976, offered unique opportunities for advocates of black history, as well other underrepresented ethnic and cultural organizations, to demand a more publicly inclusive narrative of American history.

Beginning the DuSable Museum

By 1960, Margaret Burroughs perceived that Chicago needed a more comprehensive institution devoted to both the preservation and the public presentation of black history and culture. Although starting a museum "seemed like such a daunting task," she began to explore possibilities of opening such a space.[16] Like International Afro-American Museum founder Charles Wright, Burroughs visited small ethnic museums such as the Jewish Museum in New York City (founded 1904) and the Polish Museum of America in Chicago (1935) in search of insight prior to starting the DuSable.

Original site of the DuSable Museum of African American History, 3806 South Michigan Avenue, Chicago, Illinois. Margaret and Charles Burroughs lived in the coach house behind this mansion on Chicago's South Side. In 1961, they began to run the Ebony Museum of History and Art on the mansion's first floor. Prior to the establishment of the museum, a group of African American Pullman porters used the mansion as a social club. *Inland Architect* 20, no. 1 (January 1976): 10.

Burroughs also drew intellectual inspiration from and made important contacts in the informal "salons" she had been hosting in her home for several years. During the 1940s–50s, the Burroughses lived in a coach house behind a large mansion on 3806 South Michigan Avenue in Chicago's South Side. The coach house became known among their friends as the "Chicago Salon" for its role in playing host to gatherings of prominent (and increasingly controversial) black intellectuals, teachers, and artists, including Du Bois, Robeson, Gwendolyn Brooks, and the author James Baldwin.[17] In many ways, the salon-like function of their home paralleled Carter G. Woodson's use of his residence in the Shaw neighborhood of Washington, D.C. Woodson operated his home, which he purchased in 1922, primarily as a meeting space and a storage facility for thousands of artifacts related to African and African American history and culture. Black intellectuals (including historian Lawrence Reddick, who would play a prominent role in contesting Philadelphia's interpretation of the Bicentennial), visited and conferred with Woodson in his home until Woodson's death in 1950.[18]

Like Woodson, Burroughs held her meetings in a space that encouraged intellectual freedom, as opposed to the restrictive environment imposed by the Chicago public school system. As an art teacher at DuSable High School, Burroughs always had to remain on guard for potential investigation into her political sympathies, particularly as she staunchly supported Paul Robeson even as the government blacklisted him.[19] She remembered, "God forbid that you would teach Harriet Tubman or Sojourner Truth in class. . . . While my students were painting, I would be in the middle of a discussion about the Scottsboro boys and I'd look over and see the white principal appear at the classroom door. Turning back to the class I'd say, 'And that's how Betsy Ross came to sew the flag. Now boys and girls, let's talk about Patrick Henry.'"[20] At the Chicago Salon, in contrast, there were no such limits to the conversation. Topics at the salon "routinely ran into the areas of black culture and black history. . . . For years I had been 'bootlegging' such information to my DuSable High School art students, after discovering how dangerous it could be to talk about black history around walls that could 'grow ears.'"

The Chicago Salon's dialogue coalesced around one goal: on December 20, 1960, a group of people from the salon "initiated the first structured, though informal, discussion on establishing a museum of Negro history."[21] Shortly thereafter, the Burroughses moved out of the coach house and into the adjacent mansion that had formerly been owned by a group of African American Pullman porters, railway operators, and waiters. The porters had used the mansion, constructed by architect Solon S. Beman in 1892, as a social club and boardinghouse. Thus, the physical site of what would soon become the Ebony Museum of Art and History could already claim a history of serving the black community.[22] Margaret Burroughs began to give informal tours of the African American–related books and artifacts that she displayed in the first floor of the mansion and offered to transform the floor into a temporary museum in January 1961.[23]

Under her leadership, the DuSable moved toward a radical ideology that deviated from the outwardly cautious politics assumed by earlier black cultural institutions and organizations, such as the NAACP, during the McCarthy era. Instead, the DuSable's programs and exhibits aimed to raise black consciousness, and emphasized that "art and history should teach racial self-appreciation."[24] In a 1965 interview with the Nation of Islam's newspaper, *Muhammad Speaks,* Burroughs affirmed her philosophy about the need to make black pride the focal point of the DuSable's mission: "African history and the true history of black people in America are the most vital studies a Negro can undertake, yet these subjects are almost totally neglected in the education of our youths." Because of the "low morale caused by a lack of pride and knowledge [of black history]," Burroughs argued, "Negro youths have tended to become the potential school dropouts and juvenile delinquents."[25] Burroughs's interview, together with Article III of the DuSable's first Constitution—"The Museum, gallery and research library shall be dedicated to the preservation of the culture and history of Americans of African descent, and Africans. Primarily, it shall emphasize the contributions of the Negro to American History, Life, and Democracy"—anticipated the core doctrines of the Black Power Movement as well as the mission of the Black Studies programs that sprung up on college campuses across the nation during the late 1960s and 1970s.[26] Chicago's Black Power activists intended to reorganize school curricula by rejecting concepts of black inferiority and promoting ideas about the worth of black history and culture. In subverting traditional educational curricula, activists hoped that they could enact "blueprints for change" within the Chicago school system.[27] The DuSable, then, helped establish the groundwork for these changes.

Securing the necessary equipment and finances for the opening and maintenance of the new Ebony Museum of Art and History presented a significant challenge. Burroughs recalled that "all of the expenses of the museum such as stationary [*sic*], telephone bills and stamps were paid out of my teacher's salary and Charles' salary as a laundry truck driver."[28] Thus, the networks Margaret and Charles Burroughs established through their prior activism in organizations like the NNMHF and the ASNLH became crucial resources.[29] Local businesses, libraries, and art museums donated equipment and other items that helped build the nascent museum's collection. A 4,000-volume book donation on "the Negro in Africa and the United States" from the estate of the labor leader Pettis Perry constituted one of the more substantial gifts, while well-known African American writers and artists, including Langston Hughes and Arna Bontemps, also contributed their own materials. Cultural institutions outside Chicago also began to donate items to the new museum; for instance, the Baltimore Museum of Art provided African art catalogues.[30] As the museum matured, fund-raising events included activities such as a press and radio cocktail party in December 1966, a book sale benefit, a Negro History Week benefit dinner dance, and the dedication of the DuSable Museum Library in March 1966.[31]

The DuSable sought to build recognition within the greater African American community in Chicago. By placing ads in local black newspapers that

Advertisement, "Make Negro History Live!" *Chicago Daily Defender,* August 26–September 1, 1967. Such advertisements encouraged audience participation in the creation and maintenance of African American neighborhood museums. Note the request for a small donation fee. Courtesy of the DuSable Museum of African American History.

solicited donations of artifacts, DuSable staff and volunteers hoped that individuals normally unconnected with established cultural institutions could be informed about the new museum's mission. For example, a 1967 *Chicago Daily Defender* advertisement solicited readers to "Make Negro History Live! Be a Museum Scout!" The ad called for donations of "Negro family relics from slavery time," including books, photos, and costumes. Modest monetary contributions were also welcomed: adults could donate twenty-five cents, and children ten cents.[32] While the donation success rate for this particular ad is unknown, it is clear that these advertisements worked on two levels: not only did they draw attention to the DuSable, but they also informed audiences that the ordinary material objects and artifacts of African American history—whether photographs or manumission papers or quilts—were in fact objects of immense power, worthy of inclusion in a museum. An individual who took the first step of donating an artifact might then become a museum member, further bolstering finances and increasing public recognition of the new museum.

Other African American museums that emerged after the DuSable adapted its modest donation policies and grassroots community outreach efforts. "Show and Tell" demonstrations at community meetings, for instance, helped to garner artifact donations for the Anacostia Neighborhood Museum exhibit The Anacostia Story (1977). As staff member Louise Daniel Hutchinson remembered, "We would take what we had gotten and bring it to the next meeting, and say, 'This is what so-and-so brought. . . . Now, what do you have?' They would produce Grandma's dishes, and somebody would have an aunt's favorite pair of kid gloves with the little buttons and the button hook. All kinds of things came out that we never could have gotten if we had not developed this mechanism for communicating with the community."

These Anacostia community gatherings began to evolve beyond their initial purpose: "show and tell" transformed into a social event for local residents, particularly the elderly, at a time when such interactions were made difficult because of a sense of alienation and fear concerning the changes that had taken place in the neighborhood—especially after the violent unrest that broke out in Washington, D.C., when Martin Luther King was assassinated in 1968. According to Hutchinson, "Gentlemen were getting their hair cut, ladies were getting their hair fixed, putting a little rouge on their faces, greeting one another. . . . As a result of the riot, many of the elderly were intimidated by what was going on and didn't come out as frequently. . . . But now they had a reason to come out, and they had a reason to spruce up, and they had a reason to smile and become articulate."[33] The effort that these museums made to reach the black community and the process through which museum staff persuaded neighborhood residents that they might have something valuable to contribute—even if it was a seemingly ordinary object or an old family story—speak to the shifting notions of artifact acquisition and community outreach taking place at a grassroots level in the museum field.

Black Museums and the Fight for the Neighborhood

In terms of its potential for attracting African American visitors, the DuSable Museum seemed perfectly situated because of its accessible location in the city's South Side. Better known as "Bronzeville," the South Side had long been considered the "cultural heart of black Chicago."[34] The large number of South Side schools and organizations that toured the museum during its first year, including the South Park YMCA, Wendell Phillips High School, and Dunbar Vocational High School, illustrate the appeal exerted by an African American museum in this area.

Yet there were drawbacks to the DuSable's seemingly ideal location, since the museum (and Bronzeville itself) also lay directly in the path of Chicago's ambitious urban renewal policies. After World War II, Chicago's city planners implemented programs that targeted issues such as transportation, slum clearance, and construction of public housing. White-owned businesses and factories in the South Side tried to use legislation to protect their properties from deterioration and, especially, from the migration of African Americans into the areas surrounding these institutions. Mayor Richard Daley's plan for the modernization of core areas of Chicago, particularly the business district just south of the Chicago River known as "The Loop," meant that the building and neighborhood in which the DuSable had taken root were in danger of destruction.[35] Embedded as they were within their changing neighborhoods, black neighborhood museums like the DuSable could not help but confront the changes inflicted by both segregation and urban renewal.

In 1964, Margaret Burroughs found herself fighting to prevent the city's bulldozers from tearing down the museum. Through her strenuous efforts, she ultimately saved the mansion that originally housed the DuSable, and it has since been placed upon the National Register of Historic Places.[36] Yet though Burroughs had rescued the building, urban renewal's impact upon the museum continued to reverberate in other, less immediately tangible ways. The implementation of policies such as the 1947 Relocation Act resulted in the eviction of thousands of African American residents from their homes and businesses in the South Side. Older single-family homes or low-rise apartments that lay in the path of these construction projects were torn down and replaced (although not immediately) with public housing complexes, such as the Robert Taylor Homes in the South Side and the Cabrini-Green complex in the North Side. These projects became notorious for their crime and dilapidated conditions, and the inability of residents to relocate from these often dangerous places.[37]

High levels of poverty and residential displacement, coupled with a reduction in vital city services such as trash collection, further marred Bronzeville's image. As the *Chicago Sun-Times* journalist Lillian Calhoun noted in 1966, "the [DuSable] museum is in the heart of the so-called 'Negro ghetto.' Mrs. Burroughs notes that many white visitors take pains to come early so they can leave before dark."[38] Burroughs recognized that museum visitors, especially those who were white, were likely to characterize the deteriorating neighborhood that surrounded the DuSable as dangerous or inhospitable, particularly in light of the urban uprisings that spread through American cities during the mid-late 1960s. Like the archetypal neighborhoods located on the "wrong side of the tracks," the marginalized urban space inhabited by the DuSable—or, for that matter, by the International Afro-American Museum or the Anacostia Neigh-borhood Museum—gave white visitors reason to avoid visiting these neighbor-hoods, and thereby permission to ignore the struggling institutions and people within them.[39]

Building the International Afro-American Museum of Detroit: A Black Museum for a "Black City"

In one sense, however, black museums like the DuSable offered their own form of urban renewal. In 1967, black power activists Stokely Carmichael and Charles Hamilton argued in their missive *Black Power* that "Black people have seen the city planning commissions, the urban renewal commissions, the boards of education and the police departments fail to speak to their needs in a mean-ingful way. We must devise new structures, new institutions to replace those forms or to make them responsive." During the postwar era, African American residents in cities like Chicago and Detroit increasingly witnessed this munici-pal failure. With Dr. Charles Wright's creation of the International Afro-Amer-ican Museum (IAM) of Detroit, they responded in kind, thus following Car-michael and Hamilton's decree.

Once praised as a city that powered the nation through times of war and shepherded the American consumer through seemingly limitless periods of prosperity, Detroit has since became more recognized, both in popular culture and in scholarly study, for its transformation from an industrial powerhouse to an often desperately struggling postindustrial city. Like the DuSable, the IAM emerged in an environment shaped by the city's implementation of postwar urban renewal programs, as well as by its long history of racial skirmishes and economic surge and decline. Dr. Charles H. Wright, who founded the museum in an apartment in downtown Detroit in 1965, acknowledged that the IAM had to function in a city both physically and psychologically marked by these dynamics, even as he imbued the museum's mission and outreach programs with the agenda of black empowerment.

Although the much scrutinized riot that took place in 1967 helped to define Detroit's transformation from a "Model City" to a place the media would later dub "Murder City," racial tensions were simmering there long before 1967.[40] During World War II, Detroit's population swelled as both blacks and whites migrated from the South to work in the city's factories. The population explosion spawned conflicts over the intertwined issues of employment and housing.

Original Location of the International Afro-American Museum, West Grand Boulevard, Detroit. Dr. Charles Wright converted the basement of one of the apartments in this building into the museum's first home. Later, he expanded the museum to encompass the entire building. Courtesy of the Walter P. Reuther Library, Wayne State University, Detroit, Mich.

African Americans, restricted by discriminatory real-estate and banking policies, faced limited choices of where they could live; resistance to black employment in factories prompted multiple clashes between white and black workers.[41] Tensions reached a height in June 1943, when federal troops suppressed a riot that erupted on Woodward Avenue, one of the main thoroughfares bisecting the city. Thirty-four people—nine whites and twenty-five African Americans—died.[42]

Detroit's conflicts over labor, housing, and race continued after World War II. In pursuit of more and cheaper land, the "Big Three" automakers—Ford, Chrysler, and General Motors—relocated their factories to the suburbs and, increasingly, outside of Michigan altogether.[43] City planners designed massive freeways that followed the relocation of these factories; construction that cut through the hearts of formerly self-sustaining communities had a particularly devastating effect upon black and ethnic neighborhoods.[44] The opening of the Chrysler Freeway in 1963 virtually obliterated the African American enclave known as Paradise Valley, destroying black-owned theaters, businesses, and homes. What remained, historian Thomas Sugrue lamented, was a "'no man's land' of deterioration and abandonment."[45]

Following the movement of auto factories was the decline of auto-related industries such as machine tool manufacturers.[46] With the relocation of jobs and the construction of newer homes in the suburbs, white residents followed, and Detroit's neighborhoods began to change. Between 1950 and 1960, for example, eighty-three census tracts became at least 50 percent black, whereas during the 1940s–1950s, just twenty-four census tracts were listed as 50 percent African American.[47] Clearly, the shifting demographics of Detroit's neighborhoods were not simply the result of racial tensions between blacks and whites, although this certainly contributed to "white flight." In cities like Detroit, Oakland, and Chicago, white families settled in the burgeoning suburbs because of financial incentives to do so: the federal government helped subsidize the construction of new housing, and industries that relocated to the suburbs kept taxes low. So, too, the mantra of "space"—a larger home, a larger yard, a larger car, and increased distance from those of lower incomes and darker skin—signified to white families that they had achieved the American dream.[48]

By the mid-1960s, the downward turn in Detroit's economy, coupled with its demographic shifts, seemed to indicate that the formerly prosperous metropolis had slipped out of white control. A pattern of national events, such as the increasing prominence of the Black Power Movement in urban areas, reaffirmed the perception—if not the reality—of a changing balance of power between whites and blacks.[49] Nor should the growing national and international recognition of the city's cultural scene be underestimated as a major factor in the equation of Detroit as a "black" city. In 1959, Berry Gordy's creation of Motor City Records—or, as it became more popularly known, Motown—marked Detroit as a cultural beacon powered by African Americans despite, and even because of, the city's sometimes violent racial instability.[50] The development of Detroit's black museum movement represents a lesser known but crucial cultural parallel to Motown as representative of African Americans' assertion of cultural power and political authority during the 1960s and 1970s. The birth of the IAM, and the black museum movement as a whole, constituted a defiant response to a most pressing question: Who would control the presentation and preservation of black culture, history, and identity?

As Charles Wright conceptualized the museum's mission and programs, he adapted many of the methods implemented by the DuSable Museum. In 1967, Wright cofounded the Association of African American Museums with Margaret Burroughs, who recalled in a 2004 interview with the *Chicago Tribune* that, "for many [museum founders], I met and told them how to get started. So they didn't have to reinvent the wheel."[51] As did the DuSable, the IAM received financial and material support from external organizations, including the Michigan Council for the Arts, the Detroit Public School System, and the Detroit Historical Museum. The museum also relied predominantly on volunteers for labor, financial support, and their knowledge of black history. Still, Wright's museum differed from the DuSable in several important ways. For instance, although the DuSable may have helped to define, and been defined by, Chicago's South Side, the museum did not substantially affect the popular "image" of Chicago itself. On the other hand, the creation and evolution of the IAM, along with more prominent African American organizations such as Motown, arguably played a crucial role in shaping Detroit's image as a "black" city.

Beyond "Whitewashing": Planning the IAM

The foundation of the International Afro-American Museum served as a personal milestone in Dr. Charles Wright's work as a pioneering African American doctor and civil rights activist. Born in 1918, Wright graduated from Nashville's Meharry Medical School in 1939 and served as an intern and pathology resident at Harlem Hospital in 1943 and 1944. After practicing general medicine in Detroit from 1946 to 1950, he returned to Harlem and completed an obstetrics and gynecology program in 1953, becoming a certified ob-gyn specialist and general surgeon in 1955.[52] As an ob-gyn, Wright served a population that the professional medical community often neglected. A self-described "whistle-blower," he successfully campaigned to integrate the staff of Hutzel Woman's Hospital in Detroit during the 1950s. Wright recalled that "they wouldn't allow my patient to come into the hospital if there was not a vacancy in a room [where] another black patient was. And they didn't accept black interns and residents."[53]

Wright's medical training informed his commitment to civil rights activism in Detroit and around the globe. In 1960, he and the Detroit Medical Society began the African Medical Education Fund, which funded medical training for African Americans. In 1965, he traveled to the South to serve as a resident physician during the civil rights marches in Selma, Alabama:

> The civil rights movement started . . . while I was at Harlem, and this was around the time of the [Montgomery] bus boycott. [From that] developed the Medical Committee for Human Rights (MCHR), and it was designed to involve doctors. We agreed that we would voluntarily go to any portion of the south where we anticipated trouble, to be on hand to give support to the civil rights workers . . . actually this is what got me involved in the Selma March incident when [we] had

[the confrontation] thing about voting. I was in charge of the first-aid station in the battle of Selma in 1965, and that's where I was when I had scheduled a meeting—the first meeting of the museum in 1965.[54]

Wright's conviction that a black museum in Detroit could advance the civil rights battles being waged in Selma signals how one form of activism—direct protest—could influence another—institution building. His experiences as an activist shaped his understanding of what an African American history museum must accomplish and the obstacles that it would face in rectifying traditional narratives of black history and culture.

Wright believed that the deliberate "whitewashing" of American history affected blacks and whites alike, arguing in March 1965 that "the white man in the South sincerely believes he is right. Unless the Negro can accept this concept, he cannot deal with the Southern white man. The white man is the victim of the misrepresentations of history, as well as the Negro."[55] In this, Wright must surely have been aware of James Baldwin's pronouncement in *The Fire Next Time* (1963) that whites were "still trapped in a history which they do not understand; and until they understand it, they cannot be released from it."[56]

Yet while changing the belief system of whites was important, Wright and other black museum founders did not view this as their primary task. Rather, it was influencing the psychology of African Americans that was paramount. As Wright explained, "we are trying to erase 350 years of dehumanizing brain washing and civil rights are not enough. Something has to occur inside the Negro to erase those self-degrading ideas that he has been taught." That "something," necessarily more concrete and visible than the abstract concept of "civil rights for all," could be the mission of a black history museum.[57]

Wright held the first planning meeting for the "development of a museum devoted to the past and present fight for the freedom of the American Negro" in Detroit in March 1965.[58] The attendees represented an interracial cross-section of Detroit's cultural and political leaders; even those who had previously clashed with Wright over the apparent exclusion of black history and culture from their own institutions attended. Dr. Henry Brown, director of the Detroit Historical Museum, and Willis F. Woods, director of the Detroit Institute of Arts, were among those in attendance, together with several Tuskegee Institute and Wayne State University professors. Interestingly, the turnout at these planning meetings soon dwindled to about fifteen people, according to a 1975 report on the museum's first ten years. One museum advocate posited that the reason for this drop lay in the internal power struggles between white and black committee members: "When the whites at the meeting found out that some of our black members weren't going to let them make all the policy, they dropped out. . . ."[59]

The museum's planning documents from March, June, and September 1965 illuminate how Wright and the planning committee shaped and altered the museum's mission during these first few crucial meetings. Although the group strongly supported the idea of a museum devoted to African American history, Wright expressed concern that there would not be enough material related to black history for the museum to collect and present. The lack of usable artifacts, he recognized, stemmed from the persistent neglect and diminishment of black history by most mainstream institutions: "there is a dearth of material because the Negro has been told that nothing he knows and nothing he has is of any importance."[60]

Committee members also hesitated to make the creation of an archive one of the museum's primary goals. Not surprisingly, committee member James Babcock, chief of the Burton Historical Collection at the Detroit Public Library, stressed that the collection and preservation of archival material should be a crucial task for the proposed museum. Yet while the group agreed that building an archive was necessary, "it was pointed out that we are overlooking the psychological effect. The Negro needs something grand and an archives is not an *image* provoking type of institution."[61] Museum planners believed that creating archive should not constitute the museum's primary purpose; rather, in order to secure the support of Detroit's black community, the *image* of the museum must be promoted and cultivated.

The group approved Wright's suggestion to name the museum the International Afro-American Museum, abbreviated IAM. The choice of abbreviation was not accidental: Wright explained that it stood not only for the declarative statement "I AM" but also for "I Am a Man." The abbreviation's dual meaning reverberates with an ideal that would exert a strong hold within the Black Power Movement: the reclamation of African American identity, intertwined with an assertion of black masculinity. In 1968, three years after this meeting—and just one month before Martin Luther King's assassination—striking sanitation workers and their supporters in Memphis wore placards affirming what Wright had previously articulated: "I *AM* A Man." Although the slogan, as well as King's accompanying speeches during the Memphis rallies, may be equated with an assertion of human rights, historian Steve Estes contends that strike leaders defined the slogan "in the strict sense of men's rights rather than the broader construction of human rights. . . . The sanitation workers' slogan was a direct response to the verbal and physical emasculation of black men."[62] The gendering of the IAM, then, corresponded with an emphasis on black masculinity that characterized many aspects of the black museum movement—even despite the fact that, as a female staff member later charged, it was women who ran many of the IAM's daily operations.[63]

Wright included a more comprehensive proposal for the creation of the IAM in the minutes of the June 16, 1965, meeting. The new proposal expanded upon the tentative ideas discussed in March and addressed a topic central to the black museum movement: the importance of grassroots participation from the black community. Community participation must be an absolute priority lest the project succumb to the fate of President Lyndon Johnson's War on Poverty programs, which the museum planning group criticized as having been built "from the top downward."[64] The proposal's introduction also linked the black freedom struggle with the drive to create an African American museum. Its authors again drew a strong connection between the reclamation of black manhood and the establishment of a museum, or rather, a national *monument* to all African Americans—one with global ties to the emergent internationalism of the Civil Rights and Black Power Movements: "We are here proposing a national monument to correct the false and distorted history of the Black Man, and to give him a symbol of his own identity and worth. . . . We are involved in a revolutionary movement for freedom in the United States, a struggle which is greatly affecting the rest of the world.[65] The fact that the planning group used the terms "museum" and "monument" interchangeably to describe their vision for the museum is telling. More than just a repository for documents and artifacts, the museum would serve as a monumental representation of African and African American ingenuity in the face of hundreds of years of oppression. Echoing the affirmation of identity embedded in the name's initials, the proposal concluded that the museum must present "a grand, awe-inspiring, emotion-evoking portrayal of the Negroes in the Americas. It should and must inspire respect, wonder and a sense of 'Self.'"[66]

The revised June proposal articulated five goals for the museum and placed the greatest emphasis upon the first: the museum must "dramatize the constructive existence/contribution of America's black citizens." African American audiences who came to the museum would realize not only a renewed "sense of 'Self'" but also their role in the grand trajectory of the black freedom movement. Ranked last, as per the sentiments Wright expressed in March, was the museum's goal to "provide a storehouse for artifacts and heirlooms that may otherwise be lost to history" and to "provide a valid source for research on the Negro history of the Western Hemisphere."[67]

There was little debate about what role whites should play in planning for the new museum. Sympathetic whites were not to be excluded from the process; indeed, the museum planning group welcomed their financial assistance, as well as other public displays of support. Their acknowledgment and acceptance of white support distinguishes the planning group from the defiantly separatist factions that would emerge within the Black Power Movement. Yet the group also maintained that even if whites did not offer any assistance, the project would go forth without them. For museum planners, "management must be in the hands of the Negro. Otherwise, this could become another charity that would do nothing for the Negro's image of himself."[68]

In September, the planning committee decided to significantly revise the IAM's mission statement. In the March 1965 statement of purpose, the writers had employed vivid words to illustrate the vicious impact of racism upon black men, specifically. As they maintained, "the Negro in the Americas has been denied his heritage; his skills, talents and manhood have been brutally suppressed, and his material and spiritual contributions to human culture unacknowledged. . . . We protest the distortions of our history, and of our Self, and propose to change this image."[69] After reviewing this description, however, the planning committee decided to revise the introduction and exclude charged words such as "brutally."[70] Consequently, the September 1965 proposal features marked changes in the choice of words the committee used to describe the impact of racism upon African Americans, with the authors eliminating language that could be perceived as overtly accusatory. The revised proposal read: "For over three hundred years, 'Racism' for Negroes in America has meant a denial of an identity and heritage. In the light of racist beliefs about the inferiority of Negroes, the material and spiritual contribution made by Black Men to human culture and civilization went unacknowledged. . . . As a consequence, the image of Negro peoples in history has been distorted. We feel that the time has come to correct this image."[71]

The March and June proposal drafts corresponded with the more self-consciously "militant" ideology and discourse of black power, but the September 1965 proposal, its blunt language purposefully tempered (perhaps in an effort to appeal to more conservative white supporters who might be turned off by accusations that they had "brutally suppressed" black men), echoed the discourse of the mainstream Civil Rights Movement and changed the entire tenor of the museum's approach.

Still, while the committee moderated some of the power embedded in their first declarative proposal, the museum's mission continued to reinforce the core goals of the Black Power Movement. For instance, discussion regarding museum membership centered not simply upon its role in obtaining much needed funds; rather, the weighted significance of what it meant to *belong* to a black museum was of first importance to committee members. Becoming a member was an action fraught with significance, for it signaled an individual's core belief not only in the black freedom struggle but in "human freedom." Choosing to join the museum signified not just your support of such an organization but your "personal conviction that Afro-Americans are a people of worth and dignity."[72] The committee also suggested that membership should be open to everyone— even those who could not afford it. One committee member thought that the museum should "issue a membership card to everyone who contributes any money, even if it is just a penny. Dr. Wright agreed and suggested selling one share for one cent, so that each member knows he has an investment in the organization. He is interested in the school children."[72] Ultimately, membership in the International Afro-American Museum served as a declaration of revolutionary intent, "a revolutionary movement that will help to free mankind from the bonds of racism, and establish once and for all the essential equality of all men."[73] The ways in which the museum communicated this message, as we shall see, moved well beyond the language of gradualism and conciliation suggested by the IAM's revised mission statements.

Anacostia: "In the Shadow of the National Spotlight"

If Detroit was the Motor City that powered the nation, Washington, D.C., the touchstone of American nationalism, represents a loftier side of American identity. Countless local historians and city boosters, along with millions of tourists, celebrate its monuments, museums, and memorials. Yet it also has a second, far less scrutinized identity—Washington, D.C., the city. Comprised of numerous and distinctive neighborhoods, from wealthy Georgetown to the less affluent, mostly African American areas like Anacostia, Barry Farms, and Congress Heights, these Washington neighborhoods have most often existed in the shadows cast by their powerful national twin. As a result, the spaces and neighborhoods of Washington not populated by national monuments and other popular destinations may go unnoticed by both tourists and urban planners. Even in 1995, decades after the destruction wrought by the District's urban renewal programs upon poor neighborhoods like Anacostia, the architect Robert Peck concurred that, "if it is not a monumental space like the Mall or Pennsylvania Avenue, an urban space in this town is an afterthought."[74]

One of the best illustrations of the conflict between Washington's dual identities may be found in the city's history as a slave market. During the 1840s and 1850s, slave auctions operated in the very heart of the nation's capital, until abolitionist groups, aghast at the irony of slavery literally coexisting with the democratic image that Washington supposedly represented, pressured the city to end its trade in human flesh. Almost a century later, with the black population constituting around 25 percent of the city's total population by 1920 (surpassed only by New York City, Chicago, and Philadelphia), the enforcement of segregation and the passage of urban renewal policies continued to affect those who inhabited the District's marginal spaces.

Yet Anacostia's residences, streets, and storefronts have not always been in a state of deterioration. Prior to World War II, both African Americans and some white working-class families lived in this area located in this southeast region of Washington, D.C. Single-family homes with small plots of land dominated, and early twentieth-century photographs depict a thriving main street. Mr. and Mrs. John W. Southall, Anacostia residents since 1919, remembered that "there were virtually no large apartment complexes for black citizens in Anacostia until [real-estate developer Morris] Cafritz built Parklands in 1951–52. . . . Most black citizens of Anacostia owned their homes and had gardens in which they raised vegetables and they also raised chickens."[75]

Jim Crow–era segregation placed severe restrictions on Anacostia's black community, leaving its inhabitants with limited mobility to navigate beyond, and even within, the boundaries of their neighborhood. Percy Battle, who moved from Richmond, Virginia, to Anacostia in 1937 and resided there for most of his life, reflected: "I guess when they built the Carver Theater . . . that was the only entertainment that we had. . . . Although there were two theaters that we could walk to very easily, one down on Good Hope Road and one up at Martin Luther King and Portland Street. And we weren't allowed to go to those theaters."[76]

Segregation also imposed barriers beyond the pursuit of leisure. Before World War II, Anacostia's black residents mostly worked in construction or as domestic laborers. The war opened up a few more occupations in the city; for example, the Government Printing Office and the Bureau of Engraving and Printing employed African Americans as messengers and office cleaners. Celebrated African American photographer Gordon Parks, who conducted a survey of the "back alleys" of Washington, D.C., transformed an African American charwoman laboring to clean the offices of powerful white men in the nation's capital into an iconic figure in one of his most famous photographs.[77] Many African Americans had difficulty traveling to these new places of employment, for there were only one or two crowded busses available to transport blacks to their jobs in other parts of Washington.[78]

Discriminatory education policies also affected Anacostia's black community. During the Depression, African American children could only attend certain schools in the neighborhood, such as the Birney School, located on Nichols Avenue. When they reached junior high, black students had to attend a school in the northwestern area of the District. Similarly, rather than attend the predominantly white Anacostia High School, African American students traveled to Dunbar, Armstrong, and Cardozo Senior Highs, located in other parts of the city.[79] Anacostia resident Erma Katherine Simon remembered that black teachers at the Birney School tried to make the best of the situation: "And we . . . were not aware that some of the books we got were sent down from other schools, from other white schools that is. But we got a lot of new books at Birney School also . . . the leaders at Birney Schools were strong, determined people because they saw to it that the children at Birney School had the things they needed. . . ."[80]

The constraints imposed by Jim Crow helped instill a sense of community among Anacostia's black residents. Rather than wholly depending on the outside world for goods and services, African Americans relied on black businesses and interacted primarily with black families. For instance, Erna Katherine Simon reminisced about her family's garden plot, which allowed them to reduce their reliance on grocery stores that might have refused them service.[81] Despite the obvious hardships faced by Anacostians during the days of Jim Crow, a strain of optimism and even nostalgia runs through many of these oral histories. As Simon further explained, "Then families were families. Everybody was your mother or your father. Everybody was respected. . . . So, all and all, Anacostia was like a village. Everybody—all for one, and one for all."[82]

Urban renewal disrupted this sense of community by displacing Washington, D.C.'s black citizens from one region to another and transforming Anacostia's isolation from the rest of the District into something more entrenched.

After World War II, developers razed many of Anacostia's older homes and constructed closely situated apartment buildings (with a parallel reduction in green space) to take their place.[83] In 1970, the D.C. Office of Community Renewal reported that apartments constituted 85 percent of the 38,900 dwelling units in Anacostia—an extremely high percentage indicating a lack of single-family and duplex owner-occupied housing.[84] Significant alterations in the structure and design of Anacostia's roadways also contributed to the region's housing and population changes. Highway construction projects cut through formerly cohesive neighborhoods in southwestern and southeastern D.C., thus allowing Washington's middle-class residents to speed around Anacostia without stopping.[85]

Urban renewal's destruction contributed to the characterization of Anacostia's residents as the "other" Washingtonians: poor, different, isolated. A taxi driver's comments in a 1966 *Washington Post* article reflected this sense that Anacostia's residents were inaccessible and immobile by choice, not by circumstance: "Almost nobody goes to Southeast. But sometimes, when I'm over past the Capitol, I get 'em. I hate it when that happens. Hate to go over there. Those people over there, they don't travel much. The travelin' folks, they're downtown. You come back alone when you get one to Southeast."[86] A decade after John Kinard founded the Anacostia Neighborhood Museum, staff member Louise Daniel Hutchinson recalled that this image of Anacostia's isolation persisted even among Smithsonian Institution staff members—an issue that endlessly frustrated ANM staff in their efforts to promote the museum. During her research for the ANM exhibit The Anacostia Story (1977), she visited Smithsonian staff member Silvio A. Bendini. According to Hutchinson, Bendini "was pleasantly surprised that I called and came to see him, because he had a notion that somehow we in Anacostia were black, they on the Mall were white, and we should isolate ourselves or that we desired to isolate ourselves. A part of my role. . . was to begin building some bridges to the octopus on the Mall."[87]

"For This Is No Ordinary Museum": Creating the Anacostia Neighborhood Museum

For the African American residents of Anacostia, long rendered invisible because of race, class, and separation from the heart of the city, there seemed little reason to visit the very places that granted Washington, D.C., its powerful image in American culture. The opening of the Anacostia Neighborhood

Anacostia Historical Society members gather for a photograph in front of the new Anacostia Neighborhood Museum in Washington, D.C., 1967. The Carver Theater on Nichols Avenue was one of the few theaters African Americans were permitted to enter during segregation. Community volunteers transformed the theater into the museum. Courtesy of the Smithsonian Institution Archives. Image no. 92-1705.

Museum (ANM) on September 15, 1967, in the former Carver Theater on Nichols Avenue was thus a watershed event meant to change this perception. During the opening ceremonies, Smithsonian Institution Secretary Sidney Dillon Ripley spoke with almost extraordinary optimism about the ANM's potential to transform not only museums but cities themselves. "For this is no ordinary museum," Ripley opined, "indeed it is an extraordinary museum, and because it is, it speaks to us from more than art and history, technology and natural history. . . . I suspect that museums will never quite be the same again, and perhaps our cities won't be either."[88] Two decades later, Kenneth Hudson concurred with Ripley's assessment of the museum's potential, maintaining that the ANM "must be given the credit of pioneering the concept of a museum without walls to keep it within bounds, a museum with a creative flow of ideas, exhibits and people between itself and the outside world."[89]

Ripley's welcome served as the culmination of an "experiment" he had proposed at a meeting of museum directors in Aspen, Colorado, in 1966. Ripley explained that the Smithsonian Institution must establish an experimental neighborhood museum, somewhere in Washington, D.C., as a way to entice more African Americans to visit museums.[90] As evidence of Smithsonian's neglect of this audience, he pointed to the startling results of a recent survey of visiting school groups. During the 1965–66 school year, 32,909 students from the D.C. metro area took guided tours of the Smithsonian museums, but only 1,871 of those children attended schools in Washington, D.C., itself.[91] Thus, children who visited the Smithsonian did not attend the mostly black, less affluent inner-city schools, but rather those located in the wealthier, mostly white outer-ring suburbs. Likewise, a single day-long survey (c. 1966–67) conducted at the Museum of Natural History revealed that out of 1,558 visitors, only 43 were African American. The survey admitted that "the pattern of Smithsonian visitors in no way reflects the city's actual population characteristics; in a city whose population is predominantly Negro (62%), more than 90% of the visitors to the Museum of Natural History on a recent holiday were white."[92]

As an explanation for these jarring statistics, Ripley contended that the people who usually lived in "rundown parts of cities" (which he described as often "gently dilapidated," and occasionally "violent, and, to us, jungly") generally avoided museums because they "may feel awkward going out of their district, badly dressed or ill at ease. They may easily feel lost as they wend their way along an unfamiliar sidewalk toward a vast monumental marble palace. They may even feel hostile."[93] Yet Ripley's portrayal of inner-city African Americans as naïve "city bumpkins," unaccustomed to travel and easily intimidated by the physical spaces of whiteness, was complicated by Anacostia Neighborhood Museum director John Kinard. Kinard argued that African Americans eschewed the Smithsonian not simply because of the lack of time, money, the proper clothes, or because they felt intimidated—although these factors did play some role.[94] Rather, African Americans avoided museums like the Smithsonian because "the black man did not see himself in those jobs or in those exhibits, so he wasn't going to embarrass himself by paying respect to what essentially represented cultural pressure."[95]

Since its creation in the early nineteenth century, the Smithsonian Institution has been considered an esteemed caretaker of the nation's cultural heritage. Kinard recognized, however, that the stories its curators told about history, science, and art had long been exclusive rather than inclusive; the Smithsonian's exhibits, collections, and programs insinuated, at times boldly and at other times subtly, that only certain people made valuable contributions, while others—African Americans, women, and other minority groups—remained entrapped in marginal and stereotyped roles. Indeed, the Smithsonian Institution did not systematically begin to collect artifacts relating to African American history until the 1960s. Prior to that, their only effort to do so was at special request.[96] Given this history, it is not entirely surprising that when local community organizations approached Kinard, then a pastor at the John Wesley African Methodist Zion Church in Washington, to direct the new museum, he admitted that "I don't see how a museum could have any redeeming factor in the development of this community."[97] Nor, initially, did the community of Anacostia itself.

Although the museum's grand opening sparked excitement and anticipation among museum staff and neighborhood residents, they also expressed "fear and uncertainty" about whether it would truly serve as a neighborhood museum. Some residents believed that Ripley wanted to create a neighborhood museum in order to prevent them from visiting the more prestigious ones that lined the National Mall; even some Smithsonian staff members, Kinard remembered, thought that the ANM "was a half-baked Ripley idea, that they weren't for it, didn't think it would last two weeks, and weren't going to help, anyhow." While Kinard acknowledged the validity of the skepticism surrounding Ripley's proposal, he emphasized that Ripley's intentions were sincere and were not, at least consciously, driven by racism: "No, I never saw that. I don't think anybody in his right mind, who knew Ripley, thought that, either, you know."[98]

Another major concern was whether the museum would provide jobs to Anacostia's residents, regardless of skill level. Since other Anacostia community organizations employed people from the neighborhood, it was "expected that any new project would serve the same purpose."[99] Many community members, not surprisingly, also believed that money should be spent on more practical needs than a museum. Kinard recalled, "it was felt that a museum was just not the kind of institution the neighborhood needed, that it would prove to be not only irrelevant to the issues of concern to the community but totally alien, and judging from what was known about museums, it might be so highbrow as to be an embarrassment or downright insult."[100] If the museum was to serve as a welcoming place for community members, then Kinard believed that its mission must extend beyond simply collecting and displaying objects. Instead, it must reflect the priorities of the Anacostia community and reinforce a sense of place, purpose, and history for its residents.[101]

Under Kinard's direction, together with staff and volunteers, the ANM would soon begin to tell the stories of African American life and attempt to reclaim a sense of place and belonging for the city's literally and metaphorically displaced African Americans residents. Kinard's own extensive background as a young community activist in southeast Washington with the Neighborhood Youth Corps, as well as his prior work in Africa with the Operation Crossroads Africa program and the U.S. State Department, contributed to the museum's visionary mission and strengthened the ties between museum and the Anacostia community.[102] The collaboration between S. Dillon Ripley and John Kinard also marked a period of introspective and not necessarily mutually agreeable change for the Smithsonian and, later, other mainstream museums as they began to move away from their roots as nineteenth-century institutions devoted solely to the collection and preservation of artifacts, and instead consider how to (re)-interpret once "forgotten" histories. A major impetus for these changes sprang from the groundbreaking work of African American neighborhood museums located in the marginalized black places of the nation's metropolises. African American leaders who founded these museums intended to represent and instill empowerment, self-sufficiency, and assertive pride in one's heritage. Although these institutions, and their audiences, were seemingly invisible to most white Americans, they vibrated with an undeniable energy as they carved out unique cultural and social spaces for black activism.

CHAPTER 2

"NOT IN MY BACKYARD"

The Contested Origins of the African American Museum
of Philadelphia

Compared to the civil rights movement that swept through southern cities like Montgomery and Selma, the future home of the African American Museum of Philadelphia was not as renowned for its activism—despite the fact that the city witnessed a strong civil rights campaign during the 1940s and 1950s.[1] In 1951, for example, Philadelphia passed a groundbreaking charter that established, among other civil rights practices, a Commission on Human Relations that enforced the city's antidiscrimination laws; city contracts and employment would henceforth be governed by these laws.[2] The commission's members included both blacks and whites. Clarence Farmer, an African American civic leader and entrepreneur who became executive director of the commission in 1967, would later help lead the campaign to build the African American Museum of Philadelphia.

Despite the commission's efforts, by the early 1960s many African American leaders expressed growing frustration with Philadelphia's ongoing racial tensions and discriminatory practices. While the commission modeled its work upon the practice of "biracial coalition politics," failure on the part of the city government to effectively address issues of school segregation, the impact of ill-conceived urban renewal policies, and police brutality raised questions about whether such interracial alliances were worthwhile. After riots tore through northern Philadelphia in 1964, black activists began to create their own organizations, with the notion of black power as their main driving force.[3]

One particularly effective African American group that challenged Philadelphia's dismal record of police brutality was the Council of Organizations on Philadelphia Police Accountability and Responsibility (COPPAR). Mary Rouse, an African American woman whose son had been beaten by the Philadelphia police in 1966, formed COPPAR in 1967; other African American women constituted its primary leaders. COPPAR helped initiate hearings on police–community relations held by the U.S. Commission on Civil Rights in 1971.[4] As COPPAR contested Philadelphia's tainted methods of law and order, the media directed their attention to the more "dramatic" activities of Philadelphia's male-dominated Black Panther Party, which formed in October 1968. Among the main grievances of Philadelphia's Black Panthers were police brutality, discrimination, and poor housing and school conditions—in short, the same injustices targeted by newly formed Black Panther Party organizations across the country. Philadelphia's Black Panther Party did not typically engage in such visibly confrontational activities as the armed patrolling of city streets. Instead, they focused primarily on selling Black Panther–produced newspapers, holding demonstrations against police brutality, and initiating medical clinics and breakfast programs. By 1970, the chapter had grown from fifteen members to more than one hundred.

Internal factionalism, as well as the suppression of black militant activism by federally instituted surveillance programs like COINTELPRO, hastened the decline of the national Black Power Movement during the early 1970s. In Philadelphia, by 1973 fewer than twenty-five members remained in the local Black Panther Party.[5] Yet despite the apparent disintegration of the national Black Power Movement, Philadelphia's black activists had nonetheless developed crucial tools used to both challenge and remake the city's traditional power structure. Although the practice of "all-black" radical grassroots protest was vital to this process, African Americans were also moving into political offices, such as those of neighborhood ward leader, and even state representative. As a result, Philadelphia's municipal administration during the late 1960s and 1970s began to be fundamentally reshaped.[6] This combination of pressure from radical black activist groups like COPPAR, together with increased black access to local political office, enabled African American leaders to place sustained pressure upon Philadelphia officials in the battle to open a city-funded African American museum during the nation's Bicentennial year. The debut of the

African American Museum of Philadelphia (AAMP) in 1976 represented the successful outcome of this unique, and sometimes volatile, coalition.

Unlike museums such as the International Afro-American Museum of Detroit or the DuSable Museum of African American History in Chicago, the AAMP's unveiling did not stem from the culmination of a relatively smooth and consensual planning process implemented by a small group of dedicated committee members. In contrast, the museum opened its doors only after a series of protracted debates among museum advocates, municipal leaders, and neighborhood residential organizations. For many museum supporters, the resistance that some Bicentennial planners and predominantly white neighborhood organizations leveled against the construction of the museum smacked of racism, disguised under the pretexts of funding shortages or opposition to increased traffic and zoning violations. Dissension also arose among museum advocates regarding whether the AAMP truly represented Philadelphia's African Americans, since the city—the museum's primary financial contributor—seemed, at times, to control the entire project. Indeed, many African American residents believed that Philadelphia's government granted funding for the museum only to alleviate the possibility of an embarrassing uprising during the Bicentennial year.

Laying the Groundwork

Planning for the nation's Bicentennial began in earnest years before the official celebrations began in 1976.[7] In Philadelphia, Mayor Richardson Dilworth (1956–62) initiated Bicentennial projects in 1957; Dilworth's successor, Mayor James Tate (1962–72), appointed an organizational group in 1965.[8] In 1967, the city chartered the Philadelphia 1976 Bicentennial Corporation, which had direct oversight over the acceptance or rejection of Bicentennial program proposals.[9] Predominantly comprised of white businessmen and politicians, the corporation did include some African American members, including Clarence Farmer.

Philadelphia '76, as the Philadelphia 1976 Bicentennial Corporation became known, initially adopted the theme of "human values" as its focal point, arguing in their publication *Toward a Meaningful Bicentennial* (1969) that the principles of the Bicentennial had not yet been realized: "although we have created the most affluent society on earth, with the resources necessary to orbit men around the moon, we have yet to create humane cities, and we experience difficulty in preserving the peace within our own country."[10] Borrowing, perhaps, from Jane

Jacobs's call for more "humane" cities in her groundbreaking manifesto *The Death and Life of Great American Cities* (1961), Philadelphia '76 proposed establishing action programs in poor neighborhoods in North and West Philadelphia, as well as creating exhibits that offered solutions to urban problems.[11] Philadelphia '76 also believed the Bicentennial could serve as an impetus for urban redevelopment, which had begun in Philadelphia during the early 1950s. New expressways, parking garages, pedestrian walkways, transit stations, and a downtown shopping plaza were all part of Philadelphia's "Comprehensive Plan" to redevelop the Central Business District, as well as Lower North Philadelphia and Market Street East.[12] By instituting such reforms, planners hoped to convert the downtown into a pleasant and tranquil experience for middle-class, suburban families. Such a transformation might then convert the city from what some perceived as a "dying industrial metropolis" into a "new (and newly perceived) global role."[13]

Other American cities also recognized the potential benefits of promoting the Bicentennial in conjunction with urban revitalization efforts. Urban planners in Detroit, struggling with a deteriorating economy, the 1967 riot, and white flight to suburbia, placed great hope in the Bicentennial's ability to restore the Model City. Indeed, Detroit's Bicentennial planning committee maintained that there ought to be no real debate about whether the Bicentennial should be celebrated as a "major, total community effort supporting Detroit's revitalization or merely a local city fair in a national celebration."[14] The group outlined the three primary purposes of the city's Bicentennial program in a document revealingly titled "Detroit Bicentennial: Catalyst for Progress":

1. Redirection to the still unrealized ideals—life, liberty, and the pursuit of happiness
2. Celebration of the city's diverse ethnic heritages
3. Physical regeneration and beautification of the city.

The committee integrated questions about how the Bicentennial might address issues such as crime, unemployment, housing, and police–community relations within the framework of these three goals. The Bicentennial celebrations, members argued, would benefit the city on multiple fronts: tourists headed to downtown Detroit would generate jobs, and more crowds might engender less crime, for "a crowded city, particularly downtown, is a safer city." Detroit's new housing program, to be enacted during the Bicentennial, might alleviate the city's housing crisis. Completion of the "Woodward East" housing project, explained the committee, "would be an inspiring example of citizen participation in a venture which blends the old and the new."[15] Other programs scheduled to take place in Detroit during the Bicentennial included the restoration of historic Fort Wayne; the display of the J. Edward Bailey Exhibit, which featured photographs of distinguished African Americans, and a Summer Music Festival that highlighted Detroit's African American musicians. Yet while apparently committed to an ambitious Bicentennial program, the committee recognized the limits of the holiday's ability to solve all of the city's problems. "To the extent that Bicentennial projects can generate a common citizen purpose and pride of residency," wrote the committee, "they can help to heal the city's polarization. This is not in any way meant to suggest that Bicentennial activities are a panacea for this critical problem."[16]

Like the Detroit Bicentennial committee, Philadelphia '76 acknowledged that their publicized hope of creating a more "humane city" had not yet assuaged the concerns expressed by diverse local groups disaffected with the official Bicentennial plans. What is intriguing is that, at least initially, Philadelphia '76 appeared responsive to this populist dissent. For example, the Philadelphia '76 publication *Toward a Meaningful Bicentennial* included summarized remarks made by a group called the City-Wide Black Community Council. The council argued during a December 1968 speech that, "in view of today's bitter realities, human values must take priority. [The council] added that if the United States Bicentennial concept were based upon human rights, both the external and internal symptoms of alienation in America's minority groups would disappear."[17] Another counter-Bicentennial group, whose remarks Philadelphia '76 also included in *Toward a Meaningful Bicentennial*, elaborated upon the stark polarities between the reality of urban life for black Philadelphians and Bicentennial ideals:

> The majority of Philadelphia blacks are living in the worst sections of the city. . . . Greater participation in policy decisions by members of minority groups can be the first significant step toward establishing a meaningful Bicentennial in the Delaware Valley and especially in the City of Brotherly Love, Philadelphia. . . . The validity of the Bicentennial will come from its ability to motivate representatives from all cultures—both within and outside America—to a full realization of human potential. That was the meaning of 1776 and must be the meaning in 1976.[18]

This argument constituted both a summation of the dire living conditions experienced by many black Philadelphians and a rallying cry for the oppressed to seize the opportunity presented by the national holiday to take charge of their own institutions—in short, the credo of black power activists working in the United States and across the globe. Philadelphia '76 concluded that these diverse perspectives regarding the meaning of the Bicentennial signified that the planned celebrations should represent, "not the imposition of the ideas of the few on the many, but rather decisions being made by citizens from all the communities and interests of the city."[19]

Yet the group's initially ambitious commitment to a complex assessment of the Bicentennial's meaning deteriorated during the city's actual celebrations in 1976. Although President Richard Nixon proposed that Philadelphia would serve as the site of an "international exposition" during the Bicentennial, by 1972 his administration had neutralized the city's prominent role. Some sources suggested ominous reasons for the withdrawal of federal funding to the city. According to a 1972 article in *Time* magazine, the spectacle of "lower-middle-class whites [who] staged unpleasant demonstrations, protesting against the possible influx of black laborers and 'foreigners'" heightened Nixon's reluctance to have Philadelphia serve as an international symbol of the Bicentennial.[20] Likewise, the election of Mayor Frank Rizzo (1972–80), a former police commissioner who led raids on Philadelphia's Black Panther Party headquarters in 1970, and who enforced harsh penal laws against African American residents perceived as "disorderly," marked the further deterioration of an already strained relationship between the city's administration and its black population.[21] All this, together with the increasingly vociferous protests from Philadelphia's black leaders regarding the content of the Bicentennial celebration, cast Philadelphia's suitability as a site for national celebration into doubt.

Contesting the "Official" Bicentennial

As the Bicentennial drew near, many African American critics in Philadelphia publicly objected to the diminished expectations and watered-down programs planned for the event. Theopholis Fair, an African American assistant professor of history at La Salle University, argued that during the Bicentennial celebrations "America's economic and material achievements will be equated with a smugness that views the promise of the Declaration of Independence as being fulfilled."[22] Fair maintained that one way to counter this sanitized version of history would be to present an exhibit on black history that "demonstrate[d] the importance of the principles of the Declaration of Independence and the need for continuing national commitment to the fulfillment of these ideals."[23] In response, Philadelphia '76 approved a request from members of the African American community that proposed creating a permanent "black cultural center" that would open in 1976.[24]

The Black History Exhibit Nominating Committee began to hold meetings in late April and early May 1974 to determine who would oversee this project. Gerard P. William, executive assistant to Philadelphia '76 chair William Rafsky, wrote to the Honorable Judge Raymond Pace Alexander (a prominent African American judge in Philadelphia) laying out his recommendations for who might serve on the project's board. William, who was African American, argued that the Black History Exhibit Nominating Committee should recruit esteemed members of the black community, as well as "conscientious members of the White community," in order to plan and execute an exhibition that "truly reflects the accurate historical and phonominal [*sic*] role Blacks have played in the development of the City, State, and Nation." William thus believed that white allies could serve as an effective tactical strategy in securing the success of either an exhibit or a museum. Still, he argued that it was crucial that the black community have a strong voice with regard to the election of board members, because the board was charged with "enlisting the involvement and participation from the tremendous resources of existing Black history collections, artifacts, memorabilias, etc., from a variety of major institutions and/or existing organizations as well as major private collectors."[25] In other words, if Philadelphia's black community felt alienated from the board, they would not contribute such items to the new museum.

Discord between Philadelphia's Bicentennial planners and the local black community regarding the creation and control of either a black museum or an African American exhibit immediately surfaced. In a March 14, 1974, memorandum, historian Jerry Grundfest, the coordinator of Historical Programs for Philadelphia '76, recounted the conflicting opinions that had arisen during a meeting held by Clarence Farmer, who by that point was chair of the Commission on Human Relations as well as a member of Philadelphia '76. Farmer met with members of Philadelphia's black clergy, who wanted to know whether Philadelphia '76 would maintain control over the development of a black history project. The clergy members questioned whether the city "expect[ed] the [black] community to accept it. If so, they objected strenuously."[26] The clergy members' "strenuous objection" to the expectation that they should accept an exhibit or cultural center sponsored by the city encapsulates the conflict surrounding the city's Bicentennial plan as it related to African Americans: Philadelphia's black community wanted to control the presentation of their own history regardless of what entity funded the project.

Clergy members also expressed concern regarding the role that academics might play in creating a black history exhibit, for too much emphasis placed on academic training might "exclude Black historians who were not endowed with degrees." On the other hand, they recognized that academic involvement might make it easier to attract grant money for the project. Grundfest continued: "I noted that it would be difficult to satisfy everyone. This remark hit home immediately thereafter when two of the group got into heated controversy over whether the director of the exhibit should be a Philadelphia resident or not."[27]

The issue of who, specifically, should control the project also surfaced in Caroline Golab's March 15, 1974, letter to William Rafsky. Golab, who was white, served as coordinator of "Ethnic Events" for Philadelphia '76. She agreed that planning an African American museum, from its construction to its content, must be a "totally black run, black organized affair."[28] Here, Golab's support might suggest the extent to which the core doctrines of the Black Power Movement—that is, the necessity for black institutional control over their own cultural, political, and economic productions—had infiltrated the discursive arena of Philadelphia city politics. Yet Golab's advocacy of a museum controlled by Philadelphia's African American community did not necessarily stem from her belief in the tenets of black power—or, for that matter, the legitimacy of black agency. Rather, supporting the idea (if not the reality) of black control of the proposed museum meant that Philadelphia's black community would also assume sole responsibility for whether or not the project succeeded or failed, consequently relieving the city's Bicentennial committee of such responsibility. As she noted, "if there is never any exhibit for 1976 it will have to be because of the failure of the various black groups and organizations to 'get themselves together'; if they all really want a museum/exhibit, they'll all have to make some compromises and realize the limitations of time and money. . . . the blacks of Philadelphia must do this themselves; if the exhibit never materializes, it is thus their fault, not ours; if it is a success, it is their success, not ours."[29]

Golab maintained that there should be a multiplicity of voices involved in this project. She thought, however, that these diverse opinions would inevitably translate into conflict regarding the project's creation and substance, recognizing that "just because all the persons wanting a piece of the action for the black museum/exhibit are black, doesn't mean that they will necessarily agree on everything or anything for that matter." Golab proposed a presumably facetious solution to the supposedly simmering tensions between black organizations regarding the exhibit: "We just may have to lock them up and tell them to come up with some compromise, otherwise there may never be any black museum in 1976."[30]

Conflicting stories reported in Philadelphia's newspapers regarding details leaked from closed-door meetings reinforced the qualms of museum advocates regarding the city's intentions. An October 5, 1974, *Philadelphia Tribune* article quoted Paul Garabedian, coordinator for the Ethnic/Nationalities Programs of Philadelphia '76, as saying that city funding for a black museum was unlikely. Garabedian allegedly indicated that the city would withhold funds for a permanent black museum because "many Blacks in the community all want it in a different place. . . . In addition to the usual jealousy and bitterness you have with different groups of people, some Blacks won't have anything to do with the others. Some members of the 'Black Establishment,' for example, won't have anything to do with other Blacks. Furthermore, Blacks come from so many different parts of Africa that there is no real cohesion, which you need for a historical project of this sort."[31]

Garabedian's argument that "Blacks come from so many different parts of Africa that there is no real cohesion" between them was, of course, misleading. Most of Philadelphia's black museum advocates had been born into families who had been in the United States for generations and had resided in Philadelphia for many years. If Garabedian had instead referred to the difficulty of creating cohesive exhibits on black history because African Americans originated from many different parts of Africa, this "problem" clearly had not prevented other black museums from tackling this same issue. In alluding to a division between the "Black Establishment" and the amorphous congregation of "other Blacks," Garabedian constructed a class-based conflict between these two groups. While it was true that there was precedent for strife between predominantly middle-class blacks active in local political affairs and the broader African American community, Garabedian's portrayal of a community divided by such variances did not necessarily stem from his observance of actual dissonance, but rather from perceived or anticipated divisions.[32]

Shortly after this article appeared, Garabedian contended that he had never made such comments about discord within the black community. In a private letter to John Saunders, the president and editor of the *Philadelphia Tribune,*

Garabedian complained that reporter Len Lear's article represented a "gross misrepresentation" of their interview, being "provocative, inflammatory and a distortion of the fact, implying to the community that there is a division of thought and effort in the programs being planned by organizations in the black community."[33] Garabedian stressed that he involved minority groups in Bicentennial programming to "dispel any point of view that the celebration is being conceived, developed and implemented to the exclusion of minorities [sic] citizens." Garabedian also contacted Philadelphia '76 chair William Rafsky, repeating his assertion that this "libelous" article constituted a "vicious distortion of what was discussed," and that the reporter had withheld discussion of the "actual plans being made for Black participation in the Bicentennial." As proof, Garabedian pointed to a month-long Festival of Performing Arts intended to showcase the cultural contributions of African Americans. For instance, Anton Dvožák's *New World Symphony*, which featured "distinguished Black soloists of international fame," would be conducted by Everett Lee, an African American master violinist. The festival would also present the Alvin Ailey Dancers, the opera *Porgy and Bess*, as well as other performances featuring African Americans.[34]

Still, while these programs certainly involved black participation, it is questionable whether they would truly reflect a broad section of Philadelphia's black community. Anton Dvořák was a European composer inspired by traditional African American spirituals; George Gershwin's groundbreaking opera *Porgy and Bess* drew heavily from African American jazz and blues traditions. With the exception of Everett Lee's presence and the Alvin Ailey Dancers, the African American–themed programming primarily featured the works of white artists known for their liberal "borrowing" and reinterpretation of musical forms pioneered by African Americans.

Caroline Golab, reporter Len Lear, and Paul Garabedian all expressed varied and conflicting views concerning the extent of division within Philadelphia's black community and its leadership. Regardless of the veracity of Lear's interview with Garabedian, or Golab's "joking" observation about "locking" black leaders in a room until they agreed upon a unified Bicentennial program, both the real and the imagined dissension within and between Philadelphia's black community and the city's leaders reveals a deep anxiety about the strength of Philadelphia's supposed commitment to including black history and black people in the Bicentennial. A March 1974 memo written by Philadelphia '76 official Jerry Grundfest validated the skepticism of the black community, admitting "I think that the First Continental Congress program is very weak in the area of Black and ethnic events. . . . I think it would be a mistake to release the program to the press and public without defining some kind of Black participation."[35] Robert A. Donner, an employee of the Philadelphia Department of Recreation, realistically observed that black participation in the Bicentennial would only occur "when programming and participation have their root sources in the community itself."[36]

A Black Museum as a "Public Relations Ploy"

Confronted by a celebration with no obvious roots or strong support within Philadelphia's black community, African Americans thus had no reason to back the city's Bicentennial plans, and every reason to levy resistance to such programs, or even a museum proposed on their behalf.

Lawrence Dunbar Reddick, an African American professor and historian at Temple University who served as cochair of the Afro-American Historical '76 Bicentennial Corporation of Philadelphia, was one of the fiercest critics of the city's limited Bicentennial vision.[37] Reddick's comments in his unpublished and privately circulated 1974 essay, "Will the Bicentennial Celebration Be an Accurate Picture of American Life and History and Be Fair to All of the American People?" caustically question the city's commitment to building an African American museum and delineate why blacks had to exert greater control over Bicentennial programming. First, he claimed that the city purposefully excluded black history from the Bicentennial celebrations:

> How did it happen that the plans for the Bicentennial celebration at Philadelphia result in virtual exclusion of Blacks from active participation and a distortion of the role of the Black people in the building of "American civilization?" Was it because the Bicentennial staff that has had the responsibility for generating and implementing the plans just did not have the competence to deal with the Black Experience? Or if the staff was sufficiently competent, was its action part of a deliberate design to come up with a celebration that would severely restrict and obscure the achievements of Black people?[38]

Reddick also argued that Philadelphia '76, in considering the acceptance or rejection of projects submitted by black organizations, employed unreasonably arbitrary criteria rooted in (willful) ignorance about black history and achievement. Furthermore, they offered only weak concessions in light of their ongoing rejections of black-sponsored programs. For example, in 1974 an African

American group called The National Technical Association proposed a Bicentennial program that highlighted black contributions to science and technology.
The association's proposal, however, met with considerable skepticism from
Philadelphia '76 officials. An official wrote, "one would have to demonstrate
conclusively that there is in fact sufficient material on important Black scientists
to make the expense and effort worthwhile. . . . I am, however, not discounting
the possibility that Black contributions are such a well-kept secret that existing
historians are simply not aware of them. But if they are not, who is?" A University of Delaware professor concurred, maintaining that, while Philadelphia
scientist and mathematician Benjamin Banneker was worthy of recognition,
"beyond that [he] sees no way that a worthwhile exhibition and conference
series could be mounted on Black history of science."[39] Presented with these
"facts," Philadelphia '76 rejected the National Technical Association's proposal.

What Reddick found most disturbing was the fact that nonblack organizations, both commercial and nonprofit, proposed that they too should portray
scenes and narratives from African American history during the Bicentennial.
Reddick believed that the participation of these groups in creating programs
and exhibits related to black history diminished the efforts of African American organizations to present—and thereby control—their own projects. Furthermore, such programs would likely reduce funding opportunities for black
associations. Reddick also feared that nonblack groups would inevitably revert
to stereotypes in their depiction of African American history. One suggested
plan, explained Reddick, "proposes to show 200 years of Black history, but
what assurance would the Black community have that such a money-making
oriented concern would not have a parade of cotton-picking scenes, Uncle
Toms and Black faced comedians?"[40]

In fact, Reddick labeled those African Americans who agreed to work with
mainstream Bicentennial organizations as "Uncle Toms," contending that making such concessions to the white establishment had historically resulted in the
severely compromised position of African Americans. As evidence, he recalled
the story of a black minister in the 1870s who called for greater African American participation in Philadelphia's Centennial celebration—yet officials only
included those blacks who sang approved spirituals and performed "coon
dances." The situation in 1976, argued Reddick, had changed very little.[41] The
city simply decided as a "public relations ploy" to create a black museum, "if
the Black community would thus be satisfied. A trusted friend of the Bicentennial authority, who had made a career of satisfying the white establishment and

pacifying the Black masses, put out the word and sent it down the line that the Black community had better grab the Black museum while it had a chance to do so or it would get nothing of substance."[42] This ultimately condescending gesture, concluded Reddick, constituted a meaningless and antiquated "bone" thrown to the masses.[43]

In order to rectify and expand the narrow scope of the Bicentennial celebrations, Reddick proposed several action steps that city leaders had to follow. First, Philadelphia '76 should include additional African American representatives preapproved by the black community.[44] Second, Philadelphia '76 should allow a "selected group of citizens of the Black community and consultants of their choice" to examine Bicentennial proposals and determine "if they meet the test of presenting a true and balanced picture of life and history and will inflict no injury or humiliation on any group." If these steps failed, African Americans must take their case to the state and federal levels and notify philanthropic agencies responsible for funding Bicentennial projects. These agencies should be asked if they were "aware of the misuse and abuses to which their funds may be exposed."[45]

If official Bicentennial plans continued to exclude the full participation of the black community, Reddick warned that African Americans would—and, indeed, must—publicize their cause through a variety of highly visual protest methods. Boycotts, the disruption of lectures, and even the "destruction of exhibitions and other forms of violence" all constituted valid forms of protest against the city's Bicentennial committees. Reddick's avocation of these forms of protest, from nonviolent civil disobedience to more radical "guerrilla" techniques, clearly drew from the tradition of African American public protest honed during the Civil Rights and Black Power Movements. A counterpoint to this uncompromising call for protest, however, came from Vera Gunn Harden, the director of Philadelphia's Heritage House, a predecessor of the AAMP that had opened in 1949 and presented African American art and culture to the public. While Gunn-Harden agreed that Philadelphia '76 was dragging its heels regarding the extent and the manner in which the black community must be represented during the Bicentennial, she also asserted that the Afro-American Historical '76 Bicentennial Corporation had failed to exert effective pressure upon city planners, despite Reddick's efforts as chair of this committee. Gunn-Harden contended that "when it comes to getting funds from the Bicentennial to do a job for the black community . . . we hear the same old story, that there aren't any funds. . . . It seemed as though the group was afraid to express their opinion to [Philadelphia '76 chair] Mr. Rafsky."[46]

The amount of funding Philadelphia '76 granted to white ethnic organizations for Bicentennial projects also came under fire by Reddick. Declaring it "fine" that many of the proposed projects depicted the "part played in American History of the Jewish, Italian, [and] Irish people," nevertheless he argued that only three projects addressed the "Black Experience." Although the African American community had endorsed these particular projects, they received, according to Reddick, a minimal amount of funding compared with the other "ethnically" themed programs.[47]

Leaders of Philadelphia's white ethnic groups complicated Reddick's citation of the disproportionate amount of funding that their groups received for the Bicentennial, however. For example, the president of Philadelphia's Ethnic Heritage Affairs Institute, Dr. Jaipaul, charged that Philadelphia '76 offered only token gestures to include ethnic programming in the Bicentennial events. When Mayor Rizzo's administrative assistant, Roberta White, reassured Jaipaul in June 1973 that the Bicentennial programs were "being designed to involve communities and participation at the local level," Jaipaul refused to be placated.[48] In a letter to Mayor Rizzo, he contended that the lack of "indigenous ethnic representation" in the Bicentennial caused him "great concern," and that leadership of Philadelphia '76 must be more inclusive. Jaipaul reminded Rizzo that "it is our bicentennial and must be hosted by us. . . . We urge you, therefore, to carefully consider the appointment of several ethnic representatives to the Board of the Philadelphia '76 Incorporated."[49] Likewise, in an October 1973 letter to Philadelphia '76 chair William Rafsky, Jaipaul confessed his doubt regarding the city's intentions: "We are not sure about the priority of [Philadelphia '76] in ethnic programming as part of the bicentennial celebration. It is evident from the fact that [the] Ethnic and Nationality Coordinator is probably the last one to be hired. Second, the response to our earlier correspondence as to having some representatives of ethnic interests on your Board has been cool."[50]

Some city administrators recognized that Jaipaul's displeasure with Philadelphia '76 might have political implications beyond the Bicentennial. For instance, a December 10, 1974, *Philadelphia Tribune* article reported that a Bicentennial executive named Albert Gaudiosi had warned Mayor Rizzo about the growing discontent of white ethnic groups regarding the city's proposal to fund a black history museum. He pointed out that, since it was an election year, a black history museum "would offend [Mayor Rizzo's] most zealous followers."[51]

Gaudiosi's ominous suggestion that Rizzo's base—largely white, working-class, traditionally Democratic voters—would not reelect the mayor if he provided funding for an African American museum reflects the sweeping political changes that were taking place in Philadelphia during the 1970s. As the Great Society agenda of the 1960s clashed with the realities of white flight, racial unrest, and mainstream alienation from the counterculture, white working-class families who traditionally voted Democrat began an unprecedented realignment toward political conservatism—a shift ultimately responsible for Ronald Reagan's election in 1980.[52] Mayor Rizzo subsequently heeded Gaudiosi's warning, allegedly informing Clarence Farmer to let the Afro-American Historical '76 Bicentennial Corporation know that funding for the black history museum "had been killed"—on Rizzo's orders. Furthermore, instead of building a new African American history museum, $8.5 million would go toward the construction of a "Living History Museum" that would "deal with American history without reference to any specific ethnic group."[53]

The following day, a *Philadelphia Inquirer* article ran as a counterpoint to Lear's piece. The article's title attests to the defensive stance taken by city leaders regarding the rumors that the African American museum project had been scrapped: "Black History Museum Planned, Rafsky Insists."[54] Rafsky reassured Philadelphia's African American leaders that the city would construct a permanent black history museum, though it would likely not be built by 1976 due to a lack of funding. To make up for the delay in constructing a permanent museum, Rafsky noted, the city would sponsor a temporary African American history exhibit during the Bicentennial.

In response to the news about the delayed construction of a permanent museum and the rumored withdrawal of city funding, the Afro-American Historical '76 Bicentennial Corporation's board of directors sent a protest delegation to Mayor Rizzo and the Philadelphia City Council. The AHCC stated that the city's commitment to funding a temporary black history exhibit without any concrete guarantee of funding for a permanent museum represented a merely temporary appeasement—a public relations bandage to be applied during the Bicentennial and removed once the public displays of city pride and patriotism had reached their approved conclusion. If other white ethnic groups received funding to construct museums and run their own programs, the city's refusal to fund a black museum seemed indicative of the city's true feelings toward its African American citizens. As one unnamed source charged: "There's no doubt that this monstrous decision was made by the Mayor on a purely racist basis. . . . This is a disgrace and an insult to all black Philadelphians, and it shows once and for all what Rizzo really thinks of us."[55]

Some city leaders, responding to deeply embedded associations of African American protest with physical violence (beliefs reinforced by the lingering tensions of the past decade's unrest), speculated that racial strife within the city would dramatically increase if the museum plans disintegrated. Philadelphia City Council president George X. Schwartz, who had originally opposed the construction of a permanent black museum, advised Philadelphia Bicentennial planners on December 12, 1974, that a black history museum should be immediately constructed, "or they may face a racially divided city in 1976." Schwartz's announcement came just a few days after William Rafsky told the Afro-American Historical '76 Bicentennial Corporation of the lack of municipal funds for a museum. Schwartz believed that excluding African Americans from the Bicentennial would not only bring embarrassment to the city in its most important hour but might also incite violence. Schwartz, who was white, further explained his newfound support for a permanent African American museum by referencing the fact that "one third or better of the city is black." Given their strength in numbers, "I think this [building a black museum] is important in order to make the Bicentennial successful and to allay many fears and many suspicions. People have said to me: If you go for a Mummers Museum, why can't you go for an Afro-American History Museum? I think such comments are well-taken, well-founded."[56]

In mid-December 1974, Mayor Rizzo abruptly pledged "solid support" for a permanent African American museum in order to avert the threat of a public relations debacle for Philadelphia '76—and by extension, the city of Philadelphia. In January 1975, the Philadelphia City Planning Commission approved $2.5 million for the construction of a black history museum. The vote passed 4–2, with one abstention.[57] Other Bicentennial proposals submitted by African American groups in Philadelphia also began to receive additional funding. In October 1975, Philadelphia '76 approved a $5,000 grant for the Kulue Melee Afro-American Dance Ensemble, which proposed a presentation of Afro-American folk dances.[58] Likewise, Philadelphia '76 endorsed a $5,000 grant for the Philadelphia Dance Company, an African American dance organization that planned to offer a "choreographed presentation of the history of the past 200 years of black American dance."[59] The Ile-Ife Black Humanitarian Center also received $10,000 to support a mobile, interactive exhibit on West African and Caribbean cultures. Following the example set by museums such as the Anacostia

Neighborhood Museum and Detroit's International Afro-American Museum, each of which initiated their own mobile exhibit vans, the Ile-Ife exhibit would be a "museum on wheels" that would reach "persons not familiar with the Afro-American experience. Built on a rented trailer, the museum is scheduled for eight, one-week sojourns in park areas in each section of the city. In this fashion, all ethnic groups can be reached."[60]

Rizzo's eventual willingness to construct a permanent black museum illustrates how the Afro-American Historical '76 Bicentennial Corporation, Lawrence Reddick, and other African American leaders successfully employed activist techniques to resist the city's exclusion (or token inclusion) of black organizations and projects during the Bicentennial. Their persistence aggravated some city officials, who opposed the construction of a black museum not only because of its likely multimillion-dollar price tag, but also because they felt that giving in to the relentless public pressure from African American community leaders constituted a sign of (white) weakness. Indeed, Philadelphia city commissioner John M. Elliot maintained that building an African American museum represented a case of political pandering to powerful black activists.[61] Instead of a constructing a black history museum, Elliot suggested that a black history exhibit would suffice, and that it should "be part of a single museum that would detail the contributions of all of the city's ethnic and racial groups."[62]

Elliot's charge that the city's Bicentennial groups had capitulated to black activist leaders, and his proposed solution to build a museum that would include the contributions of "all of the city's ethnic and racial groups," clashed with the views of the Afro-American Historical '76 Bicentennial Corporation, which believed that an integrative museum would instead function as exclusionary. On its most fundamental level, Elliot's proposal would remove control from Philadelphia's black community, for such a museum would likely lump all "ethnic and racial groups" together, gloss over the problematic nature of their interrelationships, and give African American history short shrift in the process. A museum devoted solely to African American history, on the other hand, ideally, would allow for an in-depth examination and interpretation of the African American presence in Philadelphia and in the nation as a whole.

Location, Location, Location: The Battle to (Re)Claim Society Hill

Following Mayor Rizzo's go-ahead to create an African American museum, an unexpectedly charged debate ensued about where to build it. Many African

American museum advocates recognized that the physical location of a museum would likely affect its reception by audiences and subsequent visitation rates. For example, although the Smithsonian Institution initially considered several sites for the Anacostia Neighborhood Museum, its original location in a highly visible storefront on Nichols Avenue remained physically accessible for most of Anacostia's African American residents. The building's prior history as the former Carver Movie Theater—one of the only theaters to allow African Americans entrance during the period of Jim Crow—further communicated a sense of familiarity and welcome to black audiences. More than its accessibility, however, the Anacostia Neighborhood Museum's unassuming facade stood in direct contrast to the monumental assertions of grandeur found on the National Mall. Such vernacular familiarity may have reassured those visitors who felt alienated by the Mall's neoclassicism. When the ANM opened a new, larger building at 1901 Fort Place in 1985, its parklike setting, removed from the bustle of the street, lent it an appearance somewhat remote from the daily activities of the neighborhood. Still, the museum remained located within Anacostia and accessible to most residents by bus.

The original locations of many other African American museums that began during this period also connected physically with their intended audiences. For example, the first site of the Studio Museum in Harlem, founded in 1968 at Fifth Avenue and 125th Street, as well as its second location at 144 West 125th Street, remained inside Harlem—admittedly to the dismay of some of the museum's board members, who wished to move closer to the Metropolitan Museum of Art.[63] Likewise, both manifestations of the DuSable Museum, and also the first site of Detroit's International Afro-American Museum, were ideally situated in communities primarily composed of black residences and businesses.

Yet advocates for the African American Museum of Philadelphia faced stiff opposition from residents at the preferred museum site, which was located in a neighborhood known as Society Hill. The contentious public and private discourse advanced by certain members of the Society Hill Civic Association (SHCA), as well as other neighborhood organizations opposed to the construction of an African American museum, such as the Washington Square East Project and the bluntly named "Neighborhood Organized to Help Ensure a Residential Environment," or NOT-HERE, suggests that for some white residents, the presence of a museum designated as African American constituted a serious concern that must be vigorously addressed in both private and public

Anacostia Neighborhood Museum director John Kinard (*second from right*) breaks ground for a new museum in 1985 as Anacostia Museum staff members look on, among them museum historian Louise Daniel Hutchinson (*first from left*) and Smithsonian Institution Secretary Robert McCormick Adams (*first from right*). Kinard increasingly clashed with the Smithsonian throughout the 1970s and 1980s over the administration's perceived neglect of the ANM. Courtesy of the Smithsonian Institution Archives. Image no. 95-1212.

arenas. Indeed, resistance to the construction of the African American Museum of Philadelphia within Society Hill grew so heated that black museum advocates were forced to consider alternative, less desirable sites.

The Afro-American Historical '76 Bicentennial Corporation hired an African American architect, Theodore V. Cam, to create an architectural study for a permanent black history museum in Philadelphia. The study, published in 1974 when the museum had yet to be approved by the city, presented a preliminary report on the potential locations and content for a black history exhibit or museum. Cam's report also included essays authored by several of Philadelphia's African American leaders, who outlined their philosophies concerning participation in Philadelphia's Bicentennial.

Multiple criteria had to be met during the site selection process, such as available building space, cost, and pedestrian and public transit access. Cam also argued that the physical character of the neighborhood surrounding the museum, together with the presence and work of neighborhood organizations, would exert a distinct impact on the museum's efficacy. In a gesture that demonstrated their intention to reach more than just the immediate black community,

Society Hill Zoning Hearing, February 20, 1975. Concerned residents of Society Hill gather in City Hall to protest the construction of the African American Museum of Philadelphia. Members of the Society Hill Civic Association argued that the proposed museum violated neighborhood zoning laws, but many museum advocates argued that racism underlay this opposition. Photograph by Robert L. Mooney. Courtesy of the *Philadelphia Inquirer* and the Special Collections Research Center, Temple University Libraries, Philadelphia, Pa.

planners maintained that the black history museum should be accessible to "rich and poor, black and white alike." As such, the area around the site should possess "an income and racial mix so that people of various income groups and racial backgrounds would feel comfortable approaching the museum. In other words, the area should not be solely poor, middle class, or wealthy, nor should it be a ghetto, white or black." Markers of a stable neighborhood included the presence of active civic and business organizations that could "complement and aid" the museum, as well as attractive physical characteristics, such as street width, vegetation, housing conditions, and the availability of parks and play-grounds.[64] The site's historical relevance for Philadelphia's black community was also an important, if less easily quantifiable, factor.

In compliance with these conditions, museum planners identified six poten-tial museum sites. The first, the Ile-Ife Museum, was located on 7th and Dau-phin Streets (Site A). However, planners soon deemed the Ile-Ife Museum too small for museum programs, and deteriorating buildings around the site also made the area aesthetically unsuitable. Site B, Heritage House, was located on Broad and Master Streets. Cam concluded that, although Heritage House had historical qualities (and, in fact, currently housed a collection of African American art and artifacts), the site had "no historical relationship to Black history." Furthermore, "buildings to the west [of the site] are not being maintained and are deteriorating."[65] The former First National Bank, located on 15th and Walnut Streets, was identified as Site C. The Curtis Building, located on 6th and Walnut Streets, represented Side D. Site E consisted of a plot of land on the northeast corner of 6th and Pine Streets—a neighborhood known as "Society Hill." Unlike the other sites, no building existed on Site E. Thus, a museum would have to be built from scratch. Finally, the Ridgway Library on Broad and Christian Streets constituted Site F.

Out of all the sites, Cam concluded that Society Hill (Site E) appeared most suitable because of its location adjacent to Mother Bethel AME Church, which had drawn Philadelphia's African American worshippers since 1794, when Richard Allen, Absalom Jones, and William White created it in response to blatant discrimination within the main Episcopal Church. Furthermore, historically African Americans had lived in the neighborhood surrounding Mother Bethel.[66] By the 1970s, however, Society Hill and other residential segments of downtown Philadelphia had undergone a radical transformation. During the late 1940s and early 1950s, city officials began to implement sweeping urban redevelopment campaigns in areas formerly dominated by apartments and rental housing. These urban renewal projects partially stemmed from concerns revealed by data from the 1950 federal census, which indicated that 10 to 30 percent of Society Hill residences had no private bathrooms; 6 to 10 percent of homes had no running water. By 1960, owners occupied fewer than 40 percent of the buildings.[67] By demolishing older multifamily structures, or offering incentives to wealthier residents to convert and remodel them, Philadelphia city planners hoped to attract new residents—and revitalized businesses—to downtown. The urban redevelopment campaign was quite successful: between 1964 and 1967, most of Society Hill's properties had been sold and its population increased from 4,478 to 4,841.

These numbers are deceptive, however, for Society Hill's black population fell by 55 percent, while the white population increased 67 percent during this same period.[68] From 1950 to 1980, the nonwhite population of Philadelphia's entire "Center City" area, which included Society Hill, declined from 23 percent to 6 percent.[69] Unable to pay the higher rents once the buildings were demolished and rebuilt, or remodeled, six thousand residents lost their homes. Indeed, the urban redevelopment plans initially proposed to solve the city's housing crisis left black Philadelphians with few options, for "all but 1,022 of the 150,000 new housing units built in postwar Philadelphia were marketed on a whites-only basis."[70] These statistics suggest how the redevelopment of Society Hill and other increasingly prosperous (and formerly minority-dominated) neighborhoods, such as Rittenhouse Square, prompted an exodus of African American families to the more distant, poorer neighborhoods of the city. Historian Carolyn Adams maintains that this black exodus was very much intentionally planned by Philadelphia's redevelopment leaders, who engaged in a rapid urban renewal campaign in an effort to check the typical "white flight" pattern from downtown to the suburbs.[71]

Some of Society Hill's African American residents took action against their probable displacement. In 1972, seven residents of Octavia Hill, a division of Society Hill located on the 600 block of Lombard Street, could no longer afford to pay rising rents and engaged in a letter-writing campaign appealing to Society Hill residents for financial assistance. The Society Hill Civic Association, a predominantly white homeowners association incorporated in 1967 and engaged with concerns such as the construction of Interstate 95 and the explosive commercial development in the neighborhood, created a committee to help these particular residents remain in the neighborhood.[72] The SHCA's willingness to assist a few low-income residents avoid displacement indicates that the group understood that the process of urban renewal inherently disadvantaged those who had lived in Society Hill long before it became a magnet for upper-middle-class whites. Their gesture also introduces an added complexity to the contentious fight that would unfold between the SHCA and supporters of the African American Museum of Philadelphia, in that portraying the SHCA's opposition to the construction of an African American museum as evidence of the inherently racist leanings of the entire SHCA obviously presents only a shallow understanding of the organization. On the other hand, allowing a few minority residents to remain in their homes likely was a much easier decision for most of the SHCA's members to support, in contrast to encouraging an "influx" of black audiences to a large, nonresidential building designated for and by African Americans.

Interestingly, the choice of Society Hill as a location for an African American museum was by no means unanimous even among African American leaders. Society Hill's conversion into a middle-to-upper-middle-class white neighborhood, coupled with its increased disassociation from Philadelphia's African American heritage, created doubt as to whether the neighborhood was appropriate for the museum. For instance, Philadelphia City councilwoman Dr. Ethel Allen, who was African American, argued that the black history museum should be built in North Philadelphia, in order to restore "community pride to black residents and tourist dollars to black businessmen." Allen also hinted at a worrying disconnect between museum supporters and the black community as a whole. While Society Hill might hold historic roots for the black community, Allen believed that these roots had been altered beyond recognition. Furthermore, "in some circles, the whole thing of a Black Museum is visualized as a gesture of tokenism. . . . There is no evidence at 6th and Pine of what black people have done in this town [for] over 200 years."[73]

Henri Lefebvre argues that space may be conceived of as not only the literal, physical place in which a building takes root but also the metaphorical space that it creates. In other words, the concept of "space" is not neutral or devoid of meaning.[74] More than just conglomerations of bricks and mortar, houses, and roads, places like Society Hill and the African American Museum of Philadelphia encompass "social, material, and ideological dimensions, as individuals develop ties to kin and community, own or rent land, and participate in public life as residents of a particular community."[75] Philadelphia's black museum advocates remained attached to their particular vision of Society Hill as a historic home for African Americans, while white residents of Society's Hill, removed from this history, held a distinctly different image of their neighborhood. Many white residents viewed the neighborhood's potential "transformation" as a personal loss, while African Americans believed that locating a black museum there would represent a defiant reclamation of Society Hill's African American heritage.

As supporters of the Society Hill museum site persisted in their efforts, those members of the SHCA who feared a reversal of progress if an African American museum took shape in their neighborhood readied themselves for battle.

A Fight for the Neighborhood

The SHCA and other like-minded neighborhood organizations, such as NOT-HERE, waged their campaign against the construction of an African American museum through petitions, private letters, and public missives sent to newspapers, city leaders, and Bicentennial committees. Although the SHCA did not object "to the concept of a Black History Museum or to the construction of a

well-conceived and properly serviced museum facility on an appropriate site"—
an assertion the organization repeated, in varying forms, throughout their crusade
against the museum—nevertheless the association strongly opposed "the absence
of any neighborhood involvement in the planning and design of the facility."[76]
One NOT-HERE member argued that Society Hill residents "just don't feel that
a popular history museum would be appropriate for the area, especially one that
would draw the thousands of daily visitors projected."[77] Black museum supporters duly observed, however, the lack of complaints about the crowds who lined
up to tour Independence Hall, just two blocks away. Gerard William, project
manager for the African American museum, argued that SHCA members would
be "against it [the black museum] even if it were the size of a matchbox."[78]

The SHCA's public objections to the creation of an African American
museum in Society Hill revolved around the ways in which the proposed
museum would detract from the residential qualities of the neighborhood. In a
1975 letter to Philadelphia '76 chair William Rafsky, John Francis Smith III,
president of the thousand-member SHCA, enclosed two resolutions recently
adopted by both the SHCA and the Washington Square East Project area committee. By a vote of 136 in favor to 7 opposed, the first resolution concluded
that the plans to build the African American museum in Society Hill had been
prepared without soliciting the input of neighborhood residents. Furthermore,
the proposed museum would violate zoning ordinances, attract thousands of
daily visitors, create traffic and parking problems, and "would generally dero-
gate from the residential character of the neighborhood."[79] Since the museum
was zoned as a business, rather than a residence, its proposed physical scale
appeared to exceed the neighborhood's zoning requirements. Smith complained
in a letter to Philadelphia City Council president George X. Schwartz that the
museum's scale fell completely out of proportion with the rest of the buildings
in the area, "excepting only Mother Bethel AME Church itself."[80] The SHCA
also believed that museum advocates had deliberately railroaded their proposal
through city committees without properly consulting Society Hill residents.
Smith reiterated this last point to Schwartz, contending that the museum proposal had been presented "only last Thursday," leaving no time for SHCA
members to review the document.[81]

In light of these serious oversights, the SHCA demanded the total redesign-
ing of the museum, this time with the full involvement of neighborhood representatives. An SHCA petition to Philadelphia '76 listed the multiple changes
that must be made in order for the museum to be built on the 6th and Pine site.

The primary physical change called for reducing the museum's floor space and square footage "to approximately ½ of the scale of the presently proposed 50 feet high, 30,000 square feet which would cover virtually the entire site."[82] Another concession included the creation of additional parking space in order to meet Philadelphia '76's projected figure of 10,000 museum visitors per day during the Bicentennial. As the SHCA president pointed out, "the present provision for parking is a nearby lot . . . which will only accommodate some 20–30 cars. Together with bus traffic, the possibility of severe congestion is apparent."[83] According to the SHCA, the museum also needed additional buses in order to transport these thousands of visitors to and from the museum.[84]

The SHCA's petition also insisted that Society Hill residents be allowed input regarding an "agreed schedule of hours which cannot be changed without neighborhood approval."[85] The number of museum visitors must be regulated, in order "to discourage waiting lines outside of the facility, and crowding and confusion among visitors about access to the facility." Throughout the museum's construction and daily operation, the petition argued, neighborhood representatives must be allowed to serve on the museum's board, and exercise "absolute veto power over changes in hours, number of visitors and other than museum uses of the facility."[86] As the petition continued, concerns regarding the physical characteristics of the proposed building at 6th and Pine Streets blended with deep apprehension about the primary audience for such a building. Would hordes of daily visitors linger in the public space outside of the museum? What impact might crowds of nonresidents have on the peaceful residential character of Society Hill? Since the museum had not yet agreed on an operating schedule, throngs of visitors arriving at all hours promised, at the very least, confusion—and perhaps a frightening disorder. Although prosperous whites might have reclaimed and gentrified Society Hill's public spaces, now those spaces were threatened with being taken over by, presumably, African American audiences.

A January 30, 1975, letter from Eugene Newman, head of the Addison Court Residents Association, to SHCA president John Smith reinforced this fear regarding not only the scale of the proposed museum but also those whom the building might attract. Newman carefully stated that the construction of a museum "depicting the history and progress of a minority group" was not in itself unacceptable. Indeed, his group "strongly promote[d] and endorse[d]" such a facility. However, Newman confided that "the negative impact to our residential neighborhood that would accompany such a museum (or any other non-residential building for that matter) gives us ample and justifiable concern." Like the SHCA's public petition, Newman's main concerns focused on land use, parking, traffic, and other annoyances, such as litter. He expressed a specific objection to the potential presence of sidewalk vendors, for they might compromise the "safety and protection" of neighborhood residents: "commercial enterprises bring with them undesirable elements and conditions that would affect our property, personal safety and the welfare of our children."[87]

For the most part, the city's responses to the petition rebuffed each of the logistical concerns about the museum. For example, Augustine A. Salvitti, executive director of the Redevelopment Authority of the City of Philadelphia, explained in a letter to SHCA president John Smith that the museum appeared to be "rushed" because Philadelphia '76 had only just received the plans for the building, and Theodore Cam's architectural design had only recently been reviewed—hence the lack of notice given to SHCA members. Salvitti further argued that the city did not intend to bypass community input; rather, "it is certainly our intention to continue to seek the fullest possible community involvement in all discussions of this project, especially the coming Design Board review of more detailed drawings."

While Salvitti was reassuring on this note, he countered the SHCA's insistence that the proposed scale of the museum violated the neighborhood's residential character, maintaining that the proposal was compliant with the city's Urban Renewal Plan. Concerns about the museum's height were unfounded, since "the three levels proposed are quite close to the height of the adjacent structure [Mother Bethel AME Church]. The coverage requirements of the Urban Renewal Plan permit building coverage of up to 75%, and this requirement will be easily satisfied by this proposal." Finally, although Philadelphia's Urban Renewal Plan did not mandate that the museum create a certain number of parking spaces, Philadelphia '76 indicated that it would discuss the possibility of using Mother Bethel AME Church's parking lot in order to alleviate possible traffic congestion.[88] Interestingly, the results of a February 1975 traffic analysis report concluded that objections to the museum based on concerns regarding traffic congestion were unnecessary; indeed, "our analysis of traffic patterns indicates excess traffic movement capacity in light of expected street pattern changes [during the Bicentennial celebrations]. This proposed development will do little to tax that excess capacity."[89]

Museum advocates thus surmised that there was another, more insidious basis for the continuing public opposition to the museum even after the logistical rebuttals offered by the city: namely, the unwillingness of many Society Hill residents to share the same space with those who might visit and work at an African American museum. At a public meeting attended by a hundred and fifty people in February 1975, African American historian Dr. Charles Wesley raised such a charge, and speculated that "the (Society Hill) protest is being raised mainly because we're black." Upon hearing this, the audience reportedly offered "groans and boos" in response. After being warned by the Zoning Board chair that "inferences or testimony as to racial or ethnic origin are not relevant," Wesley withdrew his accusation.[90] Yet while some audience members may have angrily dismissed Wesley's reasoning, Mayor Frank Rizzo bluntly confirmed in a March 1975 *Philadelphia Inquirer* article that "Many are opposed to it because it involves blacks. . . ."[91]

Accusations of racism aside, the faulty communication structure within and between Philadelphia's Bicentennial committees clearly contributed to the general disorder surrounding the museum's construction. Perry Triplett, an African American board member for the Philadelphia Bicentennial Corporation, agreed that the plans for the museum in Society Hill had been mismanaged from the very beginning, and by multiple organizations. According to Triplett, "this extreme haste and very poor planning" inevitably encouraged black museum advocates to insert racism into the debate: "racial overtones have been loosed by too many people who either don't understand zoning, construction, design, particularly of a museum which is a highly specialized building, which is most unfortunate."[92]

On the surface, the objections presented by Society Hill neighborhood organizations against the museum's construction—traffic congestion, zoning violations—appear to have been reasonable; to insert racism as the primary component of their efforts to block the construction of an African American museum seems overreaching. SHCA members were, on the whole, civic-minded residents with a growing interest in protecting the historic spaces of Society Hill from extensive commercial development. Indeed, in later years, the SHCA and the Washington Square East Project Committee continued their fight against the construction or expansion of certain area businesses at the expense of the neighborhood's historic and aesthetic character.[93]

Yet while Society Hill's redevelopment and subsequent gentrification led to the rehabilitation of deteriorating historic housing and the preservation of green space, it clearly left lower-income residents without the ability to pay the higher rents and property taxes that gentrification typically entails. The petition levied by residents of Octavia Hill in 1972 to remain in Society Hill speaks to the threat of displacement along class and racial lines that gentrification engendered; the positive response from SHCA members to Octavia Hill's request revealed their awareness of this issue. Nevertheless, as the Bicentennial approached, Society Hill neighborhood organizations continued to pursue a narrowly defined vision of how their neighborhood should look, and whom it should attract. Despite their vigorous denials, museum advocates detected and publicly decried the undercurrent of racism they felt underlay Society Hill's protests against the proposed museum—an undercurrent historically reinforced by their knowledge and experience of the "ruthless" methods with which Philadelphia officials had implemented the city's urban redevelopment program, and the resultant displacement of thousands of African Americans from their homes and neighborhoods.

Concessions and Compromise

As negotiations between the Afro-American Historical '76 Bicentennial Corporation, Philadelphia '76, and the Society Hill Civic Association continued into March 1975, the SHCA finally agreed that a museum could be built in their neighborhood. Museum supporters must make, however, certain concessions—namely, accept a fifteen-point resolution regarding the building's construction.[94] Resolutions of particular interest included:

J: There shall be an established schedule of museum hours of operation during daylight hours only acceptable to the neighborhood and which cannot be altered without neighborhood approval.

K: There shall be a limit, acceptable to the neighborhood, on the number of tour, charter group or other institutional visitors permitted to visit the museum on any one day.

L: There shall be no food sales permitted in the museum. . . .

M: The museum floor space shall be completely devoted to exhibit and archive space, provided however that there shall be a limited percentage of the total floor space acceptable to the neighborhood that shall be permitted to be used for the sale of museum shop items.[95]

That Society Hill neighborhood organizations must approve the square footage of the gift shop; that the museum must place an "acceptable" limit on the number of visitors each day; that the museum must only operate during daylight hours and at hours acceptable to the neighborhood—restrictions not in place at other prominent museums in Philadelphia—all constituted an effective removal of institutional control. Point M is particularly revealing, in that the neighborhood would dictate what function interior rooms, which were not visible to passers-by, must fulfill. Point L also encompassed the prohibition of sidewalk vendors—another potential, visible intrusion upon the desired character of the neighborhood. The numerous allowances demanded by the SHCA seemed to further insinuate that this debate had gone beyond practical concerns and instead revolved around the intertwined issues of race and power.[96]

Black museum advocates and Philadelphia '76 initially agreed to reduce the museum's square footage from 29,000 to 25,000 square feet in order to meet Society Hill's zoning regulations. Additional, agreed-to concessions included greater community representation on the museum board, regulation of museum hours, and the inclusion of architectural elements that would better blend in with the neighborhood. The SHCA, however, argued that these steps were not enough, and that the museum must stand as a one-story structure.[97] Yet if the museum were to meet this requirement, as architect Theodore Cam explained, the building would have to be downsized to "approximately 2/3 of the present floor space . . . necessitating a completely new program (space) formulation and building concept. The delay that this would cause in the development of the project would ensure that the Museum would not be completed in time for the Bicentennial Celebrations."[98]

Even as it continued to negotiate with Society Hill residents, Philadelphia '76 suggested that museum advocates explore alternative sites.[99] Museum planners thus were forced to weigh the sacrifices—a museum compromised in design but closely connected in location and historical spirit to Philadelphia's African American history, or a museum constructed according to the designer's blueprints and open in time for the Bicentennial but situated in a less-than-desirable location. Unwilling to further delay construction, museum advocates chose the latter.[100]

As might be expected, the decision to forgo the Society Hill site was not entirely conciliatory. Drawing upon theatrical displays of mourning and defiance, architect Theodore Cam and forty onlookers gathered at the 6th and Pine Street site in early April 1975 to stage a funeral-like ceremony. Cam ignited the original cardboard architectural model of the museum with lighter fluid, and the crowd (which included both museum supporters and Society Hill residents) applauded. The reporter present observed, "almost like throwing dirt on a grave,

Theodore Cam's blueprints for the Afro-American Historical and Culture Museum. Due to the fierce resistance to the construction of the museum in Society Hill, museum advocates decided to build on the corner of 7th and Arch Streets, in an area dominated by office buildings. Courtesy of The African American Museum in Philadelphia and the Special Collections Research Center, Temple University Libraries, Philadelphia, Pa.

a few other men—framed by the yellow sign that said 'New Home of the Afro American Cultural Museum'—sprayed lighter fluid on the fire. A small boy watched the flames and said, 'Mommy, look what happened to the house.'" After the model had burned, Clarence Farmer dug a makeshift grave and buried it." Farmer, who had publicly stressed that racism underlay the opposition to the Society Hill site, suggested during the mock burial, "Why don't we try to forget all the charges?"[101] In another *Philadelphia Daily News* article, however, he expressed less mollifying sentiments. Upon being asked whether the ceremonial burning represented a "monument to racism," Farmer replied, "Call it whatever you like. . . . It will give those (Society Hill) residents something to think about."[102]

On Wednesday, April 9, 1975, workers broke ground for the new African American museum on the corner of 7th and Arch Streets, a business district at the edge of Philadelphia's Chinatown neighborhood. Surrounded by office buildings, the museum was both physically and psychologically removed from the cultural institutions that bordered Philadelphia's "Avenue of the Arts" (the tree-lined avenue marked by the imposing presence of the historic City Hall at its eastern end and the Philadelphia Museum of Art at its western terminus) and from Society Hill's black heritage sites, such as Mother Bethel AME Church. Although the museum's new setting was located just over a block from the bustling renovations taking place on the fifty-five-acre Independence National Historic Park, its ahistorical, office-park surroundings undermined the site's desirability. Most crucially, the museum's final location remained isolated from the areas in which most of Philadelphia's African Americans lived and worked.

As desired, the African American Museum of Philadelphia debuted during the Bicentennial summer to enthusiastic crowds. Once the celebratory fervor had subsided, however, fluctuating museum leadership, together with questionable exhibit quality (abetted, some argued, by a compromised gallery space), subjected the museum to uncomfortable public scrutiny. Within the geography of Philadelphia's dense core, the museum lay north of Society Hill by barely a mile; yet the distance between these locales served as a reminder of the seemingly insurmountable conflicts between Society Hill's vociferous white residents, an ambivalent municipal bureaucracy, and the African American community.

Despite some public protests to the contrary, the conflict between the Society Hill Civic Association and museum advocates was still interpreted, even several decades later, as having been driven by less than honorable motives. In the museum's anniversary publication, *20 Years of Reflection: 1976–1996,* the authors argued that "Either willfully or out of ignorance, these [Society Hill] residents neglected the deep roots of the African American community in this section of the city, roots which gave the museum particular license to be located there."[103] The museum's contested physical and ideological origins arguably would play a critical role in the black community's perception of whether the African American Museum of Philadelphia truly constituted a "neighborhood" institution, created for and by Philadelphia's African American residents.

CHAPTER 3

CONFRONTING THE "TYRANNY OF RELEVANCE"

Exhibits and the Politics of Representation

In a 1973 *Washington Sunday Star* article titled "The Anacostia Tree: How a Neighborhood Museum Has Become a Source of Pride to 'the other' Washingtonians," reporter Joan Kramer cited an exchange between Anacostia Neighborhood Museum assistant director Zora B. Martin and visiting African American schoolchildren:

> "Why did black people leave Africa?" asks Miss Martin. "Because they were afraid of the animals," several children shout in unison. "No," says Miss Martin. "Black people didn't want to leave their homes. White people came to Africa, separated the families, and put them into boats. When black people were brought to America, they called them by a different name. Do you know what that was?" One child pipes up, "White people?" "No," says Miss Martin. "They called them slaves."[1]

The children's answers revealed their ignorance about why and how Africans arrived in North America, and what happened to them once they reached its shores. Since textbook authors were only beginning to rethink their portrayal of slavery as a benevolent institution, Martin and museum director John Kinard were keenly aware of these deficiencies and their potential impact upon African American (and white) audiences. Kinard explained in 1968, "Many in Washington and America are enthusiastic about the idea of giving the American

Negro his proper place in history. . . . All the history books have been untruthful about this—not with lies—but by what is excluded from the material. The result has been psychologically and physically damaging to the black man, who senses he has been ignored and is made to feel he has contributed nothing to society."[2]

The conversation between Martin and the visiting schoolchildren demonstrates the process through which neighborhood museums like the ANM transformed the "hidden" stories of African American history into a *public* history. Even with limited resources, many African American neighborhood museums began to produce increasingly complex exhibits and educational outreach programs as their creators challenged traditional methods of interpreting and presenting black history. In doing so, they served as a resource for traditional museums that struggled to remain relevant to audiences as riots, assassinations, and the evolution of the Civil Rights Movement from nonviolent civil disobedience to black power rocked the country.

Early Exhibits and Public Education at the DuSable Museum

During its first year of operation, the DuSable Museum hosted a variety of visitors, including the South Park YMCA, the Negro History Roundtable Group, the Ida B. Wells Children's Art Class, the Chicago Conference of Christians and Jews, and the African Students Reception.[3] Although exhibits and artifacts constituted an important draw for these audiences, the DuSable's early exhibit content did not represent the full extent to which the black museum movement would come to challenge traditional representations of African American history and culture. An October 1961 dedication ceremony for the new museum, for example, simply presented a watercolor exhibit on the "Arts and Crafts of Southern Plantations," lent by the National Gallery in Washington, D.C.[4] Along with displays of African and African American art and artifacts, the DuSable's exhibits during the early to mid-1960s generally emphasized the contributions of Africans and African Americans in science, industry, and the arts. Indeed, many African American museums embraced this "we, too, were here" technique, wherein the contributions of notable African American individuals were emphasized at the expense of a more complicated interpretation of social, political, and economic events.[5]

While simplified, the relative absence of even the "heroic" version of African American history in contemporary museums at the time, let alone in the textbooks to which Chicago's black schoolchildren (and their parents) were exposed, make the content of the DuSable's early exhibits crucial. The DuSable's exhibits clearly revised the then standard construction of American history through the deeds and words of white men. A December 1961–January 1962 exhibition, for example, presented portraits of prominent African Americans collected by the Association for the Study of Negro Life and History. The exhibit for February–March 1962, A Free Negro Family in 1840, consisted of a collection of papers and other artifacts from the family of Thelma McWorter Kirkpatrick, a descendant of the slave Free Frank McWorter, who founded the town of New Philadelphia, Illinois.[6] In keeping with the Burroughses' international ties and the connections black activists forged with concurrent African independence movements, African heritage and culture also became a focus at the museum. For instance, April–June 1962 featured the exhibition All About Africa—Saluting African Freedom Month, while July–August 1962 continued the African Diaspora theme with a photographic exhibit of Senegal, Ghana, and Nigeria.[7]

The exhibits staged by the DuSable during the late 1960s reflected an intensified political focus. For example, a 1968 exhibit featured a series of original paintings with several distinct themes: the kingdoms of West Africa; the periods of enslavement and slave revolts in America; the successes and failures of Reconstruction; the brutalities of lynching; and the work of activists like W. E. B. Du Bois and Ida B. Wells.[8] Also around 1968, the museum highlighted a series of dioramas by Chicago artist and sculptor Bob Jones. Jones's dioramas depicted particularly painful periods in African American history; his "Slave Ship", for example, illustrated "how slaves were crowded for months in a filthy ship in their passage to the American shores," while the "Slave Market" replicated "a market in which human beings were sold, families separated, and huge profits were made."[9]

Jones's dioramas recall an earlier body of work by African American female sculptor Meta Warrick, who was commissioned to display a series of dioramas at the 1907 Jamestown, Virginia, Tercentennial Exhibition.[10] At first glance, Warrick's works presented a linear narrative of scenes depicting the historical progress of African Americans. While seeming relatively "safe" for the largely white audiences who attended the exhibition, Warrick's narrative, rendered in physical form, represented a significant departure from the standard interpretation of black history penned by most white authors. Within these dioramas, and without the benefit of exhibit labels or other text, Warrick enfolded a "hidden in plain sight" commentary about sensitive subjects such as miscegenation and racial violence. Bob Jones thus was continuing the tradition pioneered by Warrick, though by 1968 there was less need for such contextual ambiguity; for, unlike Warrick, Jones was now working in a physical space created and defined by African Americans.

Public Outreach Programs at the DuSable

From its beginnings as one of the first major African American museums of the postwar era, the DuSable Museum represented more than just a repository for African and African American artifacts and exhibits. Rather, museum leaders believed that its educational programs could influence an audience believed to be in danger of slipping through society's cracks: black children and teenagers.[11] One of the more practical reasons that educational programs became so important in the development of African American museums was because the space to develop and display exhibits remained limited during the early years of most of these institutions. Consequently, the activities sponsored by the DuSable became critical in sustaining the museum's mission not just to "develop a center of materials on the Negro to serve the research students and schools and universities of the Midwest," but also to serve as "an instrument for community accord."[12]

Schoolchildren, who toured the DuSable at no cost, made up the museum's primary audience.[13] Attendance during the DuSable Museum's first year of operation, from October 21, 1961, to September 30, 1962, reflected their predominance: 499 children came to the museum during February—presumably drawn there by the museum's celebration of Black History Week. February also attracted the highest number of total visitors, with 572 children and adults visiting the museum.[14] In all, 2,664 people visited the DuSable during its first year—a remarkable achievement considering the fact that volunteers staffed the museum until 1968 and the building was open to the public only from 1:00 to 4:00 p.m. on Fridays and Saturdays, and noon to 5:00 p.m. on Sundays.[15]

DuSable staff designed their education programs to attract both adults and children. In 1962, the museum sponsored an essay contest titled "Why It Is Important for Negroes to Know Their History." Winners received copies of books on or by African Americans, and "every contestant . . . [would] be given a year's free membership in the museum."[16] Teachers, too, were seen as important resources. For example, interested teachers could receive a black history materials kit that contained short biographies of ten to twelve important African Americans, which could then be distributed to students. The DuSable also held teachers' training classes on black history at the museum; in 1966, twenty teachers enrolled in an eight-session class on "Negro History for School Teachers"[17]

The DuSable actively engaged with the community that surrounded the museum, with staff members offering extension lectures on African American history in easily accessible neighborhood locations, such as homes, schools, and churches.[18] The Burroughses and other DuSable staff and volunteers lectured to a variety of groups, including the Negro Labor Council, the Emma Lazarus Club, and the Jewish Community Center. Other outreach programs targeted international audiences; one such "foreign guest hospitality program" allowed international visitors who wanted to meet African Americans to "be invited into a Negro's home and get to sit down and eat with them and not feel tense about it."[19]

In another ambitious outreach move, the museum sent fourteen teams, each comprised of one adult and two high school students, into the predominantly African American neighborhoods of Chicago's South Side in 1970. The team, dubbed Operation Awareness, had received funding from the federally implemented Model Cities Program. Participants carried displays of the museum's cultural and historical exhibits and reached thousands of people, according to the museum newsletter. Students also recorded interviews with senior citizens, the transcripts of which served as a resource for both the community and the DuSable.[20] Other programs during the 1970s included a black history essay contest for junior high students and museum internships for elementary and high school students. The internships taught students black history and museum procedures, and introduced them to other ethnic museums—all in the hopes of creating the next generation of black history museum staff and volunteers.[21]

Besides being a source of much-needed revenue, the DuSable Museum store represented one way to extend the museum's philosophy beyond its walls. The store sold a variety of items themed around African American and African history, such as "10 mimeo broadsides on Negro history" (fifty cents); an ancient map of Africa; a collection of Negro History Poems for fifty cents; and the pamphlet "Problems of a Black Artist" by artist Marion Perkins, which featured a discussion of problems facing black artists and pictures of the author's sculptures. Margaret Burroughs also sold her written works, including a collection of poems titled "Africa! My Africa," a recording of "What Shall I Tell My Children Who Are Black," and "Whip Me Whop Me Pudding and

Other Stories of Riley Rabbit and His Fabulous Friends," which she described as "a new book of animal stories taken right from the heart of African and African American folklore. No dialect is used but the full flavor of all idioms is given in easily read English."[22]

For one dollar each, museum patrons could purchase prints of well-known African and African American figures such as Frederick Douglass, Phyllis Wheatley, and Alexander Pushkin.[23] The museum also offered calendars for sale; the DuSable's 1964 calendar highlighted "Negro scientists and inventors." Subsequent Heritage Calendars featured subjects such as black musicians and, in 1966, black women.[24] In addition to serving as an effective marketing tool, an item as simple as a calendar could communicate the museum's mission; visually denoting the months of the calendar year through the achievements of Africans and African Americans subverted the usual Anglicized methods of marking the passage of time.

The DuSable's growing status as an African American cultural institution allowed it to draw attention to other black organizations in Chicago that had difficulty garnering public attention or support—particularly after the divisive pressures of the McCarthy era. Burroughs wrote in 1966 that "we have tried to act as a clearing house or referral agency to publicize and direct the public's attention to such groups or institutions as The South Side Community Art Center; The Frank London Brown History Club; The Negro History Round-table . . . and all other groups interested in the promulgation of Negro History. Increasing numbers of research students have worked in our library."[25] Seventeen-year-old Brandon Smith, who attended Chicago City College, was one such student who found more than just an intellectual sanctuary within the DuSable Museum's library. In an article included in the December 1970 newsletter, Smith testified to the transformative power of the DuSable in terms of his consciousness as an African American. Smith wrote that while

> I've never been impoverished or on the brink of starvation, but anyone who lacks the self-respect, love of his people, and ambition to improve himself as I did is extremely destitute. . . . My proud heritage meant nothing to me, because I was never told that I had a heritage, and that it was something to be proud of. Besides, why should I give a damn about Crispus Attucks, Frederick Douglass, Dr. Charles Drew, etc., because they were all dead and buried and didn't have anything to do with me. Anyway, they couldn't have been much because they were "Negroes," weren't they?[26]

The resources offered by the DuSable Museum, on the other hand, contributed to Smith's heightened sense of identity and self-worth—qualities emphasized by Margaret Burroughs and the activists leading the "Black Muslim Movement," the original subject of Smith's research. Smith recalled that the lack of material on the "Black Muslim Movement" at the public library led him to the DuSable, where "I somehow became intrigued with the outstanding achievements of great Afro-Americans, past and present and I come to the Museum as often as I can. I've decided to enter the mainstream . . . of the movement directed to achieving equal rights for all American citizens."[27]

The DuSable Museum's Second Annual Educators' Committee Luncheon, held in 1974, demonstrated the powerful connections forged between the DuSable and other local African American organizations. A variety of area high schools and colleges, including Malcolm X College, Garrett A. Morgan Elementary School, Charles H. Judd School, and Martin Luther King High School, acted as the primary sponsors of the luncheon, together with churches, black sororities, and fraternities.[28] In their advertisement for the luncheon, individual sponsors Evelyn and Irwin Salk, a white Jewish couple long invested in Chicago's radical Leftist movement, linked the DuSable's achievements with its significance for black America as a whole. The Salks believed that "Afro-American history can well serve as a surgeon's scalpel in cutting open and exposing the depth of the racist cancer in the entire body politic. . . . Today Black America is the basic revolutionary force in this country."[29]

A "Museum on Wheels" for the Motor City

International Afro-American Museum founder Charles Wright likewise believed that his intent to preserve and disseminate black history could encourage Detroit's African Americans not only to serve as a revolutionary force for change within their neighborhoods but also to become active agents in a national (and, as the museum's name implied) an international freedom movement.

Like the DuSable Museum, space limitations necessitated that the International Afro-American Museum's early programs extend beyond the walls of its first location in Wright's apartment on Detroit's West Grand Boulevard. During the first few years of the museum's operation, for example, the IAM produced a radio broadcast titled "Spotlight on Black People," which aired October 12, 1967, on Detroit's WJLB radio station.[30] The museum also held an ongoing lecture series on African American and African history, distributed a quarterly newsletter about the museum, and produced two fifteen-minute career films, "You Can Be a Doctor" and "The Bank is Open to You," aimed at recruiting African American schoolchildren for these professions.[31] Museum brochures advertised "daily memorandum books with events in the history of Black peoples for every day in the year," as well as placemats that depicted scenes from African American history—another nontraditional method of communicating black history to mass audiences.[32]

Wright prioritized reaching out to African American senior citizens as part of the museum's overall educational mission. For example, the IAM sought to record the stories of elderly African Americans and include these tapes in an oral history library. Here, too, museum staff made use of mass media to impart the museum's mission. The Oral History Committee, which held their first meeting on June 9, 1966, planned to "[seek] contacts with persons able and willing to recount their experiences which illuminate some facet of the Negro's history." The committee intended to distribute these tapes to multiple audiences, including schools, clubs, and churches; these recordings were also broadcast on radio station WJLB in Detroit on Saturday evenings.[33] Although these sorts of outreach programs are relatively common in twenty-first-century public history practice, at the time the IAM's efforts to reach underrepresented audiences were groundbreaking, and further encouraged the nascent partnership between the museum and the African American community

Arguably, the IAM's most important early accomplishment came with its initiation of a mobile exhibit van.[34] The van, which opened to the public at the Michigan State Fair in August 1967, later traveled to various schools and churches —mostly black, but some white—throughout Detroit. Discussions surrounding the possibility of creating a "museum on wheels" began almost immediately after the museum opened its doors because of concerns that not enough people were "being exposed to the impressive culture of blacks." A mobile museum, staff and volunteers reasoned, could "reach those who could not visit the museum."[35] The mobile exhibit sought to achieve three goals concurrent with the IAM's overall mission:

1. Repair the distorted image of the African World—an image of jungle savagery, ignorance, brutality, and superstition
2. Create in Afro-Americans a greater sense of pride in their African heritage
3. Increase the knowledge and respect of all Americans for Africa and Africans, past and present.[36]

Establishing the mobile unit allowed museum staff to address what they believed to be the outright manipulation and distortion of African and African American history contained within most textbooks and mainstream museums. Advertisements for the museum on wheels reflected this approach; one brochure, for instance, exhorted its audience to "abolish racism from American education by supporting the International Afro-American Museum's Mobile Museum Series."[37] Detroit's major African American newspaper, *The Michigan Chronicle,* called upon African American organizations and individuals to demonstrate their support for the museum by offering the van a place to park, and drew attention to the van by linking the self-worth and identity of their African American audience to its success: "Are you concerned with 'the Negro image?' Members of the International Afro-American Museum Committee, presently laying plans for a summer mobile unit, are. Citizens or organizations interested in offering temporary location of the unit on their property are being urged to contact the committee, which hopes to base the exhibit in the Dexter–W. Grand Blvd. area and later tour the city."

The mobile museum's first exhibits included an African art collection donated by a former governor of Michigan, G. Mennen Williams, as well as oral history tapes of "outstanding Negroes."[38] The museum planning committee proposed that additional exhibit content for the mobile unit focus on three distinct chronological periods: "early history," "the medieval period," and the "modern period."[39] Although the exhibit would examine indentured servitude, slavery, colonialism and racism, museum planners also wanted to emphasize the "contributions of the African peoples to the development of the cultures in the New World."[40] As such, the mobile exhibit implemented a "heroic" interpretation of black history that highlighted achievements in art, the military, agriculture, and the contributions of important individuals, such as Crispus Attucks, Benjamin Banneker, and Phyllis Wheatley.

Staff in charge of the mobile van unit began building innovative contacts with other local organizations promoting black empowerment, such as the Black Arts Confederation of Unity—a national organization headquartered in Detroit and "dedicated to the cause of Black Nationalism, unity and self determination." The confederation sponsored a Black Arts Convention from June 29 to July 2, 1967, at Detroit's Central United Church of Christ. Other programs at this combination of conference and festival included a black arts parade, lectures on African American history, a black business trade fair, and a youth conference. Betty Shabazz, the widow of Malcolm X, attended a keynote meeting, along with H. Rapp Brown, chairman of the Student Nonviolent Coordinating Committee.[41] Rather than accept "whitewashed" interpretations of black history and culture, the Black Arts convention informed its patrons that "we need genuine Black Sociologists and Black Historians reflecting on our past, present and future. We must not allow ourselves to be fooled and hoodwinked by historians, who either overtly or covertly tell us that we have never contributed anything to civilization."[42]

The phrase "genuine Black Historians" is revealing. The confederation was as dismissive of African Americans they viewed as "Uncle Toms"—or, in their literature, "Uncle Roy or Whitey Young"—as it was of whites. The prose produced by the IAM usually did not reach this level of confrontation, as is made clear by their revision of the museum's June 1965 planning document in an effort to diminish the charged, even "brutal," accusations levied against whites.[43] Yet despite such caution, the IAM's approach to reinterpreting black history meshed with the goals of black power organizations like the Black Arts Confederation of Unity. The fact that the mobile unit, stationed on the conference grounds, raised around $160 in donations—a small amount, to be sure, but perhaps representative of the income level of most conference participants— seems indicative of this mutual support.

The deadly riot that began in Detroit on July 23, 1967, lent new urgency to the museum's mission to reach Detroit's black community. On July 23, at around 3:45 a.m., the Detroit Police Department raided a "blind pig" (an illegal, after-hours liquor establishment) in a largely black neighborhood. The police arrested eighty-two people who, according to some sources, had gathered to celebrate the return of a black soldier from Vietnam. A crowd formed when the first patrol wagons arrived to take away those who had been arrested; ten to twenty people soon swelled to two hundred. According to the subsequent Senate investigation, the growing crowd "began throwing rocks at windows, and by morning looting had begun and the riot was on."[44] President Lyndon Johnson and Governor George Romney sent 9,200 members of the National Guard, 800 state police officers, and 4,700 paratroopers to quell the rioting. By the time one of the worst riots in U.S. history was over, forty-three people (thirty-three blacks, ten whites) were dead.[45] The Detroit Police and the National Guard arrested around 7,200 people, most of whom were black. Nearly seven hundred fires destroyed or damaged businesses and homes, most of which were located in the black community.[46]

Utter devastation—economic, structural, psychological—rippled through

Help us to put· · ·
HISTORY ON WHEELS
with the NEW - - -

INTERNATIONAL AFRO-AMERICAN MUSEUM
1549 WEST GRAND BOULEVARD
DETROIT, MICHIGAN 48208 — PHONE 899-2576

Brochure for the International Afro-American Museum's mobile museum. The van brought the museum's message of black pride to neighborhoods, churches, and schools around Detroit. Other African American neighborhood museums, including the Anacostia Neighborhood Museum, borrowed from this innovative approach to educational outreach. Courtesy of the Charles H. Wright Museum of African American History.

the heart of Detroit as a nation questioned how race relations had reached such a deadly impasse in this once Model City. The aftermath of the riot left many African American museum and community leaders deeply perplexed, for here was evidence of a disenfranchised, poor, and forgotten black "underclass" now making their voices heard through often violent means. A celebration of "Black History Week," or an invitation to view African artifacts on display, would not begin to address their needs.[47] Indeed, it is evident that museum staff and board members wrestled with doubts over whether their dream of building a new, larger museum in Detroit was realistic, in light of the destructive federal and municipal neglect of Detroit's black community and the chaotic aftermath of the riot. Minutes from an August 1971 Board of Trustees meeting reveal the board's skepticism regarding the efficacy of sending the mobile unit into an area deemed the "inner city," and whether a new African American museum should be built in such a location. Upon hearing that the mobile unit had parked at an "inner-city" supermarket, Trustees questioned: "should we build in the heart of the ghetto? Will 'these' people be as interested in a museum as to a recreation . . . [*sic*]?"[48] The quotation marks around the word "these" acknowledges that the board knew they were employing exclusionary, class-based language to describe an audience unknown or unknowable to many of the museum's board members. Yet the self-conscious quotation marks do not diminish the board's profound doubts, as they likely believed that a recreational facility such as a public swimming pool might be a more sensible destination than a museum—even an African American one—for "these people."

Mobile exhibit staff also encountered some resistance at schools they visited, which may have heightened the frustration the board felt in bringing the van to certain areas of Detroit and in planning for a new museum. For example, in a letter to Charles Wright, volunteer Neomi Hill reported that students and teachers at Southeastern High School showed little interest in the mobile van's exhibits, to the point where "the students were rude and disorderly, and the teachers didn't try to control them." Interestingly enough, Hill admitted to her own weaknesses as a guide, and even perhaps to the shortcomings of the museum's volunteer training program: "the fact that I knew little about the exhibits may have been the reason why the children ignored me."[49]

Regardless of these problems, staff and volunteers still believed they must continue their innovative method of mobile activism by bringing the museum to those unable, or unwilling, to travel. By and large, their efforts met with overwhelmingly affirmative reactions. While those affected by the riot might not be able (or willing) to visit the museum itself, let alone the museums or libraries in Detroit's cultural center, the staff could bring the museum to them. In a September 1967 letter, C. Elrie Chrite, the executive director of the IAM, proudly reported that more than a thousand people "in the heart of the Detroit riot area" viewed the exhibits in the mobile unit. During that same period, Chrite reported that Wayne State University hosted the mobile unit, and that the van would soon tour Detroit High Schools at the invitation of the Detroit Board of Education.[50]

Additional indicators of the mobile unit's impact upon Detroit's black and white communities may be found in the numerous requests from pastors, teachers, and ordinary citizens, both black and white, that it visit their schools or churches.[51] Teacher Doris DeDeckere wrote a letter on February 19, 1968, that indicates one of the ways in which educators used the mobile van. DeDeckere first confirmed the mobile museum's reservation at St. Matthew's Roman Catholic Church, and then asked, "May we also have a selection of material to be presented to the students before their tour of the van? We want them to be as prepared as possible so they will derive the most from the displays." Three parochial schools with mostly white student bodies—St. Matthew's, St. Clare Grade Schools, and Dominican High School—participated in this event, and DeDeckere requested that the IAM provide three hundred copies of museum material to distribute to the students.[52]

Clearly, a simple visit to a mobile African American history exhibit could not fully ameliorate the obstacles faced by Detroit's black communities. Yet even in the desperate months and years after July 1967, the mobile van attracted enthusiastic audiences. By bringing the mobile museum to churches, schools, and other community centers throughout Detroit, the museum exposed Detroit's schoolchildren, as well as older audiences, to a new and accessible interpretation of African American history and culture. Many of the students' reactions to the exhibit revolved around a similar theme: "Its about time someone thought enough of Negroes to tell us something about ourselves!"[53] The connection between the riots and lack of education was not lost on people like Margaret Burroughs, who commented in July 1967, "if you're going to stop riots on the West Side or Watts, you've got to give these people what has been denied them—a background."[54]

The mobile unit attempted to expand museum access by acknowledging the real barriers that many of Detroit's African American families came up against, such as unreliable public transportation, or the inability to pay a museum admission fee. But perhaps the mobile van's deeper power lay in its ability to address obstacles more intangible—and more hurtful: the potential for racial discrimination and exclusion that African American audiences, particularly schoolchildren, had to encounter when they visited "established," mainstream museums and other cultural institutions. One such disheartening experience for black children visiting the Detroit Institute of Arts occurred in 1968. Four teachers who taught mostly African American students at Ferndale High School (located about eight miles from downtown Detroit) complained to Detroit mayor Jerry Cavanagh (1962–70) about their most recent visit to the art museum. On July 11, 1968, the teachers had taken fifty students to the Detroit Institute of Arts and the Detroit Historical Museum. At the Art Institute, the students were a bit loud and made some questionable comments about the artwork. According to the teachers, a guard then "descended upon us and ordered our departure." The teachers reasoned: "Considering all the problems that face such children in these times it would certainly be better judgment on the part of the Art Institute to lean over backwards to welcome the culturally less fortunate. . . . That this was a black–white confrontation may be born[e] out by an incident that occurred while our group was being escorted out. Another small group of Negroes were standing at the side of the room; they were also herded along despite their protestations of innocence. It was not until we [white] teachers interceded for them were they allowed to remain."[55]

As a result of the attention garnered by new museums like the IAM, as well as the dialogue prompted by the Civil Rights and Black Power Movements, staff at the Detroit Institute of Arts slowly began to address patterns of discrimination embedded in their organization. For example, during the tenure of director Willis F. Woods (1962–73), curators integrated African art into the main collection. Woods also helped create the Friends of African Art support group, and in 1966, he dedicated a gallery to African art.[56] The institution also began to hire and train minority employees in an effort to reassess their approach to underserved audiences.[57] This would not be the last time, however, that the International Afro-American Museum and the Detroit Institute of Arts would be pitted against each other in the intertwined battles over culture and race in Detroit.

"I AM A Man": Gendering the International Afro-American Museum

Like most museums, the International Afro-American Museum engaged in continuous fund-raising and membership recruitment in order to promote growth. In the summer of 1972, for example, the museum staged a month-long summer program for children called "IAMARAMA," which "encourage[d] youngsters to be informed and curious about Afro-American history and literature." In addition to being "inundated" for one hour each day with exhibits, films, and lectures on African American history and culture, the children would "receive a year's membership worth $1.00 in the IAM; a button to wear with the Museum's logo and a brochure depicting IAMARAMA of 1972." The museum expected one hundred schoolchildren to attend the program each day.[58]

Staff and volunteers increased awareness of the museum and its work through conference sponsorships. In March 1969, the IAM held a conference celebrating the fourth anniversary of its founding. The theme of the conference was "Black Awareness, New Directions," and its charge was to "seek a Community Answer to 'How Might the concept of THE MUSEUM' be developed and expanded to address itself to the current pressing needs of the Black Community?"[59] To recruit attendees, museum staff sent an individually addressed letter to leading figures in professional fields such as education, the arts, religion, and business, and argued that "it [is] important, if not imperative, that you serve as a resource person to deal with problems relative to Black participation in the developing Black museum as it seeks an effective role in the life of the community." Although the IAM constituted the conference's primary focus, staff also drew connections between the "Black liberation" struggle and the role that African American museums might play in this movement.[60] The museum positioned itself as a unique facilitator for these discussions, thereby breaking down the notion that museums must remain static institutions distant from social concerns.

Another IAM-sponsored conference on "Black Historical Museums" began in September 1969 at Wayne State University. Charles Wright solicited the attendance of African American-themed museums around the country, both large (such as the DuSable Museum) and small (such as the Old Slave Mart Museum in Charleston, South Carolina, founded in 1937).[61] The conference brochure stressed community identification and involvement with the museum and its future: "OUR AIM as the Detroit Committee of I.A.M. is to ADOPT the COMMUNITY'S IDEAS in our planning for the FUTURE. You are cordially invited to join with us in our attempts to define: THE LIVING MUSEUM." Local African American leaders, including Wright, Congressman John Conyers (D-MI), and Congressman Charles Diggs (D-MI), presented lectures on a variety of topics, such as the correlation between the black museum movement and the growth of black studies programs. Richard Austin, the county auditor of Detroit and an African American mayoral candidate, concluded the conference with a speech on "The Impact of Black History Museums upon the City."[62]

In spite of these fund-raising and marketing efforts, however, Wright's private correspondence and the minutes of board meetings revealed a worrisome trend. In 1969, just four years after the museum's debut, expenses were "running neck and neck with the income." Revenue from January through June of

1969 totaled $14,634.04, while the expenses ran to $14,658.07, leaving the organization with a small but growing deficit.[63] The fragile state of funds for many African American neighborhood museums was symptomatic of the poverty within the communities that typically surrounded these museums. Yet Wright also blamed the apathy of people who belonged to the "Black Establishment," as well as the fact that the media—even the black media, such as the *Michigan Chronicle*—failed to publicize his museum.[64] In a bluntly worded press release from July 1968, Wright suggested that a new, larger museum could be built if African Americans simply redirected their spending toward more worthy goals. Charging that only "about one in every 500 black Detroiters" had supported the museum financially or in-kind since its inception, Wright bemoaned the fact that the "black leadership in Detroit only gives us a casual glance, if they see us at all. . . . If we the smokers and beer drinkers would contribute to the International Afro-American Museum what we spend in one month we would break ground for our museum this year. . . . Come and see what we are doing and join with us to produce the only real emancipation— freedom of the minds of black people."[65]

Charles Wright and his staff targeted African American men specifically, stressing a "particular" brand of leadership they could offer the black museum movement—a type of leadership black women seemingly did not possess. An August 1968 letter to board members compared the contributions of black women on the board to the significantly smaller efforts of black men:

> One of our primary goals in IAM has been to reflect a strong, black male image. Yet, the female members of our board have made, and are making a significantly larger contribution to your organization than the male members. It is imperative that the male members of the board demonstrate their confidence in the future of IAM by a creative rededication to it and its programs. . . .The future of IAM is in your hands.[66]

The museum's gendered method of recruitment reflected concern over the sexual division of labor between black men and women. Ideally, black women were expected to embrace the feminine role of raising children while allowing black men to (re)claim their position as head of the family and primary breadwinner.[67] Of course, in 1965 Wright had designed the museum's very initials as a declaration of black manhood—an affirmation replicated much more publicly in 1968, when striking sanitation workers in Memphis wore placards that declared "I AM A Man."[68]

Thus, even though women ran much of the museum's daily operations, the IAM's promotional efforts revolved around concerns about black masculinity. Museum member Verona Morton penned a direct plea to the museum's male audience in an article titled "A Man's Reach Should Exceed His Grasp, Else What's a Heaven For?" for the 1975 newsletter.[69] Morton referenced the tensions that surrounded the appropriate private and public roles for black men and women, and while her overall tone was encouraging, she nonetheless called attention to the gap between the slogans of the Black Power Movement and the actual work needed to achieve these ideals. Morton exhorted her audience that, "since black men rap about doing something for their own—Then Get To Doing It! There are few, if any men at the tables selling museum wares; few are seen in the membership drives. But there are plenty of women."[70]

Morton did not call for black women to quit their jobs in order to elevate the masculinity and social standing of black men, as she recognized that many black women worked outside the home in order to make ends meet. Instead, she argued that African American men must find leadership positions that allowed them to move beyond being caught in the trap of repetitive jobs with little hope of advancement. Volunteering at the museum could accomplish this, for "Black men want their 'dues.' They want to get a piece of the action their ancestors sweated over 300 years for. And the black men claim there is no outlet for their creative, managerial, leadership talents; and they're right to a certain extent. G.M. [General Motors] isn't about to budge. The Metro Museum of Modern Art isn't about to budge. So why not use these talents at our museum where it is not necessary to become mixed into the mediocrity of middle management. There is a black museum awaiting all this black, male ability."

Morton also acknowledged that some African American men might believe that the IAM was not prestigious enough to deserve their full involvement. She countered this belief, however, by asking "who else is going to build that prestige? There's enough myth about 'Momism' and inept black males to inspire more black men, of all ages, to stop in the museum and demand the opportunity to be a part of its next Decade of Progress."[71] Conscious of the power and sense of belonging that one's job title could confer (or deny), Morton informed potential male volunteers, "everyone will admire and recognize your position. Your title will be clear and self-explanatory, Director or Curator or Historian— no assistant to or 'co-ordinator to the or third vice-chairman.'" While racism might indeed function to strip black men of their masculinity, Morton reassured her male readers that black women had faith in their abilities: "since we [women] know you black men can perform, you don't have to prove to us that you can. Thus the internal job pressures are off, and all of your energies can be concentrated in dealing with external pressures." Any residual anxieties between the sexes, Morton maintained, could be alleviated by men seeking greater involvement with the museum.

Although the black museum movement represented a chance for African Americans to establish equitable footing within the museum profession, an inherent contradiction existed in the movement's ideals and practice. African American women like Verona Morton and Margaret Burroughs took on the positions of organizer, volunteer, and staff member at many black neighborhood museums. At the same time, however, the IAM's publications suggest that the black museum movement (at least in its early years) emphasized that it was men, not women, who should assume the crucial leadership roles within these institutions.

Furthermore, despite women's overrepresentation in volunteer and staff positions at African American neighborhood museums, they were typically underrepresented in the exhibits produced by these institutions. The exclusion of black female artists from exhibitions was an early trend at the Studio Museum in Harlem, as it was within the Black Arts Movement as a whole.[72] The Studio Museum of Harlem exhibition Harlem Artists '69, for example, featured African American artists from all over New York City; yet out of fifty-four artists, just five were female.[73] Likewise, during a symposium held by the Metropolitan Museum of Art, artist William Williams reiterated Studio Museum founder Edward Spriggs's equation of art as solely the province of the black male by emphasizing that black artists should serve as a "male image, symbols of attainment for the community."[74]

In a 1972 Smithsonian Institution oral history interview, Doloris Holmes pressed African American artist Cliff Joseph on the reasonable extent to which black artists could expect to be represented at shows held by the Whitney Museum of American Art or the Metropolitan Institute of Art since, after all, the art world rarely bestowed recognition upon female artists (regardless of race). In a rare admission—in these sources, at least—Joseph agreed that black female artists faced greater difficulties than black male artists in gaining recognition for their work. Joseph acknowledged that "women have gotten very badly shaken in this field as well as other creative fields or industrial fields or whatever. And certainly I believe that black women have come up with the shortest end of the stick."[75]

Lawrence Reddick's reaction to Philadelphia's plans to depict women's history during the Bicentennial parallels Joseph's observations to a certain extent.

Arguing that it would "shock the public" if they learned that more money had been appropriated to celebrate the history of women in Philadelphia than had been spent on the depiction of African American history, Reddick also thought that the city's focus on the achievements of white women seemed particularly overbalanced. After reviewing Philadelphia's Bicentennial exhibit plans, Reddick pointed out that "we could not find a word about Black women or Puerto Rican or Native American women."[76]

The comments by Verona Morton, Cliff Joseph, and Lawrence Reddick all reveal the contradictory dimensions of the black museum movement. Even as African American museums battled the constrained and stereotyped roles assigned to black history by mainstream cultural institutions, they themselves also restricted many black women based upon the belief that the contributions and leadership of black men were inherently more valuable. Thus, while African American museums may have represented a "free space" for African Americans suffering from discrimination and poverty, the categories of gender, race, and class still delineated the composition of these free spaces. Such restrictions would inevitably inform the ways in which various audiences (women, middle-class African Americans, whites, etc.) perceived the work and identity of black neighborhood museums.

The Anacostia Neighborhood Museum and the Smithsonian Challenge

Compared to independent neighborhood museums like the DuSable and the International Afro-American Museum, the Anacostia Neighborhood Museum's direct affiliation with the Smithsonian Institution significantly distinguished the museum from its counterparts. Indeed, perhaps due in part to its relationship with the Smithsonian, the ANM's exhibits during its opening year barely hinted at the museum's future identity as a uniquely "black" cultural institution—despite being located in a predominantly African American neighborhood.

Louise Daniel Hutchinson, the director of the Research Center at the ANM from 1974 to 1986, reflected that the Smithsonian initially viewed the ANM as a "facilitator to move people from one point to the other, to introduce them to museums and then carry them into the total museum experience on the Mall."[77] In 1966, Smithsonian staff suggested a series of artifacts for the new museum that reflected this generic "outpost" identity: a hot-air engine, a crystal detector radio receiver, and a collection of bells from the neighborhood that visitors could ring.[78] The museum's first permanent exhibits, borrowed from the Smithsonian's collection, included a model of a 1890s general store, a small petting zoo, animal skeletons, and other artifacts designed to withstand repeated touching and use.[79] These were unremarkable objects apart from the fact that they were designed to be frequently handled. Some Smithsonian staff members assumed that any valuable objects lent to the museum would be vandalized, given the poverty of the area and the association of "slums" with crime.[80]

The museum's first special exhibit, Doodles in Dimension (November 1967), featuring sculptures inspired by the pen-and-ink doodles of President John F. Kennedy, also did little to suggest the museum's potential to transform the field through its focus on the needs and concerns of Anacostia residents. Indeed, in a January 1968 letter to Charles Blitzer, who served as Director of Education and Training at the Smithsonian, Wilcomb Washburn lamented the apparent lack of "groundbreaking" exhibits at the new museum; he blamed inexperienced director John Kinard and the tight control he exerted over ANM. Washburn, who headed the American studies program at the Smithsonian, admitted that while he "admire[d] the sentiment of allowing local autonomy . . . the exhibits installed so far (such as the Kennedy doodles) do not inspire confidence."[81]

The museum's failure immediately to produce innovative exhibits may have also been an extension of the communication problems between the ANM and the Smithsonian.[82] Much to the frustration of some Smithsonian employees, S. Dillon Ripley often sided with the ANM in its attempts to assert its own identity as a black museum apart from the Smithsonian. Ripley chided two Smithsonian staff members in a 1968 memo:

> I was really depressed to hear recently (not from Kinard I assure you) that for his exhibits at the ANM, the curators of MNH [Museum of Natural History] and MHT [Museum of History and Technology] had been unable to bring themselves to lend anything with the sole exception of some African drums for the current show. Is this the way to bring our exhibits to the people? As someone who has been a curator for twenty-nine years, I cannot understand why a colleague would not be greatly impressed by this experimental one-of-a-kind museum and its unique opportunity to bring museum techniques to people who otherwise do not visit the main museums on the Mall, and thus eventually to get them over to visit those very museums. What is the trouble?[83]

Museum of History and Technology Assistant Director Silvio Bendini responded to Ripley's accusations with incredulity. Stating that, in fact, the Museum of

Natural History and the Museum of History and Technology had willingly lent multiple objects to the ANM, Bendini asked "what can be done to improve communications with the staff of the Anacostia Museum so that our own staff can engage in greater participation with better cooperation? Our show of willingness to cooperate and our efforts to do so will continue to prove fruitless as long as communication within the Smithsonian itself is liable to misinformation."[84]

Despite the ANM's less-than-promising beginning and the evident communication barriers between it and the Smithsonian, the neighborhood museum's staff and volunteers gradually broke away from presenting "traditional" exhibits and programs. Kinard began requesting funding to produce exhibits that featured pressing social commentary about the living conditions of the poorest African American residents of Washington, D.C., as well as the history and culture of the African Diaspora.[85] A major catalyst for the museum's shift from the ordinary to the groundbreaking came with the assassination of Martin Luther King, Jr., in April 1968 and the chaotic unrest that followed in Washington, D.C. and other American cities. Indeed, it was not until after King's murder that the museum's status as an "African American" museum would be fully realized. With King's death, Hutchinson recalls, "the community began to articulate new concerns for the museum . . . [they] began to look at themselves and say, "Where do we fit into a museum experience? . . . If we go downtown, are there any exhibits about us, about people who look like us? Anything about our past, our heritage?" The answer was a resounding no."[86]

The methods the Anacostia museum employed to initiate such exhibit and program changes borrowed from the template created by earlier African American neighborhood museums. For example, taking a cue from the International Afro-American Museum's "museum on wheels," the ANM instituted a mobile museum to increase attendance and museum exposure in 1969. The mobile division consisted of a van that traveled to schools, hospitals, and playgrounds in Anacostia to present exhibits and lectures. Mobile exhibit kits featured interactive objects, such as a twenty-one-piece puzzle map that formed the neighborhoods of Anacostia (an interesting tool for teaching children to become conscious of their "place" within Anacostia), a black history puzzle map, as well as exhibits on topics such as pollution in Anacostia and the "Black Man in Science." During the first three years of the mobile division, according to museum staff member Fletcher Smith, more than 75,000 people viewed its exhibits.[87]

The Anacostia Neighborhood Museum began to present a rotating collection of special exhibits with a strong emphasis on internationalism. For example, in

January 1968 the organization introduced children's art from Brazil; in February 1968 the museum's Negro History Week celebration featured a collection of portraits of distinguished African Americans from the Harmon Collection of the National Portrait Gallery. Education curator Zora Martin remembered that after viewing the exhibit one child exclaimed, "I've never seen so many Negroes in one place in my whole life!" In May 1968, the exhibit This Is Africa offered a food fair with African cuisine, a fashion show, performances by the African Heritage Drummers and Dancers, and lectures on African history and culture.[88] Exhibits on Makonde sculptures (October 1968) and a Jamaican Festival (September 1969) both established and reinforced a shared identity between Anacostia's African American residents and African communities around the world.

A Turning Point: The Rat—Man's Invited Affliction

An exhibit titled The Rat—Man's Invited Affliction (November 16, 1969–January 25, 1970) marked a key turning point in the Anacostia Neighborhood Museum's exhibition history. Staff designed the exhibit to realistically present and analyze a decidedly unpleasant issue faced by a wide swath of the Anacostia community, namely the problem of rat infestation brought on by overcrowded apartment buildings and haphazard trash collection—the legacy of urban renewal and municipal neglect. The Rat influenced the content and method not of only future exhibits at the museum but also of exhibits at museums across the nation and internationally. Indeed, Kinard and Esther Nighbert argued that The Rat "convinced the advisory committee and the staff that the museum could no longer afford to present exhibitions dealing only with life in the past. Such exhibitions, it was strongly felt, must have relevance to present-day problems that affect the quality of life here and now in Anacostia."[89]

The exhibit's conceptual origins reveal how exhibit ideas at the ANM now traveled from the bottom up—from schoolchildren to senior museum staff. For instance, staff noticed that mice were disappearing from the museum's small petting zoo; in the meantime telltale bones surfaced in the snake cage. When asked, neighborhood children responded that "it was those bad boys" from the neighborhood who were responsible. The staff surmised, however, that the children's hatred for rodents, rooted in their daily living experiences, was the real reason for the disappearing mice. Hence, staff proposed mounting an exhibit that addressed Anacostia's rat problem.

To determine what the museum should present in the exhibit, the staff

Young visitors attend The Rat: Man's Invited Affliction exhibit at the Anacostia Neighborhood Museum, November 1969. This groundbreaking exhibit addressed locally pertinent subject matter that mainstream museums typically ignored. Courtesy of the Smithsonian Institution Archives. Image no. 2004-63044.

surveyed children about what they had learned about rats from daily life. Their responses startled Kinard: "Rats can give you rabies. Rats tear up things at night. They bite you. They can do many tricks." The children suggested things they wanted to see portrayed in the exhibit, including "Show why they see very well in the dark. Tell the different diseases they carry. Show how to poison them."[90] Accordingly, when visitors arrived at the museum's new exhibit in November 1969, they found panels on the history of rat infestation and the impact of rat bites and learned about pest control. A model of a backyard featured live rats in cages, and a CBS-TV film titled *Who Do You Kill?* portrayed a black family living in a one-room apartment; their child had died from a rat bite. As the museum's Calendar of Events described the film, "the parents' struggle to deal with life in the ghetto demands that the viewer seek answers to poignant questions." Anacostia teenagers also presented an original skit called "Rats" based on their day-to-day experiences.[91]

As part of their public outreach program connected with the exhibit, ANM staff invited representatives from the National Park Service, the mayor's office, and other city offices to tour Anacostia in order to determine the source of the neighborhood's endemic rat infestation. The representatives informed Kinard that rats were difficult to eliminate in Anacostia because of the overlapping jurisdictions between the municipal offices; nobody knew which office was responsible for rat control in Anacostia, and therefore nothing was done.[92] As was the case with the district's urban renewal programs, bureaucratic neglect of a basic necessity led to real misery for people living in one of Washington, D.C.'s poorest neighborhoods.

The grim subject matter portrayed in The Rat prompted some Anacostia community leaders, including those who had campaigned for Kinard's hiring at the Anacostia Neighborhood Museum, to protest the museum's choices. Marion Conover Hope, one of the leaders of the Greater Anacostia Peoples Corporation, complained to Kinard that "people will despise [the exhibit] and not like it. It will be the beginning of the end of this museum." Kinard, however, argued that the museum was not exaggerating the issue, nor was it trying to be a "prophet of doom."[93] Rather, it was attempting to help Anacostia's residents combat the problems of urban life—and to remind Washington's policymakers that its citizens would not suffer in silence. Kinard argued during the November 1969 seminar at the Bedford Lincoln Neighborhood Museum, held the same month as the The Rat's debut, that the museum "can and must speak forthrightly, without fear of retribution, on such social evils as rats, water pollution, and racism, and that if it does it will become a new creature. Other museums—the marble halls and the huge architectural structures—if they take this challenge, will also become new creatures to enhance the quality of life in this country."[94]

The public responded strongly to The Rat, with the exhibit attracting high attendance and extensive local and national news coverage. Other museums also noticed Kinard's achievement. Kinard took the film *Who Do You Kill?* to France for viewing at the 1971 International Council of Museums conference, and those who saw it were astonished: after viewing the film, one attendee told Kinard, "That ain't no museum."[95] The Rat's success paved the way for future exhibits that tackled the issues facing Anacostia's residents, such as the two-part exhibition Evolution of a Community, which received grants from the Carnegie Corporation and the Department of Housing and Urban Development. The first half of the exhibition, which opened in February 1972, examined Anacostia's early history; the second half, which debuted in September 1972, dealt with current problems faced by Anacostia and other economically depressed communities. Slide shows, information from various community agencies, drawings, photographs, and oral history interviews conducted with Anacostia residents were among the highlights of the second half of the exhibit. Interviewers asked community members to define which they considered to be most serious problems in Anacostia and how to solve them, then incorporated their answers into the exhibit.[96]

Although the second half of Evolution of a Community addressed the community's major concerns—unemployment, transportation, and education—attendance began to decrease. The declining number of visitors bothered Kinard, "because this is what the community said they wanted us to do. They wanted us to amplify their concerns."[97] Puzzled, Kinard closed the museum for three days in order to examine how the exhibition might be "turning the community off." Staff soon realized that, "inadvertently, we had mirrored all of their concerns, but we had not offered any solution to the concerns. . . . We said, 'Then all right, what is the most positive approach? What is it that the community has been most responsive to?' The history. That's when we decided to do 'The Anacostia Story.'"[98]

Kinard discovered that, in retrospect, the ways in which Evolution of a Community interpreted Anacostia's history were "replete with omissions" concerning the role of African Americans in building Anacostia. These omissions, in turn, negatively affected the psyche of Anacostia's black citizens. Consequently, The Anacostia Story, 1608–1930 (1977) revisited the first half of Evolution of a Community by exploring Anacostia's history from 1608 to 1930 and offered residents an active opportunity to remember and celebrate their community's heritage.[99] In the preface to the exhibit catalogue, Kinard lauded The Anacostia Story as "designed to inspire concentration on the significance of local history. It is the first effort of its kind on the history of Anacostia."[100] By incorporating the voices of Anacostia's citizens, including oral histories drawn from descendants of the original settlers, the exhibit went beyond simply documenting an often forgotten community's history. Instead, it "has been written to inspire a sense of pride and to heighten the aspirations for dignity and self-assurance of every person, no matter his station in life." The ultimate goal of The Anacostia Story and the museum itself, maintained Kinard, was to "return this rich history to the people of Anacostia—for it is their story."[101]

Transforming the Visitor Experience

By producing exhibits like The Rat and The Anacostia Story, as well as implementing a mobile museum and innovative outreach programs, the Anacostia Neighborhood Museum differed starkly from most traditional museums at this time, many of which remained oblivious to the struggles of the communities in which they were located. The contents of the museum's suggestion box reaffirmed its community mission. Of the few surviving records, one reads: "I like this museum. It's good to feel you're part of something. A lot of times I go into different museums and enjoy the items on display but there's an empty feeling. This place gives you a chance to feel history."[102]

The museum's transformative leadership within the black museum movement and the field of museology as a whole also emerges in the records of the ANM's Office of the Director. Numerous letters from museum administrators appealed to Kinard and his staff to advise them about how to include black history in their current exhibits and about viable methods to initiate museum extension programs within minority communities. A letter from the Curator of Education at the Norfolk Museum of Arts and Sciences in Norfolk, Virginia, represented a typical plea. The curator invited Kinard to address a group of sixty female docents about the "obligations of museums such as my own to Afro-Americans," confiding that "as a group, they are intelligent, but have led very insulated lives as to your experiences."[103]

These requests reflect an increased concern among some museum directors and curators that significant changes in museum interpretation and outreach were on the horizon. The focus of the American Association of Museum's annual meeting in 1969, "What Are We Doing to Justify Our Existence?" tapped into this growing anxiety, as did the federally commissioned publication of *The Belmont Report*, which detailed the state of American museums in the midst of tumultuous social change.[104] In a special 1972 *Washington Post* series on "The Urban Museum Crisis," journalist Elisabeth Stevens lamented the lack of progress that most mainstream museums had made in addressing the needs of "inner city" audiences. For Stevens, the failure of these institutions to reach minority audiences was not simply a problem confined to the museum world. Rather, museums' efforts (or lack thereof) to serve neglected audiences exerted a ripple effect on broader social problems. Even after the dire warning issued by the Kerner Commission's *Report on Civil Disorders* (1968), Stevens pointed out that "only a few of the big urban museums are trying to attract inner city people with outreach and other programs . . . and many of these efforts may well be doomed to insignificance, even failure. And others have failed to grasp the implications of their roles as 'white institutions.'"[105] Yet as these large museums floundered, Stevens also observed a new and hopeful trend: "in the heart of the ghettos, small, new and often remarkably successful small-scale museums run by and for blacks, Puerto Ricans and other minority groups are cropping up."

Success stories that Stevens cited included the Studio Museum in Harlem and the Anacostia Neighborhood Museum, as well as Brooklyn's MUSE, El Museo del Barrio, and the Store Front Museum in Jamaica, Queens (1971).

The Smithsonian Institution scrambled to adjust the content of its exhibits in response to the increasingly publicized work of the Anacostia Neighborhood Museum, not to mention the tumult of national and local events. The directive for change at the Smithsonian emanated from its leadership. S. Dillon Ripley corresponded with African American historian John Hope Franklin shortly after the 1968 Washington riot about the Smithsonian's responsibility toward the African American community. Acknowledging that the Smithsonian fell short in its inclusion and interpretation of African American history and culture, Ripley asked Franklin to assist the institution in its efforts to provide a more balanced narrative. Ripley admitted, "although we are proud of our experimental neighborhood museum in Anacostia and of our training programs, and some of our newer exhibits' technique and content, I am very much aware of how much remains to be done."[106]

Ripley's description of the Anacostia Neighborhood Museum as an "experimental neighborhood museum" is illuminating. Clearly, the ANM was proving its worth as an institution in its own right, connected to yet independent from the Smithsonian. Yet Ripley, who by all accounts remained a dedicated advocate of the ANM until the end of his administration, still perceived the museum as an experimental outpost of the Smithsonian—not quite in the same league as established institutions like the National Museum of American History. Furthermore, not all Smithsonian employees shared Ripley's enthusiasm for the ANM's work and his conviction that the Smithsonian had a "moral responsibility to consider its exhibits for the effect they may have upon all sorts and conditions of people."[107] Indeed, some Smithsonian staff members questioned the ANM's emphasis on African American history, arguing that such a focus precluded the staff's objectivity in designing exhibits. Upon reviewing the ANM exhibit Negro History and Culture (1968), for instance, John Anglim, the chief of the Smithsonian's Office of Exhibits, criticized it for "lacking expertise and objectivity . . . [and for] its lack of organization and emotional connection to exhibit topics."[108] Smithsonian employees also took issue with relatively inexperienced ANM staff members who were unfamiliar with the technical aspects of the museum profession, such as writing exhibit scripts. Anglim complained, "any remarks [that criticize the choice of scriptwriter], no matter how mildly phrased, receives an immediate response from John Kinard that bristles with defensiveness."[109] Yet

Kinard's defensiveness was, perhaps, necessary: in order for the ANM to fulfill its identity as an African American "neighborhood center," African Americans had to run it—even if they did not have extensive experience as museum professionals.

Although the ANM's exhibits did not yet "measure up" to the Smithsonian's professional standards, maintaining institutional relevance for diverse audiences seemed to be increasingly crucial for the survival of mainstream museums. The only way for the Smithsonian to accomplish this was to learn from the successes of the Anacostia Neighborhood Museum and to understand the sweeping changes taking place in the community and across the country. Some Smithsonian staff members other than Ripley recognized that museums like the one in Anacostia might hold the key to the Smithsonian's renewal. For instance, a July 1968 memo from Frank Taylor, the director-general of the Smithsonian Museums, urged all curators to add black history to their existing exhibits. Taylor stated, "I cannot over-emphasize the urgent need the Smithsonian faces to make visible its sincere and continuing concern for the recognition of the Negro in American history." Taylor included a bibliography on black history and provided content examples that curators could add to existing exhibits, such as information on black inventors and scientists, or a lithograph of the Boston Massacre that featured Crispus Attucks. Even if curators believed that they could not locate appropriate black history–related artifacts within the Smithsonian collections, Taylor instructed curators to revise exhibit text in an effort to incorporate this "new" perspective on American history.[110]

Determining how the Smithsonian should integrate elements of African American history into their exhibits became a process fraught with complications. For example, staff at the National Museum of American History feared that presenting separate exhibits on African American history, rather than including narratives of African American history within existing exhibits, would highlight how few resources related to black history the museum actually had. On the other hand, curators wondered whether these "integrated" exhibits would attract black audiences. Left unspoken in these records, perhaps, was a more pressing fear: Would exhibits devoted solely to African American history attract white audiences and their financial resources?[111]

Responding to the "Tyranny of Relevance"

A 1969 *New York Times* article titled "Museums Respond to New Needs" tracked these shifting dynamics within mainstream museums by examining the changes taking place at the Detroit Institute of Arts (DIA).[112] Local *Times* readers invested in the survival of their own long-standing, tradition-bound cultural institutions, such as the Metropolitan Museum of Art and the Whitney Museum of American Art, may have been interested to read reporter Jerry Flint's assessment of how museums like the DIA could no longer remain oblivious to what was taking place in their own communities.

Flint first situated the Detroit Institute of Arts geographically to help readers understand why the museum faced such challenges. If the art institute had been located in Detroit's suburbs, it is likely that the museum would have been able to continue in a state of relative oblivion to the dynamics of urban change. But the museum was located in Detroit's "inner city," with "poor blacks to the east, college students to the west, more poor Negroes and equally poor whites to the south." In effect, black residents and other undesirables were "crowding up around" the museum. The impact of the still raw wounds inflicted by the 1967 Detroit riot "reminded Detroit museum men of their vulnerability. Their memories were refreshed this spring when a handful of Negroes raced through the museum at Flint, 60 miles to the north, breaking some windows and damaging some works." The *Times* reporter did not speculate about why this group targeted a museum—in this case, the Flint Institute of Arts—nor did he connect the similarities between Detroit and Flint, two cities firmly rooted in the (now declining) automobile manufacturing industry and a shared history of racial unrest.

While additional security expenditures at the Detroit Institute of Arts might prevent this sort of criminal activity, museum leaders believed that maintaining the public health of the institution meant rethinking and expanding their outreach programs. Jazz concerts on Tuesday nights were one such popular addition to traditional programming that drew "non-traditional" audiences to the museum. In the tellingly detached language of DIA public relations director Robert Rodgers, the jazz concerts successfully attracted "great undigested lumps of people that come from somewhere." These "undigested lumps," Flint went on to explain, were Detroit's blacks, "Appalachian whites," and "Spanish-Americans." In short, those who attended the jazz concerts had long labored in Detroit's factories or, like Wright, had perhaps even owned their own businesses, but they were an audience who had been—and likely still remained—largely invisible and inexplicable to museum men like Robert Rodgers. The behavior of these nontraditional visitors was, of course, scrutinized: Flint reported that for the most part, those who attended the concerts behaved as they should, except for the "occasional listener carefully saving a cigarette butt, which could mean the weed smoked in the sculpture court isn't tobacco; but then, it might mean the listener is just tidy."

Flint explained how other museums were attempting to respond to the suddenly "new" needs of unexpected and formerly invisible audiences by designing programs and exhibits that seemed more "relevant." For instance, Chicago's Museum of Science and Industry planned a Festival of African American Arts, while the Chicago Historical Society renewed their efforts to collect African American-related artifacts. As did both the Anacostia Neighborhood Museum and Detroit's International Afro-American Museum, the Oakland Museum of California instituted a traveling van that brought African American artifacts to black churches and redevelopment centers. Reflecting on the upcoming one-hundred-year anniversary of the Metropolitan Museum of Art and its efforts to revitalize its programs, art critic John Canaday argued that such museums must not fall into the current vogue of making art "relevant" for today's audiences. Instead, art should be relevant for art's sake.[113] The director of the Oakland Museum, historian J. S. Holliday, also let slip an admission of his feelings about the changes his museum was undergoing, declaring that museums must reconcile with the "tyranny of relevance [that] demands that [they] serve the needs of today and nourish the interest of all, rather than only the interest of the few for whom museums have been a traditional experience." Yet while Holliday, who was white, may have felt burdened by dealing with this new directive, he rejected Canaday's dismissal of the need to transform museums into welcoming spaces for diverse audiences. Indeed, two years after assuming the directorship of the Oakland Museum, the museum's governing commission fired Holliday because of the extensive changes he made to programming and, more specifically, his efforts to involve Oakland's black community in the governance of the museum.[114]

The Smithsonian's reaction to the Anacostia Neighborhood Museum's "emotional," and therefore (in the eyes of some staff members) "unprofessional" exhibits, together with Emily Harvey's shocked impressions of African American dissidents at the 1969 seminar at the Bedford Lincoln Neighborhood Museum, clearly reveal that not all museum administrators welcomed the tyranny of relevance—a burden often coupled with drastic critiques of museum operations. At the American Association of Museums conference in 1972, Evan Turner, director of the Philadelphia Museum of Art, bristled at the charge that museums were elitist and racist institutions uninterested in responding to the needs of underprivileged communities. Indeed, Turner believed that most museums were already initiating public programs for minorities, and whether the museums developed these programs out of a "sense of moral conscience or out of a sense of self-preservation doesn't affect the very fact that these programs exist."[115]

John Kinard's handwritten comments on the pages of Turner's speech offer a terse rebuttal of Turner's justification, and illuminate the ways in which Kinard understood the Anacostia Neighborhood Museum's mission. Kinard wrote that it *did* matter whether museums created programs for minorities either "out of a sense of self-preservation" or out of "moral conscience," because the reasons *why* museums developed these programs exercised a direct impact upon their survival and success. Through the creation and presentation of exhibits that challenged and inverted the historically obsessive representation of the deeds and material culture of white America, African American neighborhood museums like the DuSable, the International Afro-American Museum of Detroit, and the Anacostia Neighborhood Museum spoke to the needs and interests of formerly neglected audiences. Although Evan Turner may have abhorred museums that engaged in "social confrontation," black museum leaders like John Kinard viewed social confrontation as a vital part of everyday life—and a necessary function of museums. Social confrontation, according to Kinard, could and should extend beyond "protest ideals, demonstrations, bombings or any particular outward show of force." Rather, it must resonate in the ways in which museums both initiated and responded to social and political change.[116] Whether by establishing groundbreaking educational programs or by offering students a welcoming space in which to study black history, black neighborhood museums consistently worked to generate these social, cultural, and political changes through deceptively quiet measures.

Protesting Invisibility in New York City

Evan Turner's dismissal of the need to reshape the Philadelphia Museum of Art continued to persist within the mission and mindset of many cultural institutions during the 1970s. Yet it seemed increasingly evident that such dismissal would be met with public protest; to refuse to address issues of race and representation would, at the very least, embroil the museums in a public relations disaster.

In New York City, home of upstart neighborhood museums like the Studio

Museum in Harlem and El Museo del Barrio, mainstream museums responded inconsistently to the demands levied by nonwhite audiences. These audiences responded in kind. For instance, in 1968, African American artists and supporters picketed a Whitney Museum of American Art exhibition titled The 1930s: Painting and Sculpture in America because it excluded black artists.[117] Henri Ghent, director of the Brooklyn Museum's Community Gallery and cochairman of a group known as the Black Emergency Cultural Coalition (BECC), which formed in 1968 to protest the exclusionary tactics of mainstream art galleries and museums, led the demonstrations.[118] In their defense, Whitney officials maintained that they designed The 1930s to expose artistic trends other than social realism, which dominated the Depression era. As such, most African American artists from the 1930s would invariably be excluded from the exhibition. Staff pointed to the fact that the museum had featured black artists in previous shows, and that an "Art Resources Center" had been opened for minority students on the Lower East Side.

These steps (or, as some viewed it, concessions) were not enough for Ghent, who organized a Studio Museum in Harlem show titled Invisible Americans: Black Artists of the '30's as a counterresponse to The 1930s.[119] Works by Jacob Lawrence, Hale Woodruff, and Henry O. Tanner were represented among the fifty paintings and sculptures on display, as well as many other lesser-known African American artists of the 1930s. *New York Times* art critic Hilton Kramer admitted that it was difficult to review Invisible Americans, since he did not want to "[inflict] further injuries on the sensitivities of artists who have undoubtedly suffered much." Nevertheless, Kramer felt that the exhibition was "an extremely feeble one. The work is mainly banal, academic, and incompetent. . . . Mr. Ghent is inviting us to judge black artists by standards greatly inferior to those we bring to the appreciation of—the term is absurd but unavoidable—white artists." Ghent and the Studio Museum in Harlem, argued Kramer, did not advance the status of black artists by continuing to place art "at the service of a political ideal."[120]

Ghent, not surprisingly, took issue with Kramer's charge that he promoted political ideology over aesthetic quality. In a letter to the *New York Times*, he angrily contended that Kramer applied the hegemonic standards of white European culture to a subject that resisted such applications. The Studio Museum did not invite the audience to judge the artists of Invisible Americans in the same ways as it judged European masters of the period; therefore, Kramer had inherently misunderstood the goals of the exhibition.[121] The fundamental purpose of Invisible Americans, argued Ghent, was to present work by artists who, by virtue of their race, have been "functionally invisible to the white establishment and therefore *not considered* for inclusion in a major survey of a period when their contribution was indeed considerable."[122]

Some highly respected museums in New York did attempt to create exhibits that integrated the narratives and artifacts of African American history and culture; whether the black community responded positively to these efforts remained another matter entirely. In January 1969, just two months after Invisible Americans opened, the Metropolitan Museum of Art's exhibition Harlem on My Mind: The Cultural Capital of Black America, 1900–1968, debuted. Harlem on My Mind represented one of the more infamous examples of the complex public response accorded to the early attempts of mainstream museums to incorporate the voices and stories of nonwhite audiences.[123] Metropolitan Museum of Art director Thomas Hoving and New York State Council on the Arts visual arts director Allon Schoener placed great hope in the exhibit's transformative potential, believing that it could present the Met as a "regenerative force in modern society" by inviting "new" audiences to feel welcome at the museum.[124] The heavily anticipated show spawned heated controversy and a series of public relations disasters and mass demonstrations, which seemed to catch Hoving and Schoener off guard, despite the similar outcry against the Whitney's The 1930s: Painting and Sculpture in America exhibition two months earlier.

Contending that the Met had ignored the voices of Harlem community leaders in favor of promoting Harlem on My Mind as "entertainment," as evidenced by curators' emphasis on photographs and music segments, Harlem's leaders dropped their endorsement of the exhibit.[125] Henri Ghent again led the Black Emergency Cultural Coalition in organizing mass demonstrations as the show began attracting record-breaking crowds in January 1969.[126] Picketers outside the Met carried signs reading "That's White of Hoving!" "Tricky Tom at it Again?" and "Visit the Metropolitan Museum of Photography."[127] Several African American artists speaking at a symposium held by the Met argued that Harlem on My Mind isolated and rejected black artists. For them, the exhibition represented an "example of total rejection on the part of the establishment, of saying 'Well, you're not really doing art,' or of not dealing with the artists that may exist or do exist in Harlem. These shows deal with the sociological aspects of a community, a historical thing."[128]

Calls for the exhibit's closing began to issue from organizations other than the BECC. Robert J. Mangum, Commissioner of the State Division of Human Rights, argued that the exhibit should close "until it reflects a more accurate record of the aspirations, achievements and goals of the black people of New York."[129] Thomas Hoving, under fire for the apparently anti-Semitic remarks penned by an African American high school student in the exhibit catalogue's introduction, withdrew the catalogue completely at the end of January after continued pressure from the New York City Council, which threatened to withhold funding from the Met.[130] Nevertheless, the exhibit continued to attract protests—and large audiences—throughout its stay.

The battle over exhibits such as the Whitney's The 1930s and the Met's Harlem on My Mind, together with the inconsistent and tentative approaches toward black history and culture taken by organizations as esteemed as the Smithsonian, underscore several important points. While such cultural institutions might once have appeared neutral by virtue of their remove from the everyday currents of politics and community dynamics, they now had to choose whether to acknowledge, at least in part, their uncomfortable position as a staging ground for highly public debates about race, power, and representation.

CHAPTER 4

"TO SATISFY A DEADLINE BUT LITTLE ELSE"

The Public Debut of the African American Museum of Philadelphia

As the nation approached its Bicentennial year, the tentative efforts of mainstream museums to include multicultural perspectives, establish outreach programs, and build decentralized museums that targeted racially and ethnically diverse groups failed to alleviate the sense of exclusion that remained among nonwhite audiences. The protests surrounding exhibitions like the Whitney's The 1930s: Painting and Sculpture in America (1968) demonstrate that the transformation of the mainstream museum world continued at a slow pace during the late 1960s and early 1970s, despite the efforts of activists who pressured tradition-bound institutions to revise their collections policies, dismantle their staid and stereotypical representations of black history and culture, and acknowledge the critiques leveled by grassroots community museums.

In 1976, the Whitney Museum of American Art staged an exhibition titled Three Centuries of American Art that commemorated American artistic traditions. Yet just as during their contentious The 1930s exhibition, the Whitney again found itself the target of protests because curators "included the work of only one woman artist and the work of no Black artists at all."[1] In partial acknowledgment of such criticisms, Whitney director Thomas Armstrong eventually renamed the exhibit American Art from the Collection of Mr. and Mrs. John D. Rockefeller to designate its actual focus and provenance. The simple gesture of a name change was Armstrong's only concession, however, as he did not include additional works of art by African Americans and female artists.[2]

While it was mostly large art museums that seemed to bear the brunt of public scrutiny regarding their exclusionary practices, history museums were of course not immune from such criticisms. Anacostia Neighborhood Museum director John Kinard took particular issue with what he perceived to be the Smithsonian Institution's ongoing, problematic treatment of black history even as it prepared to commemorate the Bicentennial. A pamphlet created by ANM staff advertised four upcoming Bicentennial exhibits at the museum and revealed Kinard's goals for the holiday:

> As this nation gears up its preparations for the celebration of its 200th anniversary, it is mandatory that the history and culture of America's ethnic groups be honestly interwoven in the fiber of this country's growth and development. Traditionally, the history of a country has been recorded, interpreted and disseminated by the dominating force of that society. This has left the roles of the dominated of that society untold or, more often, distorted. In an attempt to correct these inequities, the Anacostia Neighborhood Museum is preparing a number of exhibits, materials and programs that will be available during the Bicentennial year.[3]

Kinard's ideas about the misrepresentation of black history and the perpetrators responsible for this distortion reveal the museum's continuity of ideological mission since its inception in 1967. Although the national leadership of the Civil Rights and Black Power Movements had fragmented by the mid-1970s, the cultural and political impact of these movements continued to reverberate within institutions founded by African Americans.

Like Kinard, African American activists in Philadelphia and other cities across the nation understood that the Bicentennial represented more than just an opportunity for citizens to display their civic and national pride, for the content of the Bicentennial celebrations signaled who was to be included in the official vision and interpretation of local and national history—and, most critically, how their stories would be told. Philadelphia's Bicentennial celebrations represented an opportunity to build upon, or to weaken, relationships between the city and those who dwelled inside and outside of its real and imagined boundaries. Those citizens who found themselves excluded from the dominant interpretations of the Bicentennial's meaning would, in turn, create other methods to publicly reclaim the holiday in order to address their own histories and grievances.

To this end, the debut of the African American Museum of Philadelphia in June 1976 offered a defiant counterresponse to the status quo perpetuated by museums such as the Smithsonian and the Whitney. Fresh from its battle against the Society Hill Civic Association, here was to be an institution that reminded Philadelphians that African Americans were as much a part of Philadelphia's history as Benjamin Franklin, the Liberty Bell, and Independence Hall. Yet simmering conflicts regarding the museum's finances, leadership, and identity threatened to undermine its long-term survival, as both critics and supporters felt that the museum had been conceived and built in haste, without the full support of Philadelphia's black community. In turn, these immediately local concerns represented a national undercurrent that would preoccupy many African American neighborhood museums across the country during the 1980s and 1990s.

A Fractured Celebration: Claiming the Bicentennial

The pageantry surrounding the nation's Bicentennial celebrations failed to mask the distinctly ugly state of race relations in many American cities in the months leading up to July 1976. For instance, on April 5, 1976, white demonstrators protesting integrated bussing in Boston attacked an African American businessman, Theodore Landsmark, who happened to be walking near the demonstration at Boston's City Hall. The protesters used the staff of an American flag to attack Landmark. A Pulitzer Prize–winning photo by Stanley Forman titled "The Soiling of Old Glory" captured the scene as Landsmark tried to protect his face and body from the onslaught. As the attackers beat Landsmark, they shouted "Nigger! There's a nigger! Kill him!"

A wave of retaliatory incidents, led by both blacks and whites in Boston, ensued.[4] Reflecting on the incompatible timing of the Bicentennial and Landsmark's beating, *Ebony* magazine lamented, "we cannot celebrate the country or its technological achievements if we do not confront the meaning of the Landsmark incident and of what we have not done and must do to be worthy of the Revolutionary heritage."[5] To express their disillusionment with the holiday, *Ebony* coined the "Bicentennial Blues":

> I went up to Boston to see what I could see
> I went up to Boston to see what I could see
> They were stoning black children on Bunker Hill
> And whipping black men with pieces of the liberty tree.

I went to Philadelphia to hear the Freedom Bell.
I went to Philadelphia to hear the Freedom Bell.
But the way Rizzo was talking I might as well have been in hell.

If you see Crispus Attucks and the blacks who died to make us free.
If you see Crispus Attucks and the blacks who died to make us free.
Tell 'em it's business as usual in Boston and the land of liberty.

Got the Bicentennial Blues, blue as I can be.
Men and women marching from sea to shining sea.
And after 200 years, there ain't no freedom for me.[6]

Ebony joined other African American publications, such as the *Negro History Bulletin* (published by the Association for the Study of African American Life and History) in fielding questions from readers about the appropriateness of celebrating the Bicentennial.[7] While recognizing the hypocrisy of commemorating the holiday when blacks were still suffering from the legacy of slavery and Jim Crow, the *Negro History Bulletin* argued that the roles played by African Americans in American history, and in particular the Revolutionary era, must nevertheless be recognized. Accordingly, ASALH created a National Historical Marker Project (May–July 1976) that placed bronze markers at birthplaces and historic sites associated with African American leaders.[8] The sites were spread throughout the country, including the Freedom House in Baltimore and Harpers Ferry in West Virginia, as well as at lesser-known locations such as the Boley Historic District in Boley, Oklahoma, an all-black town founded in 1903.[9] ASALH thus reclaimed the physical landscapes of buildings and towns throughout America in their drive to make visible the historic presence and work of African Americans in these places.

African American cultural institutions and community organizations were not alone in feeling estranged from the narrow vision of American history promoted by most local and federal Bicentennial organizations. Numerous grassroots organizations across the country led counterdemonstrations and parades that skewered the iconic imagery of the American Revolution and reprimanded the officially endorsed versions of the Bicentennial. Demonstrators protesting in and around spaces as varied as the Whitney Museum, the U.S. Capitol, and Chicago's Marquette Park recognized that the Bicentennial was a fitting moment for mainstream cultural institutions to reevaluate their missions. If the nation was celebrating the anniversary of its independence on July 4, 1976, how could—and would—it begin to account for the hundreds of years of discrimination against African Americans and other minorities during this very celebration? How would those cities staging elaborate Bicentennial events interpret the economic, cultural, and scientific contributions of those people who were still being denied the very rights of citizenship outlined in the Declaration of Independence?[10]

The Peoples Bicentennial Commission, a national organization founded in 1971, represented one of the most active counterorganizations.[11] On July 5, 1976, thousands gathered in Washington, D.C., on the National Mall to celebrate "the People's Bicentennial." Protesters standing in front of the U.S. Capitol Building employed the powerfully iconic images of American nationalism as a backdrop for their demonstration. A *New York Times* article set the scene: "Under a large banner proclaiming 'Independence from Big Business,' a series of speakers played out variations on a central theme: The country has fallen considerably short of fulfilling its 200-year-old promise of freedom, justice and equality for all."[12]

Although it was not yet a full-fledged settlement when Philadelphia inherited its Liberty Bell in 1776, the city of Chicago also laid claim to the Bicentennial promise—and fought over how it should commemorate this heritage. Some local African American organizations criticized the lack of attention Chicago's Bicentennial planners had devoted to Jean Baptiste Point DuSable, who had helped found Chicago and actively participated in the American Revolution.[13] For instance, Lillian O'Neill, a member of the Jean Baptiste du Sable League, complained that "there seems to be an unwritten mandate to keep the lid on the name du Sable." O'Neill then cited how the Chicago public school system consistently "uses textbooks with inaccurate information if any at all about the role of Du Sable." In response, the league intended to create a historical marker to honor DuSable, and was preparing documentation for this purpose.[14]

Other public demonstrations in Chicago raised red flags among city officials who were concerned that unruly crowds chanting nonconformist messages would interfere with official Bicentennial programs. For example, city police three times denied a permit for an African American organization called the "Dr. Martin Luther King, Jr., Movement" to march in the "racially troubled Marquette Park area," located in southwest Chicago.[15] According to the *Chicago Tribune*, the group was refused the permit because a police official and a city attorney "predicted that the parade would cause racial trouble and that 1,000 policemen might be needed to protect it," despite the group's statement that they—following King's dictum—believed in "nonviolent direct action." They were finally granted a permit to hold their march on July 17, well after the July 4th celebrations. Although no "racial incidents" were reported during the July 4th weekend because, as the *Chicago Tribune* reported, people apparently "got caught up in the Bicentennial spirit," the Commission on Human Relations nonetheless advised Chicago's Interagency Task Force on Race Relations that they should not be "lulled into believing our problems are over."[16]

It is apparent that local officials interpreted public demonstrations led by disenfranchised citizens as the antithesis of the Bicentennial ideal. For them, being enveloped in the "Bicentennial spirit" must entail an absence of protest rather than a continuation of the original radical spirit that made the fight for American independence possible. Indeed, Bicentennial planners across the country hoped to "reinforce citizen loyalty to a nation-state" by reducing potentially divisive local or regional attachments. Public deeds once praised as demonstrations of justified rebellion against an oppressive regime would now be purposefully muted and transformed into "dramatic stories in which great men made irrevocable decisions that now deserved praise, and ordinary people deferred to higher authority and fought heroically for political dogmas."[17]

Yet containing popular expressions of both celebration and dissent consti-tuted a nearly impossible task for many city officials. In Philadelphia, for exam-ple, an alternative interracial Bicentennial group called People's '76 joined with other community activist organizations to protest the officially sanctioned Bicentennial celebrations. Arguing that the planned events constituted both a "hypocrisy and a sham," People's '76 declared that "our goal is to recover the often-forgotten revolutionary currents of 1776, the ideal of a people rising against oppression, an oppression which is again . . . being reproduced today."[18] Drawing upon the structure and language of the Declaration of Independence to advertise their resistance, one People's '76 meeting called for a "reading of a Bill of Grievances, detailing Violations of Civil Rights and Civil Liberties in Philadelphia."[19] The violations cited, among them the "systematic brutality by Police, and lack of accountability for such Brutality," matched many of the same concerns expressed by advocates of the African American Museum of Philadelphia as well as other Philadelphia civil rights organizations, such as COPPAR.[20] In addition to these activities, the organization planned bread marches, neighborhood history projects, and "People's Sunday," a gathering "by and about community groups trying to solve their problems of jobs, health, social services, sexism, education, racism and police brutality," in order to draw attention to their cause.[21]

The more conservative African American cultural, religious, and social organizations in Philadelphia did not usually stage events as publicly contentious as
the "carnivalesque" activities of radical groups like People's '76.[22] Still, the daily
operations and special Bicentennial events promoted by these organizations also
shaped the public dialogue about the varied meanings of the Bicentennial and
highlighted the need for greater representation of African Americans within the
official interpretations of the holiday.[23] For instance, Philadelphia's Church of
the Brethren featured a dramatic "roll call honoring Afro-American Men and
Women," to be held on March 28, 1976, while Philadelphia's mid-city YWCA
held an exhibition titled Rites of Passage: Through Our Own Eyes, which
employed photographs, documents, and artifacts to illustrate the black community's cultural heritage and impact upon Philadelphia.[24] Mother Bethel A.M.E.
Church, which unexpectedly found itself at the heated center of that battle over
whether the African American museum should be constructed in Society Hill,
received funding from Pennsylvania State University and the NAACP to create
an African American history exhibit. Based on a book by Charles Blockson
titled Pennsylvania's Black History, the exhibit toured Philadelphia in a mobile
trailer until early October 1976.[25]

At the University of Pennsylvania, Acting Assistant Dean Harold Haskins
proposed an exhibition titled Three Dimensions that featured works by local
and national African American artists, as well as pieces by international artists.
Haskins, who was African American, remarked that Philadelphia's Bicentennial
planners had not only failed to include the contributions of African American
artists in their programs, but that this lack of attention contributed to the
artists' exodus from the city. As Haskins argued, "Philadelphia, which is on the
threshold of becoming a city of great magnitude, should take the initiative to
exhibit and record the black art contributions to this city if it is to honestly
portray its cultural heritage to the world in 1976."[26]

Black Museums Interpret the Bicentennial

Perhaps the best illustration of how African American cultural institutions
across the nation publicly responded to the Bicentennial within an "approved"
presentation—yet one that nevertheless subverted this same format—may be
found in the work of African American museums. Some of these institutions
originated from grants distributed by state and federal Bicentennial organizations; indeed, John Bodnar maintains that federal Bicentennial groups began to

recognize that encouraging positive expressions of multicultural identity might help to promote the Bicentennial as a whole.[27] Museums, then, represented one of the "safest" conduits for these forms of expression. Thus, a grant from the U.S. Bicentennial Commission allowed the Great Plains Black Museum in Omaha, Nebraska, to open in 1976. The museum featured a collection that focused on the role of African Americans in the settlement of the American West. Likewise, the Museum for Education and Research in American Black Art, Science and History in New Jersey, which opened in 1972, received a $5,000 grant from the New Jersey Bicentennial Commission to create an exhibition on the history of African Americans in New Jersey. According to the commission, the "MERABASH" Museum "was the only one in the state dedicated to the history of blacks and their contributions to the arts and sciences."[28]

African American neighborhood museums already in existence planned their own programs in response to the Bicentennial. In Detroit, for instance, International Afro-American Museum staff presented Blacks in the Age of the Revolution, which they enthusiastically billed as "the only exhibit of its type which will highlight the role of blacks during the Revolutionary period. The unit will contain information and visual presentations about blacks who were soldiers, heroes, artists, scientists, educators, explorers, and religious leaders." The museum also commissioned Ida Roberta Bell, a renowned African American doll maker, to create black figure dolls for the Bicentennial. The dolls included Crispus Attucks, Benjamin Banneker, Bishop Richard Allen, Prince Hall and Elizabeth Freeman. As had many of the museum's exhibits, Blacks in the Age of Revolution toured sites across Detroit in the museum's mobile van.[29]

Although the Smithsonian Institution planned Bicentennial exhibits and programs that emphasized America's cultural diversity, critics like John Kinard argued that the interpretive scope of these exhibits remained limited. For example, A Nation of Nations, displayed at the Museum of History and Technology from 1976 until 1991, highlighted the diversity of immigrant experiences in America and emphasized the ways in which immigrant groups merged to create a unified national identity. The exhibit also attempted to address the thorny issues of slavery and racism, and displayed drawings of slave ships and shackles. Curators shied away from displaying actual artifacts or replicas of the iron shackles, however. In choosing to display only drawings rather than the crude physicality of actual artifacts, or even replicas, Smithsonian curators avoided possible confrontation and accentuated themes and history believed to unite all immigrant groups, regardless of origin or circumstance.[30]

The Anacostia Neighborhood Museum produced exhibits specifically intended to counter the blandly inclusive Bicentennial exhibits staged by the Smithsonian. Its presentation of four exhibits—Blacks in the Westward Movement (September 1975–January 1976), Black Women: Achievements against the Odds (1976), The Frederick Douglass Years (1976), and The Anacostia Story, 1608–1930 (1977)—emphasized the distinctiveness of the black experience in America and implicitly took the "official" purveyors of the Bicentennial to task for their homogenization of this history.

An intriguing document of comments collected from the Anacostia Neighborhood Museum's suggestion box during the Blacks in the Westward Movement exhibition has survived—a rare and revealing artifact that offers a glimpse into the mindset of one specific audience that toured the exhibit during the Bicentennial year: the Andrews' Air Force Base Race Relations Program. Black and white service members (all presumably male) participated in this program.[31] While small in number, the body of negative comments about the exhibit often reflects conflicts concerning class—in particular, increased black access to wealth or objects that denoted wealth. A group member complained that his visit was "a waste of time. As a method of brainwashing a captive audience, it is a success. Another item of interest, is all the newer model Lincoln's, Buick's, Pontiac's, etc. amongst the run down neglected apartment buildings with their grassless lawns in this area." A different visitor confessed that his own economic background, described as "poor white trash," prevented him from finding anything of worth or interest in the exhibit. Another wrote: "I think it is too bad we don't have more black cowboys on TV. But if it will make you happy, we will put more on TV. You've got everything else you want." Finally, one visitor abruptly stated that staff should "turn the building into a rat apartment house." It is unclear whether his comment referred to Anacostia's pervasive rat problem or pejoratively encompassed the exhibit, museum, or the entire neighborhood.[32]

Although these negative impressions are striking, out of twenty-nine comments from the AFB group, eighteen expressed mostly favorable opinions regarding the exhibit—even from those who identified themselves as white. For example, one visitor praised Blacks in the Westward Movement for "open[ing] my eyes to much more of the problems of blacks being left out of history. It open[s] my mind to think of this country not as mine as white but ours as both white and black." Another attendee wrote: "Nice. I'm impressed. It sure is about time these people get proper recognition. And of all the Westerns I've seen I've never realized the absence of blacks. Just goes to show how blind people can be how they take things for granted." One audience member, who also identified himself as white, stated that the "presentation is quite informative. I myself come from a high income white family. I had never before been exposed to this type of black culture. God only knows we need more places like this. Thank you for the experience."

Those who identified themselves as African American tended to praise the exhibit. Still, one commenter revealed the tension he felt—possibly between himself and other members of the group—regarding the museum's presentation of black culture and its reception by white service members. Writing that he was "very upset to find out that some of the people I work with . . . think that black culture is a waste of time," he reminded readers that "those people fail to realize that my black body may save their life during time of war." Some AFB members also hedged their praise with criticism of the museum's interpretative scope. As whites, they were not in a position of power to present and interpret the information; this new sense of imbalance created an uncomfortable sensation. One admitted that while the "exhibits are good," the "presentation seemed somewhat overstated. It is difficult for me to empathize with the black need for a sense of historical importance and community. But I'm learning." Likewise, another confided that, although he found the exhibit "informative," it was nonetheless "slightly biased. There are also white slums and white people suffering." One service member, race unknown, took issue with who presented—and thereby controlled—the interpretation: "Very informative. I feel it would be better received if presented by a white instructor. So the impression would not be given 'see what we blacks have done.'"

There were, perhaps, reasons behind what some service members interpreted as the lecture's "pointed" approach. One AFB member conceded that the museum staff likely had "felt the shortcoming of our history more than most and that is why you seem to take such a hard line approach to your lecture. I can't say I blame you much." Another visitor admitted that while he enjoyed the exhibit, he would not return to the museum alone—and assumed that the museum staff would understand why: "A good exhibit, but I wouldn't come here by myself. You know what I mean." If we presume that this commentator was white, we can read this statement in multiple ways. The writer was either concerned about his personal safety in Anacostia, or he felt too ill at ease as a white man visiting a black museum. Finally, one visitor confessed to feelings of self-consciousness. As a (presumably) white man now physically surrounded by an environment filled with African American staff, African American artifacts, and a narrative that clearly deviated from mainstream interpretations of American history, he disclosed that he felt "like I've been in a zoo—and I was the animal being stared at."[33]

The AAMP: A Compromised Space?

The frank admissions from those who visited the Anacostia Neighborhood Museum's Blacks in the Westward Movement, as well as the audiences and critics who visited the Smithsonian's A Nation of Nations, reveal the complicated reactions surrounding the attempts of both African American and mainstream museums to introduce discussion of race and "nonwhite" history into the idealized Bicentennial story. Yet while mainstream museums like the Smithsonian may have floundered in their efforts to engage in this dialogue, they were, at the very least, acknowledging that the dialogue needed to occur. Many municipal organizations founded expressly to direct city-wide Bicentennial activities, such as Philadelphia '76, hesitated to engage in this conversation. Indeed, although Philadelphia '76 initially allocated funding for cultural events that attempted to highlight the city's multicultural heritage, in the end the celebrations portrayed Philadelphia in its most patriotic and unified light rather than presenting a more complicated picture of the ways in which Bicentennial ideals had yet to be fulfilled. Despite their ambitious early plans to create a more "humane city," nonsensical pageantry staged by Philadelphia '76 and other city officials ended up dominating the holiday. Overflowing toilets, lack of water, and waterlogged campsites (curiously reminiscent of a more recent cultural event, the Woodstock music festival) all merged to imbue the celebration with a rather dispirited tone. As Andrew Feffer has written, some crowd members, "overcome with the event's commemorative spirit, tore pieces off unattended [Conestoga] wagons for souvenirs."[34] City leaders who avoided discussing the difficult living conditions faced by the city's poorest residents also shunned dialogue about the implications of divisive national events like Watergate and Vietnam. Instead, they crafted celebratory speeches and programs meant to "heal the wounds" left open by the past decade.[35]

This pervasive emphasis on ceremony over content during the officially sanctioned Bicentennial celebrations precluded any discussion of the complex events and issues of Philadelphia's past and present—namely, the ideological dissonance engendered by the coexistence of both slavery and freedom at the signing of the Declaration of Independence and the present-day realities of

African American life. In the face of national events like the beating of Theodore Landsmark in Boston, not to mention the daily upheavals closer to home, the debut of the Afro-American Historical and Cultural Museum in Philadelphia in June 1976 thus met with significant welcome and high expectations on the part of many of the city's African American residents. The museum's mission to preserve and promote Philadelphia's African American heritage, and, beyond that, to respond to the ongoing social and economic injustices taking place within the city, offered a crucial counterpoint to a celebration perceived as lacking in meaning.

While some museum backers still smarted from the previous year's fight against the Society Hill Civic Association over where the museum should be located, advocates were pleased when the museum's gala opening drew more than six thousand visitors. By the end of opening weekend in June 1976, thirteen thousand people had toured the new museum—on par with the numbers originally projected by the city and (more worriedly) by the Society Hill Civic Association.[36] By December 9, 1976, eighty thousand people had visited the museum, bringing in $56,000 in admission revenues and an additional $69,000 in contributions—although the museum still retained a $200,000 deficit by the end of December 1976.[37]

Museum staff and supporters intended the AAMP's first exhibits to present the antithesis of the city's limited historical vision. Consequently, when visitors walked through the museum's doors in June 1976, they toured an exhibition that interpreted the course of the black freedom struggle from its inception through the present day—a format previously seen in the exhibits staged by Chicago's DuSable Museum and the International Afro-American Museum in Detroit. The exhibition denoted four major themes: "African Heritage" (1440–1860), "Captivity and Resistance" (1861–1919), "Struggle for Freedom" (1920–Present), and the "Quest for Equality." Curators designed the exhibition's content to help visitors expand their knowledge of African American history and culture and thereby lessen "the acceptance of historical and cultural myths that promote stereotypes and racial animosities."[38]

Theodore Cam's architectural report for the museum detailed the philosophy of the "Captivity and Resistance" portion of the exhibit, which stressed a "heroic" narrative of African American history while simultaneously illuminating its grim aspects. Just as it was necessary to negotiate alliances with white politicians during the museum's construction, "Captivity and Resistance" also highlighted the mutual interaction between African Americans and white abolitionists that took place during the early nineteenth century. Still, the report emphasized that African American initiative to abolish slavery and seek freedom must serve as the exhibit's primary focus.[39]

Beyond the opening, most of the museum's early exhibits presented collections of art related to the African Diaspora, such as Art from Zaire: One Hundred Masterworks from the National Collection. During the exhibit Great Kings (1977), which featured paintings of African leaders, staff instituted a tactic similar to that employed by the DuSable Museum: visitors received free reprints of the original paintings.[40] Black Experiences, which debuted in January 1978, focused on black family life and included thirty-one works of art by Allan Crite, Ellen Powell Tiberino, Richard Watson, and other black artists.[41] Genetic Memories (1978) featured ceramics, prints, and drawings by Philadelphia artists Winnie Owens and Winston Kennedy; its mission was to "express spiritual thought and emotion rooted in the African American Experience." Curator Deirdre Bibby explained in that the works featured in Genetic Memories "are not merely masks or wall hangings, but are strong statements on racism and its continual destructive effect in America."[42]

Like other African American museums across the country, the AAMP focused on developing educational outreach programs in order to connect with Philadelphia's black community—even if the museum itself remained physically at a distance from most of the city's African American residents. In 1978, director H. Alonzo Jennings reflected upon the necessity of bridging the perceived and real distance that separated the museum from the community. Acknowledging that "all too often, community people feel that museums are 'dry, dusty places' with which they needn't involve themselves," Jennings emphasized that the AAMP "wants the community to view it as a living and breathing institution. We want people to become personally involved with the Museum. We want them to view it as a second home."[43] In this spirit, planned lectures and workshops for 1978 included a seminar on African Americans in Philadelphia, an observance of Dr. Martin Luther King's life and work, and a celebration of black history month.[44] Jennings also proposed bringing children from Philadelphia and the Delaware Valley area to attend a weekend class on black history and culture. One hundred and twenty students were expected to attend each weekend; the estimated cost of the program was $30,000.[45] Visitors of all ages could also enjoy "Evenings at the Afro," which featured films and plays "by and about blacks," as well as jazz and classical concerts.[46]

Advertising the museum's resources represented a crucial activity for staff.

Compared to the early efforts of museums such as the DuSable and the International Afro-American Museum, which typically placed solicitations for volunteers and artifact donations in local black newspapers (with occasional ventures on black radio stations), the AAMP instigated a much larger advertising campaign. For example, the 1978 budget proposal included plans for advertisements in newspapers, magazines, theater playbills, and on billboards and transit boards. At an annual cost of $10,000, Jennings indicated that the museum also hoped to place ads on five hundred local buses and trains that would "go into the heart of the Black Community."[47]

Even before the African American Museum of Philadelphia had officially opened, however, supporters and critics alike questioned whether it could stand as a reputable institution with the potential for long-term success, or if it would simply serve as a panacea to silence Philadelphia's black community during the Bicentennial. After the excitement of the museum's grand opening had faded, together with the initially ambitious plans for Philadelphia's Bicentennial celebrations, these concerns persisted. The museum fell short of garnering significant mainstream media attention or substantial attendance, apart from schoolchildren, during its early years.[48] Critics also complained about the mediocre quality of the content and presentation of its early exhibits, which failed to approach the level of innovation represented by the Anacostia Neighborhood Museum's The Rat, or the International Afro-American Museum's mobile van (both of which were produced within the first two years after these organizations opened). A Philadelphia newspaper editorial published around the time of the AAMP's opening noted that, although the battles over the museum's location had finally subsided, prominent African American leaders continued to criticize its proposed exhibit content. The editorial reasoned that their reservations "cannot be dismissed with charges of racism—as some backers of the museum tried to dismiss objections to the original Society Hill site—because they come from blacks."[49]

Poorly executed exhibitions threatened to undermine the museum's standing in the city's African American community as well as the broader community of museums in Philadelphia. For example, in 1977, the *Philadelphia Bulletin* art critic Nessa Forman reviewed the AAMP's display of the African art collection of the diplomat Robert DuMas. While Forman appreciated the maps of Africa depicting the origins of DuMas's seventy works of art, she also observed that "this is not the most startling collection of African objects ever assembled, and in fact, several visibly damaged wooden pieces have been glued together. This points to the need for professional conservation advice."[50] Forman detected that museum staff were unable to exert much authority in exhibition design, as Clarence Farmer, who headed the museum's board of directors, ran the institution "like an absolute monarch, leaving no decision-making authority to the 11-person professional staff, now headed by [Adolphus] Ealey."

As further evidence of the staff's lack of creative control, Forman cited a March 1977 exhibit on black scientists and inventors that the Philadelphia Electric Company had donated to the museum—over the objections of many museum staff members. The exhibit consisted of portraits of twenty-four African American inventors and scientists; curators hung each of the portraits in vertical columns on a wall along with accompanying biographies of the inventors. Forman chastised the exhibit's curators, writing that "there are no little sketches showing the inventions. There is no case with models of inventions. All is characterized by a tonal nondimensional flatness that depends on a viewer's willingness to stand and read."[51] By October 1977, the exhibit was languishing in a basement lecture hall.[52]

The museum's first critically successful exhibition, titled Of Color, Humanitas and Statehood: The Black Experience in Pennsylvania over Three Centuries, 1681–1981, debuted in 1981. Curator Charles Blockson, whose archival collections at Temple University comprise an extensive span of Philadelphia's African American history, called it "the largest single exhibition ever assembled on Pennsylvania's African American history."[53] Much as the museum itself presented a bold counternarrative to the city's Bicentennial celebrations, Blockson designed Of Color, Humanitas and Statehood to serve as a counterpoint to the statewide celebration of another symbolic holiday—the state's tricentennial.

Blockson divided the exhibition into six distinct chronological themes:

Part I.   Slaves amidst the Peaceable Kingdom, 1681–1776
Part II. Blacks and the Newborn Nation, 1777–1800
Part III. Prophets of Equality, Patriots of the Union, 1801–1865
Part IV. The Search for Equality, 1866–1900
Part V. The Black Talented and Toiler during Pennsylvania's Industrial Age, 1901–1940
Part VI. Troubled Minority in the Modern Commonwealth, 1941–1981

The sixth section offered a pointed critique of the state of American race relations. Despite the gains made by the Civil Rights Movement, Blockson argued in this section that Philadelphia's black citizens still faced "far from encouraging" conditions. Although the movement had created a "wellspring of black pride" and opportunities for African American political leaders, patterns of racism and discrimination "still lurk beneath the surface of some white political movements"—a reference, surely, to the rise of Reagan conservatism. The exhibition text also discussed how resource-stricken schools and deteriorating slums presented ongoing problems for Philadelphia's African American residents.[54] This exhibit—and, by extension, the museum itself—was thus willing to venture beyond a presentation of the "heroic narrative" of African American history (such as that demonstrated by the earlier exhibit on black inventors), to a critique of present-day social and economic conditions in the city.

Despite the success of Blockson's exhibition, long-term problems continued to plague the new museum. While weakly executed exhibits contributed to its struggles, a second, less obvious limitation may have been the museum's lack of an archive. Although existing research facilities, such as the Schomburg Center for Research in Black Culture in New York City and the Moorland-Spingarn Library in Washington, D.C., offered adequate resources, AAMP planners initially believed that it was critical to develop and maintain their own research collections related to blacks in Mexico, the Caribbean, and Philadelphia.[55] Indeed, according to architect Theodore Cam, the institution had to "serve the function of furthering knowledge and understanding of the Black man in the New World through the establishment of a research facility (library and manuscript collection), designed to serve both the general public and scholars."[56] Perry Triplett, an African American construction inspector for the Philadelphia School District and a Pennsylvania Bicentennial Commission board member, likewise argued in 1976 that if the museum did not build a "truly professional archive meriting respect from historians" it would face "rejection by the black community."[57] After reviewing the museum's construction, however, Triplett had grave doubts. He warned Philadelphia '76 chair William Rafsky, "It will be disastrous to the people of Philadelphia to continue to have them believe they are getting a facility that will qualify as a museum. . . . The rejection by the Black Community of this or any facility which is not equal in merit and professional stature and character of any other like facility, will be so swift and derisive as to make me shudder and wonder as to the motives of those who are pushing this concept for that site."[58]

Charles Blockson also stressed the importance of accruing archival materials for the museum rather than simply building a "slapdash exhibit hall [to satisfy] a deadline but little else."[59] Yet when the museum opened its doors in 1976, there was no archive—much to the dismay of many who had supported the AAMP's creation. Due to the extensive costs of the museum (initially estimated at $2.5 million, the final cost reached more than $3.5 million), the fourth floor, which was supposed to house the library, archives, and school group lunchroom, was never completed.[60]

The absence of a professional archive may have slowed the research output of the museum staff; indeed, the museum's one-year plan for 1978 noted that research "has been one of the AAH&CM weakest areas."[61] Lack of a proper archive in turn hampered the public's access to a wide array of materials on African and African American history. As DuSable Museum visitor Brandon Smith had related in his 1970 letter to founder Margaret Burroughs, audiences usually had difficulty finding these sources at most public libraries, and even some universities, during the 1960s and 1970s—which is why Smith found collecting institutions like the DuSable so invaluable.[62]

The African American Museum of Philadelphia's failure to prioritize the establishment of an archive paralleled the experience of Detroit's International Afro-American Museum. During the museum's advertising and fund-raising campaigns, Charles Wright characterized the IAM as an "image-provoking" monument to black history and culture rather than drawing fund-raising attention to the presumably more mundane need for an archive. An archive, planners presumed, would not attract the same audiences as would full-scale exhibits and an impressively designed museum. Yet the IAM's choice to forgo the creation of a proper archive may have resulted in the staff's lack of opportunity to learn how to preserve fragile documents. Although the museum now boasts a solidly professional archive, a striking example of the Detroit museum's lack of effective archival training for its staff and volunteers occurred as late as November 2006. The owner of fifteen sheets of an unpublished portion of Alex Haley's manuscript for *The Autobiography of Malcolm X* sued the museum because of the significant deterioration of the document, which had been on display to the public from 1997 to 2002. The pages had a white stripe down the middle from the band that had held them in place, and the paper had turned from white to brownish-yellow. According to a *Detroit Free Press* reporter, David Ashenfelter, officials at other national museums "expressed amazement that a museum would jeopardize its reputation by allowing valuable documents to be damaged. They said the dispute might make it harder for the Wright museum to borrow other African-American historical treasures in the future."[63] In the case of both the African American Museum of Philadelphia and Detroit's Museum of African

American History, inaccessible, poorly maintained, or absent archives detracted from the primary mission of African American museums—namely, to educate and serve their audiences.

One year after its inauguration at the edge of Philadelphia's Chinatown district, public uncertainty about the African American Museum of Philadelphia's physical location also persisted. From the outset, critics felt that the museum's final site in a neighborhood dominated by office buildings rather than residences ran contrary to its desired image as a grassroots neighborhood institution.[64] The ongoing challenges presented by the museum site might have diminished its ability to resonate fully with Philadelphia's African American community in a way that the International Afro-American Museum's mobile unit and the first, immediately accessible locations of the Anacostia Neighborhood Museum, the Studio Museum in Harlem, and Chicago's DuSable Museum managed to achieve.

The AAMP's cramped interior further complicated the dilemma surrounding the museum's seemingly compromised external space. The museum's floor plan, bisected by a multilevel ramp, potentially hindered the mounting of large exhibitions. To some, such as journalist Nessa Forman, the museum's layout also reflected divisions between and within museum officials and the city. Writing that the "internal bickering was made physically visible (inadvertently, one supposes) by the form of the building itself," Forman dismissively observed that the museum's interior "is cut in thirds by a sprawling rampway, which negates any viable exhibition space. Thus, at the outset, Philadelphia's model museum . . . was physically nothing more than a building with compromised spaces."[65] In his study of the role of space in the built environment, cultural geographer David Sibley contends that "spatial structures can strengthen or weaken social boundaries, thus accentuating social division or, conversely, rendering the excluded group less visible."[66] Imposing buildings such as the Metropolitan Museum of Art, or the convoluted series of security roadblocks that marked the streets of New York City and Washington, D.C., after September 11, 2001, are examples that underscore Sibley's argument. In other words, one may design the built environment both to include and to exclude certain groups of people, physical movements, and concepts.[67] Architect Theodore Cam surely did not intend to exclude audiences and limit exhibit design when he mapped the AAMP's interior spaces. Nevertheless, in retrospect, rather than inviting the viewer's eye, the rampway acted as a visual, physical, and, perhaps, mental barrier to envisioning the full potential of the space.

Confronting the Limits of Compromise

The AAMP's less than ideal location and building design, together with its tentative early exhibits, did not necessarily present insurmountable obstacles; indeed,
many other museums, both African American and general-purpose, have managed to remain successful when faced with similar drawbacks. Instead, the apparent failure of museum advocates to actively recruit African American citizens to
become involved in the early stages of the museum's creation may have mired the
museum's success and reputation far more than its architecture and exhibits.
Although prominent African American leaders such as Lawrence Reddick and
Charles Blockson had offered crucial input throughout the museum planning
process, the responses provided by the museum's executive director, Gerard William, on a 1976 questionnaire reveal the lack of community involvement during
this process. In two contradictory statements about the museum's formation,
William indicated that, while community members had served on committees
with decision-making and advisory powers, the question "[were] citizen reactions to plans . . . actively solicited?" received a negative response.[68]

The compromises, however unwilling, that museum advocates made with
Philadelphia's Bicentennial planners, local politicians, and vociferous neighborhood organizations like the Society Hill Civic Association also contributed to
a sense of general community isolation from the museum. During a period
when many African Americans viewed relationships between white politicians
and black organizations as suspect, the museum's close (albeit contested) relationship with both white and black city leaders during the Bicentennial may
have worked to undermine its desired identity as an African American neighborhood organization fully responsive to the interests and needs of the black
community. In 1977, journalist Nessa Forman argued that the museum did not
even possess a true identity other than to function as a "political response to
Philadelphia's divided black community in celebration of America's 200th
anniversary."[69] In 1983, Teri Doke, the seventh executive director of the
museum, arrived at a similar conclusion in her summation of the obstacles
facing the institution. According to Doke, the "greatest challenge in the public
relations areas is to overcome the negative image the museum has in the Philadelphia community . . .[where it is] viewed as an entity doomed for failure . . .
the black community by and large view it as political, bearing no relationship
to the community itself, and . . . they view it as being ill-conceived, built and
run in isolation."[70] Forman's and Doke's comments reinforce the sense that

much of Philadelphia's African American community perceived the museum as an explicitly political, "establishment" project rather than an institution created by and for the city's African American citizens.

The results of a preliminary survey conducted by a New York advertising firm, Ruder & Finn, also accentuated the museum's negative association with political compromise. In commissioning the study, which was organized during the late 1970s, staff sought ways to reach a broader audience, as well as to gauge the impact of the museum upon Philadelphians. Concluding that the AAMP did not actually *possess* an "image" in Philadelphia other than one suspiciously enveloped in local politics," the survey maintained that citizens "know that the museum was started as a political response. They assume that it is being run politically."[71] Furthermore, although the fierce advocacy of black activists prior to the Bicentennial ensured that the museum would function as a full-fledged, permanent institution, its supporters exerted less immediate and unfiltered control over the creation and maintenance of the museum than did leaders of other African American museums like Charles Wright or Margaret Burroughs. In this sense, AAMP advocates shared a difficulty with Anacostia Neighborhood Museum director John Kinard, who often found himself locked in battle with the Smithsonian Institution regarding the ANM's autonomy.

The charged relationship between Philadelphia city officials and the African American Museum of Philadelphia also morphed into another problem for the museum as it struggled to establish its identity. Because the city's Bicentennial committees had primarily funded the construction and maintenance of the AAMP, the museum's leadership and finances remained tied to decisions made by the city. Consequently, the museum's administration shifted numerous times during the institution's first several years—in marked contrast to the strong directors retained by the Anacostia Neighborhood Museum, the DuSable, and the International Afro-American Museum in Detroit during their early, crucial years of institution building. Gerard William, whom Philadelphia '76 named as the first executive director of the African American Museum of Philadelphia, resigned his post in February 1977, just one year after the museum opened. Adolphus Ealey, curator and then assistant director, replaced William.[72] Ealey, who owned the esteemed Barnett-Aden collection of African American art in Washington, D.C., believed that he must "make the Afro-American Museum a legitimate museum." He maintained that the AAMP's diminished legitimacy had resulted from the "rush job" surrounding its opening in June 1976, as well as from the museum's "overly commercial emphasis." To improve its reputation,

Ealey suggested that the AAMP "drop labels" and "promote contemporary black art as American art. It's quality that I'm after. I don't know whether I'll be beaten down or not for my aims. All I can do is try." Ealey also referred to the AAMP as the "first public museum in the country to deal with Afro-American heritage." His dismissal—whether knowing or not—of other African American museums that had existed prior to the AAMP that had been at least partially funded by city, state, or federal dollars signaled a troubling disconnect with a network of institutions that could have provided substantial advice to the new director.

Just ten months after becoming executive director of the museum, Ealey resigned and returned to Washington, D.C., in order to manage the Barnett-Aden collection; Gerard William once again returned to serve as acting director of the AAMP.[73] Philadelphia newspapers found Ealey's resignation suspicious; as one reporter commented, "The question was inevitable. 'Did you jump,' Adolphus Ealey was asked, 'or were you pushed?'"[74] Clarence Farmer, chair of the museum's board of directors, had reportedly clashed with Ealey over his apparent inability to raise funds for the museum and to "get things going around here." Ealey denied the existence of such problems, but admitted that he and Farmer "haven't always agreed on the function of a director. He expects a director to be a fundraiser, while I contend a director's mission is principally cultural."[75]

Clarence Farmer's difficult relationship with the museum, city officials, and Philadelphia's African American community had complicated origins. He had played a key role in keeping to a minimum the amount of violence in Philadelphia after Martin Luther King's assassination in 1968. The relative peace that reigned after King's death had not resulted from the successful "law-and-order" strategies implemented by Deputy Police Commissioner (and future mayor) Frank Rizzo—tactics that administrators of other embattled cities also pursued with vigor. Rather, it was the contacts previously established by Farmer with local black activists that helped defuse the tense situation. For example, he organized a public memorial and rally at Independence Hall shortly after King's death; this peaceful yet highly visible demonstration of grief and anger, staged at one of the most symbolic locations in Philadelphia, eased some of the tensions within the city as well as among the more militant black power activists.[76]

Farmer was not, however, a traditional "black power" activist in the sense that supporting the goals of black power meant that one must cut all ties (in name, if not in reality) with the white establishment. For in addition to his responsibilities as chair of the AAMP's board of directors, he had served as one of the five incorporators of the Bicentennial Celebration Corporation (Philadelphia '76) and as chair of the city's Commission on Human Relations. It is not surprising, then, that after becoming museum director Farmer expressed sympathy for the city's right to direct aspects of the museum's finances, exhibition content, and administration. Indeed, he argued that, since it was the city that had primarily funded the African American Museum of Philadelphia, the museum must maintain an agreeable relationship with it. As Farmer informed reporter Laura Murray, "We rely on the city for funding. . . . Everything we do should be related to the city. The city has to participate."[77] Adolphus Ealey, on the other hand, had contended that museum staff must seize the reins of leadership and sever all ties with the city: "Politics has played its part. Now it's time for the politicians to exit. Will the people in power allow it? . . . I've done all I can. I didn't need the job. I didn't need the money or the recognition. I believed and still believe in Philadelphia's Black Museum."[78] After Ealey's resignation, another key museum staff member, Roland Savior, also resigned. While their resignations may have been coincidental, reporter Nessa Forman noted that their departure "underscores the Center's inability to decide what it wants to be and how it wants to get there. Even a $15,000 study last winter by the New York advertising agency Ruder & Finn hasn't helped."[79]

To be sure, clashes between a museum's board of directors and its staff regarding the balance between fund-raising and program development are familiar stories for many nonprofit organizations. However, the Philadelphia museum's struggle to define itself as an autonomous African American institution was further complicated because it appeared that Farmer controlled not only the museum's personnel but also the *content* of some potentially controversial exhibitions. A disturbing anecdote emerging from the flurry of newspaper articles surrounding Ealey's resignation concerned Farmer's desire to manage the museum's image on its opening night. At the last minute, Farmer told museum staff to place black velvet over a blowup of a Reconstruction-era newspaper cartoon by noted editorial cartoonist Thomas Nast. His objection to the cartoon, titled "Struggle for Freedom," was that it depicted a white man with his foot on a black woman's neck. Mayor Frank Rizzo was scheduled to attend the event, and though Farmer asserted that he did not cover up the cartoon to protect Rizzo's feelings, he did say that he "wanted the new museum to get off to a good start and he did find the piece a bit strong for opening night." As he went on to explain, "A black woman, and a white man's foot on her neck . . . I thought it might offend some people. . . . We have white children coming there. . . . I want the museum to tell a story but tell it in a way that won't offend anybody."[80] Farmer's obvious censorship of the poster did not bode well for the museum's reputation as an African American museum independent of the sensitivities of white audiences.

H. Alonzo Jennings, who became the museum's executive director in 1978, attempted to move the institution beyond these heated power struggles. In an interview with Philadelphia *Evening Bulletin* reporter Thomas Burton, Jennings emphasized that the conflicts among Gerard William, Adolphus Ealey, and Clarence Farmer were in the past: "I am running the museum. This has been made clear (by Farmer and the board of directors). We have an understanding that the administration of the museum is up to me. I do not anticipate a recurrence of these problems."[81] Notwithstanding Jennings's resolution, however, the damage had already been done. Issues concerning exhibition quality, audience retention, finances, and leadership continued to plague the African American Museum of Philadelphia during its most crucial institution-building years, even as it attempted to cement its identity as a museum relevant and accessible to Philadelphia's black community.

The African American Museum of Philadelphia's distinctive origins as an institution specifically conceived in response to the celebration of the nation's Bicentennial may in fact have significantly contributed to the numerous problems it faced both before and after its opening. Yet it would soon become apparent that the museum's difficulties were not, in themselves, unique. Many African American neighborhood museums that had begun as independent, black-controlled institutions faced significant struggles with regard to finance, attendance, and administration during the 1980s and 1990s. When confronted by, among other factors, a far more conservative political climate, internal ideological and financial conflicts, and declining attendance, some black museums were forced to reduce their staff and operations even as the number of newly created African American museums began to steadily increase. In extreme cases, some black neighborhood institutions that had set out with such energy and urgency during the 1960s had to close their doors—thus raising questions about the stability and longevity of the black museum movement as a whole.

CHAPTER 5

ROCKY TRANSITIONS
Black Museums Approach a New Era

By the mid-1980s, the small vanguard of African American museums that took root during the 1960s had grown into a network of more than one hundred African American museums across the country in locations as varied as the African American Museum in Dallas (founded in 1974) and the Black Holocaust Museum in Milwaukee (1988).[1] During the early 2000s, the number of African American museums surpassed two hundred. Like the pioneering black neighborhood museums based in metropolises like Chicago, Detroit, and Philadelphia, many of these institutions emerged in cities where African Americans wielded an increasing amount of political power; this power often enabled the allocation of funds to expand existing museums or build new ones. Yet whether the black museum movement could support the proliferation of new and expanding museums became increasingly questionable.

In an interview conducted in 2000, Rita Organ, president of the Association of African American Museums, revealed some of the problems faced by African American museums to *St. Louis Post-Dispatch* reporter Lorraine Kee. At last count, the association had "documented 211 African American museums nationally, from storefronts to stand-alones." Many of these museums, however, were in difficult economic straits: "for every three that open up, at least one closes."[2] In 2005, Earl Moore, a trustee of the DuSable Museum of African American History in Chicago, reaffirmed Organ's observation: "Philly is in serious trouble. Atlanta [The African American Panoramic Experience Museum] had serious trouble. . . , At the annual Association of African American Museums meeting, [fundraising is] always one of the topics."[3] Moore's reference to the African American Museum of Philadelphia is telling: the museum saw its attendance fall by 15 percent from 2002 to 2003. In 2002, its deficit stood at more than $150,000. In 2006, the AAMP received $454,000 in funding from Pennsylvania Governor Ed Rendell in an attempt to help the financially burdened museum develop its programs.[4]

Concern over financial disorder, dwindling attendance, and unstable leadership threatened to undermine African American museums from within and even render their initial successes invisible. Of course, African American museums were not the only cultural institutions to suffer during this period. The drastic reduction in federal funding to the NEA and the NEH during the late 1980s and early 1990s added to the decline in local and state support for many cultural institutions.[5] The financial inability to maintain new exhibits and increase collections contributed to a drop in attendance levels, even at popular cultural attractions in major cities. Between 1992 and 1993, for example, attendance at Chicago's Adler Planetarium, the Shedd Aquarium, and the Museum of Science and Industry dropped between 17 and 25 percent.[6]

Yet African American museums bore a double burden, for they had to compete with mainstream institutions for the same funding sources—in a race that they often lost. In 1999, DuSable Museum president Antoinette Wright speculated that African American museums faced an inherent disadvantage in vying with established "mainstream" museums: "we're competing for the same dollars . . . as well as other social agencies that do minority outreach work . . . our base of support is smaller and not as rich as the white community."[7] In 2005, Wright also contended that donors often hesitated to support African American museums for reasons beyond the purely financial. "Any time you tell the truth you have some people who appreciate the truth and some people who don't," reasoned Wright. "Some people don't want to know the ills of slavery or the hardships [faced by] our community."[8]

In an effort to reach broader audiences and improve their finances, some African American museums altered their mission statements, expanded, relocated, or changed their names. Occasionally, they engaged in a combination of all four techniques. The expansion and physical relocation of African American museums from their original sites was, on the one hand, a sign of progress for the black museum movement—an indicator of the success that many museum advocates had in negotiating the politics of their cities and attracting the financial support of museum members. However, some museum advocates found that defining their mission in relation to the local African American community became more difficult once the institutions had expanded or moved. Critics also questioned whether these formerly grassroots organizations had moved too far from the civil rights and black power campaigns that had motivated their creators. In making changes they believed would ensure the survival of their institutions, museum leaders had to field criticism that they had betrayed the working-class African American communities that had originally helped to inspire the creation of these museums.

"Looking beyond the Periphery"

The story of the African American Museum of Art and History in Minneapolis (AAMAH), which opened in 1969, encapsulates many of the issues that began to inundate black museums during the 1980s. Founded as part of the Sabathani Community Center in Minneapolis, the AAMAH afforded one of the few havens for African American artists in the Twin Cities. After splitting with the center, which was located in a black neighborhood in South Minneapolis, the AAMAH moved to Fourth Street and Hennepin Avenue in downtown Minneapolis, and then again to its third and final location on Eighth Street and Twenty-Fourth Avenue near the University of Minnesota. These disruptive moves, combined with internal disagreements about the museum's mission and identity, exhausted its staff and alienated its core audience.[9]

At the heart of the debate surrounding where to locate the museum was the question of whether the museum should remain focused on its original, predominantly African American constituents in South Minneapolis, or expand the institution both literally and figuratively in order to attract new, more diverse audiences. The museum's well-intentioned but vague mission statement—"to promote the cultural heritage of all Black people"—also created confusion for both staff and potential donors. The museum could not decide whether to focus on "traditional" African culture, or to include contemporary African American culture in its collections. AAMAH staff tried to develop programs and exhibits that addressed all of these viewpoints, but were unable to do so effectively. Faced with declining finances, together with an inability to resolve this crisis of institutional identity, the museum closed its doors in 1985.[10]

The difficulties that AAMAH staff and volunteers had in determining its location, and the belief that relocation would solve waning attendance and financial troubles, were not atypical problems within the black museum network. As we have seen, deciding where to build an African American museum in Philadelphia had beleaguered its advocates and galvanized its detractors in the 1970s. The issue of location also plagued the staff of the Anacostia Neighborhood Museum, who had long perceived an enormous gulf between their institution and other Smithsonian-affiliated museums in Washington, D.C. Although the Anacostia Neighborhood Museum's exhibits and outreach programs had made significant strides in drawing national and international attention to this predominantly black neighborhood in southeastern Washington, D.C., a 1979 *Washington Post* article on "Anacostia's Forgotten Museums" observed that Anacostia still remained the "forgotten fifth of the District of Columbia, across the river and out of mind. . . . It's a place where motorists tend to keep their windows up and their doors locked and their eyes straight ahead of traffic lights." The cultural and economic impact of Anacostia's "isolation" appeared obvious:

> If the Frederick Douglass Home and the Anacostia Neighborhood Museum were anywhere but in Anacostia, the tourists would be standing in line. But they are in Anacostia, which in this town is to say they are all but ignored. Climb the steep brick steps of Cedar Hill and you have plenty of time to admire the view from the Douglass porch, because the National Park Service isn't expecting visitors and it takes a while for them to answer the door. Enter the Neighborhood Museum and a guard will be surprised to learn that you came to visit the museum rather than to seek directions on how to get back to the 11th Street (Anacostia) Bridge.[11]

John Kinard both acknowledged and countered this perception of isolation. While Kinard admitted that "we, in Anacostia, have grown accustomed to seeing ourselves parochially and as occupying only a small place geographically," he reminded observers that "when viewed from a world or global perspective, increasingly, we are beginning to see ourselves as not just a part of Washington, D.C. . . . but as an integral part and consequential part of the world community. We must look beyond the periphery, for we have a story to tell."[12] Kinard nonetheless also believed that the museum's location in a former movie theater limited its potential, leaving it secondary to the other Smithsonian museums on the National Mall.[13] To combat the potential shortcomings of the original museum site, Kinard began campaigning for the museum's expansion and relocation. In 1985, the museum moved into a newly constructed building on Fort Stanton Road; the building's architectural features emphasized the institution's permanence and professionalism, as well as its ties to African American culture. Above all, the museum still remained in Anacostia, albeit within a park-like setting and away from the main streets.[14]

"Saving" the DuSable Museum

Compared to the uproar that surrounded the relocation of the African American Museum of Art and History in Minneapolis, there was little vocal neighborhood opposition to the DuSable Museum's move from the home of Margaret and Charles Burroughs at 3806 Michigan Avenue, to the Chicago Park District's former administration building at 740 E. 56th Place. Despite the relocation, which took place in 1974, the DuSable remained in Bronzeville and in a mostly residential neighborhood (though close to the University of Chicago).[15] Still, the entwined areas of finance and leadership became volatile problems for the DuSable during the late 1980s and early 1990s, threatening to weaken its standing among not only Chicago's prestigious community of museums but also within the network of African American museums across the country.

The DuSable's transition from a museum helmed by volunteers and community organizers to one managed by academics, museum professionals, and corporate representatives contributed to this turmoil. In this sense, it reflected a larger administrative shift taking place within the black museum community. The formation of the African American Museums Association in 1978 presaged the beginning of a movement from volunteers to professionals within African American museums. By the late 1990s, this shift was in full swing—though volunteers still played a crucial role.[16] In adopting a more "professionalized" approach, once radicalized community museums became "established" organizations.[17] For critics—some of whom worked and volunteered in the DuSable itself—this change was seen as an unforgivable betrayal of the community museum's original intent.

The few accessible institutional documents regarding the internal crisis that rocked the DuSable during the 1980s, such as a series of interviews conducted by an unidentified individual or individuals with DuSable staff members, paint a vivid picture of the turbulent state of the museum. In a February 18, 1988, interview, for example, the museum curator, Ramon Price (brother of Chicago's first African American mayor, Harold Washington), argued that the most serious problem facing the DuSable concerned "the steady deterioration of the museum's reputation in the community." According to Price, "career building" rather than "institution building" now served as the museum's dominant philosophy. Although Price believed that most of the staff remained devoted to the DuSable's core mission, their morale needed boosting because of widespread "cronyism and nepotism" within the museum. Indeed, Price held that museum staff and volunteers did not work as a team "because of the divisiveness (either by design or accident) which tends to pit one employee against the other." The museum's main priority must be "to serve Chicago's grass-roots community in the capacity of a resource/information center," and it could not do so unless the board of trustees addressed the museum's internal problems.[18]

An undated document (c. 1987) titled "The Future of Du Sable Museum is a Matter of Concern" attests that troubles within the museum were beginning to spin out of control. The document, penned by unidentified authors, presented twenty-five questions to the DuSable Museum's board of trustees regarding issues that had arisen at the museum during the last several years. Along with deteriorating exhibition quality, the authors cited several disturbing trends: there had been no newsletter, annual report, or annual meeting for the past two years; the museum's annual "Heritage Calendar," which Margaret Burroughs had started early in the DuSable's existence, was not produced in 1985 and 1986. The questionnaire also suggested that nepotism contributed to declining staff morale. Question 12, titled "Staff Unity and Dedication and Morale in the Past 16 Months Destroyed," inquired: "How can the President justify taking established titles and jobs from qualified personnel and relegating same to totally inexperienced employees whose background, training and expertise is questionable?"

These critics also believed that the DuSable's administration appeared to place more emphasis on hosting parties and other social gatherings than on running the museum and responding to community needs. Question 24, titled "Du Sable Museum's Image and Mission Distorted," asked "Why is the image of Du Sable Museum which was founded as a grassroots peoples Museum being changed to an institution which is being narrowly operated as a private social club?" Fund-raising activities at the DuSable reflected the administration's apparent shift in focus from its original "grassroots" constituency to a "bourgeois" mentality. As question 17 queried, "Why have grassroots activities such as the 'Walkathon' been replaced with elitist $100.00 per ticket Cocktail

Parties?"[19] While these accusations focused specifically on the DuSable, similar criticisms had been (or would soon be) leveled at other African American and ethnic museums. Critics of El Museo del Barrio, for example, derided the institution for engaging in fund-raising activities that seemed to contradict their interpretation of the museum's mission. As one community member angrily charged, El Museo "was not built so that some people can advance their careers, socialize or drink champagne."[20]

At their August 1994 meeting in Chicago, concerned leaders of the African American Museum Association expressed their misgivings regarding the DuSable's institutional strength. Although changes in the museum might have stemmed from the sometimes unstable periods of museum growth and development, the association wrote that "they may also indicate more profound problems of board/staff relationships which jeopardize institutional stability. In this context, AAMA is very anxious over the fact that the DuSable Museum has had four executive directors in a period of only six years."[21]

The DuSable's internal leadership conflicts exploded onto the public scene in 1994 with the board's dismissal of Executive Director Gwendolyn Robinson. Robinson, who had directed the DuSable since 1991, was a Chicago native and former director of the Smithsonian's program in African American culture at the National Museum of American History.[22] The reasons underlying Robinson's dismissal were murky. Some board members told the media that Robinson had decided not to renew her contract—a charge that her lawyer called "an out-and-out lie."[23] Dr. Danille Taylor-Guthrie, former DuSable board member and an assistant professor of Afro-American Studies at Indiana University Northwest, publicly decried the board's actions to the local media, arguing that the board "has no concept of what a museum can be. They never attend the exhibits or functions, they have no art or history backgrounds. . . . They talk about expanding and adding new wings and these are people who have no idea of the cost of such projects or even what to put in them."[24]

A campaign led by a group called "Committee to Save the DuSable Museum" argued that the board's dismissal of Robinson demonstrated their stubborn refusal to act in the museum's best interests:

> We are *outraged* by their attempt to *arm-twist* Dr. Robinson out of her office on August 1, 1994 (before the end of her contract) in order to replace her with Mr. Carl Perrin, an employee . . . of Coca Cola, who has no experience in museum management and no credibility in the museum and arts community. Mr. Perrin

had until a few weeks ago been Chairman of the Board of Trustees. We are *alarmed* by the consequences for the museum! The Board of Trustees seems to be on a destructive path of hiring qualified directors only to fire them soon after they have been hired.[25]

Committee members maintained that Carl Perrin's promotion to the position of executive director set a dangerous precedent for the museum, not only because of his lack of experience and, presumably, his corporate ties, but also because the committee felt that the standards of the American Association of Museums deemed such an appointment unethical.[26]

Several members of the Committee to Save the DuSable Museum spoke with the Chicago media regarding Robinson's removal from office. Lisa Brock, Chairperson of the Department of Liberal Arts at the Art Institute of Chicago, informed the *Chicago Sun-Times* that Robinson's termination, as well as the dismissal of her predecessor, Amina Dickerson, hindered the DuSable's ability to compete with other cultural institutions in Chicago and further underscored the board's desire to "control the museum for their own aggrandizement and social status." Oscar Brown, committee member and a former curator of the performing arts at the DuSable, also spoke with the *Chicago Sun-Times* in 1994. Brown bluntly asserted that the DuSable was "in danger of dying from a self-inflicted wound, because without a qualified competent director in place, donors will understandably lose confidence in the institution's ability to professionally administer its gifts."[27] In a self-produced pamphlet titled "The Road to Cultural Revolution," Brown ventured even further, portraying DuSable board members as the unwitting tools of white supremacists: "In Chicago where blacks really have 'no place to be somebody,' the DuSable Museum appears to be a hole in the dike of cultural repression and DuSable's Board of Directors whose members—though black, represent corporate white supremacy—are slavishly behaving like that fabled little Dutch boy, trying somehow to plug the leak and prevent a flood."[28]

Brown's portrayal of the DuSable board as slavish and deluded "Uncle Tomo" was, perhaps, extreme for the situation; he also made an exaggerated comparison between Robinson's dismissal and the arrest of Rosa Parks. Yet his comments reflect the contentious environment that surrounded the DuSable's administration in the early 1990s and the lingering radical metaphors of the Black Power Movement. Institutional change, in the form of the board's abrupt firing of Robinson, as well as the museum's extension into social fund-raising activities that seemed to undermine its original commitment to the black working class, were deemed by critics like Brown to be not only elitist but also a complicit acknowledgment of, and a concession to, the white power structure that still controlled the city.

The Committee to Save the DuSable Museum signed a petition that presented three demands to the museum's administration: that it reinstate Robinson as executive director, renew her contract, and evaluate the DuSable's board of trustees "in order that greater community accountability can be established."[29] Robinson's contract, however, was not renewed, and Perrin remained interim president until Antoinette Wright was hired in 1997.[30] Although the thoughts of director emeritus Margaret Burroughs regarding Robinson's dismissal are limited in the available sources, Burroughs did explain to the *Chicago Sun-Times* that she believed the complaints of the committee—whom she described as a "small group of dissidents"—were "nonsense," and that the board had terminated Robinson's contract because "we wanted to go in a different direction." Furthermore, Burroughs contended that the DuSable's naysayers were misguided, for the museum was "in better shape than it has ever been."[31] Indeed, even in the face of the museum's internal leadership problems, the DuSable successfully raised $1.5 million and added a 26,000-square-foot wing to the museum in 1993, named after Harold T. Washington. The total expansion project cost $3.5 million; corporations and the Chicago Park District donated the remainder. Significant corporate funding of the DuSable's expansion project, as well as corporate presence in the form of interim president Carl Perrin, further demonstrated the DuSable's transition from a decidedly grassroots and politicized community presence to an institution with significantly enhanced ties to for-profit organizations.

"Mainstreaming" African American History

Notwithstanding the DuSable's successful expansion, Lisa Brock's earlier observation about the museum's loss of staff, funding, artifacts, and exhibits to better financed (and internally stable) cultural institutions continued to ring true for the museum throughout the 1990s.[32] For example, in 1994, the Joyce Foundation delayed the distribution of a promised $51,250 grant because of the museum's leadership struggles.[33] In 1999, DuSable president Antoinette Wright indicated that the museum had been set to obtain the papers of Carol Moseley Braun, an African American lawyer from Chicago, and the second African American elected to the U.S. Senate. Yet because the DuSable lacked adequate archival space, the Chicago Historical Society secured the papers first. Wright also admitted that because the DuSable had a smaller budget it continued to "lose good people to mainstream museums since we don't have the money to compete with salaries offered by white institutions."[34]

Antoinette Wright's admission illustrates how the presentation of exhibits on African American history and culture had become more commonplace in so-called white institutions by the 1990s. During the 1960s and 1970s, black museum founders had based their missions and fund-raising strategies upon the conviction that their museums offered the public something that could not be obtained at traditional institutions. Now that museums with significantly larger budgets sought to "mainstream" African American history and culture in their programs, some black museum leaders believed that the ability of African American museums to stage groundbreaking exhibits and attract audiences was threatened—perhaps intentionally.[35] At the ideological heart of the conflict over mainstreaming rests the very question that drove the creation of institutions like the DuSable and the Anacostia Neighborhood Museum: who had the "right" to present exhibits to and for African American audiences other than African Americans themselves?

This debate continued to be closely linked with whether the concept of museum decentralization—that is, the practice of larger mainstream museums establishing branch museums in previously underserved or underrepresented communities—signified a racially condescending, and ultimately meaningless, gesture. During the 1969 Bedford Lincoln Neighborhood Museum seminar in New York City, African American cultural leaders discussed the growing rift around the then new concept of decentralization, and whether "white" institutions had the right to interpret black history. African American museum director Colin "Topper" Carew argued that building community-oriented branch museums in African American neighborhoods amounted to an irrelevant enterprise, for "community museums have always existed in the black community, on street corners, in backyards, on stoops. It's just that it's a living museum." Likewise, activist June Jordan predicted that the branch museum model "may well become a hip cop-out for the regular museum establishment. . . . It is possible to set up some rinky-dink operation in what is called the ghetto and let it be run by permission only. Give money out on a conditional basis and say, Fine, we've taken care of the Negroes."[36]

Jordan's belief that mainstream museums might "cop out" in presenting black history was not, of course, without basis. In her 1972 essay "The Anacostia Experience: A Personal Perspective," Anacostia Neighborhood Museum staff member Zora Martin scolded mainstream museums for their unwillingness to initiate change beyond the surface level even as they celebrated the outreach programs and challenging exhibits pioneered by the ANM and other African American museums. For example, she recalled a disturbing incident that had occurred with the museum's traveling exhibit The Frederick Douglass Years (1970). In one city, the panels on slavery were "temporarily removed from the exhibition for fear, it was said, of 'offending the blacks.'" In another incident, a museum borrowed the Anacostia Neighborhood Museum's groundbreaking exhibit The Rat (1968). This museum's docents, however, sanitized the gritty content for their audiences, thereby eliminating the entire context of the exhibit. As Martin remembered, "I heard a docent say by way of introduction to a tour group, 'And now, children, I have a surprise for you. In the next room we have some LIVE RATS!' (Squeals and end of tour)."[37]

Rather than initiating token efforts to create entirely new neighborhood museums, John Kinard stressed that mainstream museums should scrutinize their institutions from within by diversifying their staff and making more services available to the public.[38] Since Kinard directed an African American neighborhood "branch" museum directly affiliated with the Smithsonian, his critique of museums that employed the decentralization technique belies his somewhat precarious position.[39] Nevertheless, while at the 1969 conference, he bluntly argued that those at the Smithsonian Institution still refused to fully embrace community involvement for fear of what the black community would tell them. What white museum staff members needed, argued Kinard, was to be able to "sit down with the black man and listen to him or appreciate him when he calls you a honky or a pig and describes categorically how you have denied him . . . and allow him to come to some resolution within himself about how to deal with this unique problem so that the two of us can work together."[40]

Kinard's thoughts on the relationship the Anacostia Neighborhood Museum maintained with the Smithsonian remained somewhat pessimistic well into the 1980s. Regardless of his success in bringing African American history to Anacostia and the world beyond, in his view the Smithsonian Institution continued to give short shrift to the ANM—and to black history told from the perspective of African Americans:

> I recognize even now that [the Anacostia Museum] should be, based on twenty
> years of experience, much larger than it is, much more vital to the Institution, the
> Smithsonian, than it is, but I recognize why it isn't. It isn't because the black man's

role in America is not respected. His *view* is not respected. His history is not respected. Until that comes about, you will have small operations which represent smallness. Why isn't that kind of thing done down on the Mall? Why don't we tell American history? For example, they don't talk about Indians in the [Museum of American History]. In the Museum of American History, how could you even call it that and not treat the American Indian? How is it that you could treat the American black as a side issue in something called "Migrations?"[41]

Kinard's complaint about the National Museum of American History exhibition Field to Factory: Afro-American Migration 1915–1940 (February 1987–March 1988) is telling. The Smithsonian Institution had once clung to the idea that a museum represented a "tomb where the past and its taste remain preserved."[42] By the 1980s, however, the Smithsonian had expanded its interpretation of African American history, thanks in no small part to the work of grassroots black neighborhood museums and the parallel revolution in new social history. Yet its attempt to portray African American history through exhibits such as Field to Factory created unease among ANM staff, who had always clashed with the many degrees of separation between their museum and the rest of the Smithsonian system. It was not just that Kinard believed that the exhibit presented an incomplete picture of black history (even though the exhibit, curated by African American historian Spencer Crew, was notable for its innovative depiction of the variety of black experiences during the Great Migration).[43] Perhaps the more distressing factor for Kinard was the fact that the National Museum of American History, with a budget far above that of the Anacostia Museum, could now easily produce, or "mainstream," exhibits such as Field to Factory. The ANM, on the other hand, was still struggling, thus casting its place and worth within the Smithsonian community of museums in serious doubt.

Anacostia Neighborhood Museum staff member Louise Daniel Hutchinson shared many of Kinard's concerns about the museum's future, commenting in 1987: "I think there's been a continuing question in the minds of many as to whether they [the Smithsonian] will continue that museum. . . . People are very careful in their public utterances, what they won't say and what they will reveal." Still, Hutchinson praised the ANM for its groundbreaking achievements; in this, she found hope for the continued survival of the institution. Hutchinson believed that a mainstream museum exhibit like Field to Factory did not lessen the community's need for the Anacostia Neighborhood Museum

—nor indeed, for any African American museum. Rather, she reasoned that "I think it's the same kind of question as, 'Does the integration of American colleges negate the need for black colleges?' I think certainly we need them both. I don't see it as an either/or."

Even with the Smithsonian's slow shift toward multicultural exhibitions, Hutchinson maintained that it had not yet arrived at the point where, compared with its other blockbuster exhibits, curators and exhibit designers willingly engaged in both a critical interpretation and a thoughtful presentation of African American history. She specifically cited Black Wings: The American Black in Aviation (1984) as an example of the institution's still cautious approach. The Smithsonian placed Black Wings in a hard-to-reach area of the National Air and Space Museum, "where the public couldn't see it, and the guards had trouble telling you where it was. It got more attention on television than it got at the museum, and subsequently has become much more popular as a traveling exhibition, because it was just so darn hard to find in the museum itself."[44]

Like her counterparts at the Anacostia Neighborhood Museum, DuSable Museum founder Margaret Burroughs also sparred with a mainstream cultural organization regarding its decision to interpret and present African American history. In 1994, the Chicago Historical Society (CHS) planned an exhibit about the African American community who had historically lived in Chicago's South Side. The exhibit, titled Douglas/Grand Boulevard: The Past and the Promise, was part of a larger exhibition called Neighborhoods: Keepers of the Culture, which documented the past and present heritage of four distinct neighborhoods in Chicago. Burroughs objected to the Chicago Historical Society's plans to chronicle the Douglas-Grand Boulevard neighborhood, contending that the "Historical Society is treading on ground that rightfully belongs to the DuSable."[45] "When this project goes public," Burroughs warned, "it will be interpreted by the African American community as an instrument to undermine the DuSable Museum, consciously or not."[46]

A *Chicago Tribune* editorial opined that Burroughs resisted the CHS's plans because institutions like the DuSable feared that funding, audiences, and institutional identity would be compromised if "mainstream institutions—with their overwhelmingly greater resources—address ethnic subjects."[47] As there was, in fact, "no divine right to cultural history," the *Tribune* editorial maintained that the DuSable's administration "would do well to concentrate on upgrading its marketing and fund-raising skills so that it can adequately compete for exhibits in its area of specialization. The Historical Society's success need not be mirrored by the DuSable's failure. There are myriad stories to tell, and history enough for all."[48] Yet while there may indeed be "history enough for all," a museum's ability to tell "myriad stories" depends, at least partially, upon its financial success. In objecting to the Douglas/Grand Boulevard exhibit, Burroughs could not fail to realize that the DuSable's fluctuating leadership and financial difficulties made it fare poorly in comparison to the more extensive resources of the Chicago Historical Society.

There were more deeply entrenched issues that lay behind Burroughs's insistence that the CHS had no right to create and present exhibits without the active input of the African American community. The *Tribune's* statement that museums have no "divine right to cultural history" belies the fact that for centuries the dominant institutional purveyors of European culture had indeed claimed this right. Museum collections, Ivan Karp asserts, "are bound up with assertions about what is central or peripheral, valued or useless, known or to be discovered, essential to identity or marginal."[49] By publicly resisting the Historical Society's efforts to interpret the diverse history and peoples of Chicago's South Side, Burroughs was fighting against the legacy of mainstream museums that had long made it a practice to misinterpret, misconstrue, and marginalize black history in favor of promoting "essential" stories and artifacts. The fact that these institutions now seemed disposed to offer multicultural interpretations did not, in the view of black museum founders like Burroughs, grant them the right to usurp the cultural territory—and resources—of African American neighborhood museums.

Notwithstanding Burroughs's public opposition, the Chicago Historical Society continued with their plans to exhibit Douglas/Grand Boulevard: The Past and the Promise, which debuted in April 1995. In concession to Burroughs's outcry, however, the CHS loaned the exhibit to the DuSable in October 1995.[50] Yet when the DuSable opened the exhibit, its content had markedly changed. DuSable curator Ramon Price, who had previously derided the DuSable Museum Board for their seeming betrayal of the museum's grassroots origins, eliminated exhibit text that documented the history of white settlers in early Chicago to focus instead only on Native American settlement.[51] Price thus deliberately skewed—and, arguably, falsified—the historical accuracy of Douglas/Grand Boulevard in favor of a narrow and more defiantly political interpretation that meshed with his personal interpretation of the DuSable's core mission and audience.

As more mainstream public history sites like the Chicago Historical Society began to incorporate the voices and stories of nonwhite, and non-male, audiences rather than unilaterally focusing on the deeds of white men, curators hoped that new audiences would therefore follow. In many cases, however, minority attendance at even well-established, financially sound sites remained relatively stagnant. Colonial Williamsburg, for example, admitted to having ongoing difficulty attracting African American tourists despite having made significant strides to end their interpretive silence about the realities of slavery and colonial life. In an effort to counter the "whitewashing" of colonial history at this popular living history site in Virginia, its curators re-created a public slave auction, in which costumed African American and white interpreters took part. While this event, which took place in 1994, provoked strong emotions on the part of both audience and interpreters, critical reaction was mixed and included boycotts from regional chapters of the NAACP. Did the auction, in its attempt to offer both a compelling and historically accurate experience, exploit both the actors and the audience by creating a disturbing but ultimately limited glimpse of a sordid and tragic past? Was this "edutainment," or education?[52]

Colonial Williamsburg also opened the "Great Hopes Plantation," a ten-acre living history farm that depicted the lives of free and enslaved blacks as well as poor white farmers. The site attracted more whites than blacks, however. In 2005, spokesperson Tim Andrews took issue with the criticism that the Great Hopes Plantation presented a "sanitized view of slavery," arguing that Colonial Williamsburg had to strike a balance between exhibiting the potentially grim results of "historical authenticity" and offering its audience a "compelling and enjoyable experience." Yet the site's effort to present an enjoyable experience was perhaps the reason one African American couple told the *Washington Post* that they avoided places like Colonial Williamsburg. Instead, "they prefer to learn about the Colonial era by visiting such places as the National Civil Rights Museum in Memphis, a more solemn venue in which the photos of limp men dangling from trees capture the true horror of what many blacks had to deal with and overcome."[53]

Tensions Grow at Detroit's Museum of African American History

The difficulty of maintaining an interpretive balance between uplifting, "vindicationist" portrayals of African American history and the need to present its "truths"—or reconciling the tension between what historian Gary Nash has termed the "commemorative voice" versus the "historical voice"—contributed to the struggles that mainstream public history sites encountered in their endeavors to meet the expectations of certain audiences and improve minority attendance.[54] Yet even at prominent African American museums, such as the Museum of African American History in Detroit (formerly the International Afro-American Museum), efforts to negotiate the uneasy interpretive balance between "uplift" and "truth" created a state of institutional turmoil. Ultimately, Dr. Charles Wright, as director emeritus, would find himself on the fringes of a museum that he himself had founded.

The International Afro-American Museum's first relocation and expansion took place in 1987, when the newly renamed Museum of African American History (MAAH) moved out of Dr. Charles Wright's modest apartment on West Grand Boulevard and inaugurated a building on Frederick Douglass Avenue, in the heart of the downtown area designated as Detroit's "cultural center." The campaign to create a new facility for the museum encompassed more than just the museum's need for larger, more professional quarters and the potential for greater attendance. Rather, museum supporters hoped that the institution's relocation meant that the history and material records of Detroit's African American community had finally been accorded equal status with the relics of European culture, such as those contained in the Detroit Institute of Arts (DIA).

In 1993, just six years after staff had settled into their new building, the MAAH received city approval to build a $38.4 million, 120,000-square-foot museum. Many museum supporters—in particular, Coleman Young, who became Detroit's first African American mayor in 1974, argued that the organization had outgrown the building on Frederick Douglass Avenue. Both advocates and critics of the building project perceived Young's vocal and financial support of the MAAH's expansion as a powerful reminder of his administration's priorities. For Young, advancing black political and cultural power in Detroit was the first priority—but this came at the expense, DIA supporters charged, of well-respected but financially strapped cultural institutions such as the Detroit Institute of Arts.

Advocates of the MAAH, on the other hand, argued that the art institute catered only to white suburbanites who did not live in Detroit. Indeed, Charles Wright had founded the International Afro-American Museum in 1965 explicitly because he believed that institutions like the Detroit Institute of Arts intentionally excluded African American culture and history, and black audiences, from their galleries. Incidents of security guards escorting African American schoolchildren out of the art institute because of their supposedly unruly behavior further reinforced the sense that the DIA did not welcome African Americans. Thus, supporters of the MAAH maintained that the city's backing of a new African American museum located in the heart of downtown Detroit was long overdue.[55]

Michigan's auto industry underwent a steep downturn during the 1970s–1990s, further transforming Detroit from an industrial powerhouse into an often surreal landscape marked by vacant buildings and lines of unemployed. The Detroit Institute of Arts and other cultural institutions in the city suffered a severe economic blow, thus exacerbating tensions with the well-funded MAAH. One possible solution to the art museum's financial and administrative distress would have been to transfer its management from the city of Detroit to a private foundation such as the DIA's Founders Society. Mayor Coleman Young, however, refused to allow the art institute, which the city had owned since 1919, to be managed by any organization other than the city itself.[56] Those most interested in owning the DIA—notably, the wealthy white patrons who belonged to the Founders Society—were thus unable to take it over. For Young, to cede control of the DIA to an organization like the Founder's Society would have been a sign of weakness and an unnecessary concession to middle-class whites who had long since deserted the beleaguered city for its suburbs.[57]

Dennis Archer, an African American lawyer who succeeded Young as mayor in 1994, differed from his predecessor in that he supported the transferal of the art institute's management to the Founder's Society.[58] Yet the DIA's unionized janitors, guards, and maintenance workers, who feared losing their civil servant status, convinced the Detroit City Council to oppose the transfer in a 6–3 vote in March 1997, just one month before the new Museum of African American History opened. Bret Ceriotti, chief union steward for AFSCME Local 542 and a maintenance worker at the art institute for sixteen years, admitted: "I personally would rather see the museum close than go to (a nonprofit corporation)."[59] The results of this vote inflamed many DIA supporters, who perceived "reverse racism" in action. One *Detroit Free Press* reader wrote to indicate her disbelief over the "mean-spirited, shortsighted and racist attitudes of DIA union employees and Detroit City Council members, and at their efforts to prevent the DIA from having the same independent, nonprofit status as the [Museum of African American History]." She recommended that all suburban residents and institutions, including schools, "boycott the Museum of African American History until the DIA has equal status."[60]

In the midst of the DIA's highly public struggles, the Museum of African American History opened an impressive new building in April 1997. The museum now functioned, Detroit newspapers declared, as a "magnificent, if unofficial, eastern gateway to the Cultural Center."[61] It thus became easy for the media to contrast the fate of the two institutions, fueling the debate about the perceived racial favoritism of city officials. Details about the construction of the third incarnation of the African American museum (and its stunning $38.4 million price tag) followed articles about the art institute's loss of more than $40 million in state funding since 1991.[62] The deteriorating physical structure of the DIA, a Beaux-Arts style building built in 1927, paled against the architectural opulence and African design elements of the new Museum of African American History. In the suggestively titled *New York Times* article "A Rich Museum in Detroit and Its Poor Cousin," reporter Keith Bradsher painted a stark physical contrast between the two institutions. As DIA employees vainly attempted to "place sponges and mop heads just below gallery windows . . . to catch the condensation dribbling down the single panes of thin glass," a few blocks away at the MAAH, "the double-paned glass dome over the rotunda . . . is specially designed to admit light while keeping the building at a steady temperature and humidity. . . . The towering decorative masks over the main entrances are partly plated with 14-carat gold."[63]

Determining the specific extent to which the DIA's financial hardships directly stemmed from the "racial favoritism" displayed by city officials toward the Museum of African American History, as opposed to other issues, such as the faults of the DIA's own management structure and Michigan's statewide cuts in cultural funding throughout the 1990s, is not as crucial as understanding how the observers and participants interpreted the political, racial, and cultural symbolism of these two institutions and their mutual battles.[64] Deep-rooted conflicts regarding the transformation of power, race, and class in Detroit lay at the heart of the debates regarding the physical and discursive space occupied by the MAAH and DIA. Critics of the MAAH argued that "corrupt black urban machines" were primarily responsible for the DIA's hardships; these machines had arisen from, and contributed to, increased black access to local political office in Detroit—and the declining power of whites. Supporters of the MAAH, on the other hand, maintained that it was due time for their museum to reap significant political and financial support from the city, given the long history of racial injustice suffered by Detroit's black citizens—and the fact that Detroit's population was now predominantly African American.[65]

A "Ghetto on the Block" Institution?

For Mayor Coleman Young, ensuring the Museum of African American History's successful journey from Dr. Wright's apartment to an architectural masterpiece in the heart of the city was synonymous with the survival of Detroit and its black inhabitants, even in the face of the city's ongoing social and economic crises.[66] No better symbol of the inextricable connection between Young and the new MAAH can be found than in the image of Young's body lying in state under the grand rotunda of the museum in November 1997. His final resting place reinforced the museum's status as an icon of black achievement and power.[67] Yet even as the tide appeared to shift definitively in favor of Detroit's African American cultural institutions, the initial flush of excitement over the newly built Museum of African American History began to fade. In the process, the MAAH found itself entangled in a series of crises: administrative, curatorial, and membership retention issues all converged to threaten Wright's original mission.

One of the museum's more visible problems concerned the controversy over its permanent exhibit, Of the People: The African American Experience, which opened as the centerpiece for the MAAH in April 1997. The exhibit's main feature constituted a life-size replica of the harrowing journey taken by slaves on the Middle Passage. Intending to bridge the past with the living present, renowned exhibit designer Ralph Applebaum modeled the plaster casts of the slaves upon the faces and bodies of Detroit's African American children, teenagers, and adults. Despite its grandeur, however, Of the People generated criticism as soon as the exhibit opened. Some audiences argued that it literally positioned African Americans as perpetual victims unable to emerge from a desolate, brutal past, and that the sculpted, static forms of the African American slaves worked to reduce interaction between the audience and the exhibit. In choosing to emphasize slavery and the Middle Passage, Applebaum had bypassed a "sufficiently uplifting portrayal of black history" and instead victimized African Americans. The fact that Applebaum was white also upset some critics, who argued that he did not have the right to portray such a traumatic subject.[68]

On the other hand, scholarly reviews of the exhibit charged that it lacked a critical voice because it promoted an "overly celebratory" tone. In a 1999 *American Quarterly* review, Christopher Clarke-Hazlett stated that the exhibit presented a triumphant narrative of African American history (or what another reviewer referred to as a "Roots Response," after Alex Haley's popular book and television miniseries) at the expense of a critical examination of the realities of this history. Still, Clarke-Hazlett also recognized that it was difficult for curators to strike a balance between "affirm[ing] the value and the struggles of past generations of African Americans without sacrificing the complexity of lived history and without ignoring or obscuring the deep, sometimes bitter conflicts that arose among black people who were otherwise united in resistance to racism and oppression."[69]

Scholar Alison Landsberg countered this criticism, maintaining that the exhibit succeeded in creating a "prosthetic memory," in which "the person . . . takes on a more personal, deeply felt memory of a past event through which he or she did not live. The resulting prosthetic memory has the ability to shape that person's subjectivity and politics."[70] In other words, by interacting with a skillfully created exhibit like Of the People, audiences were granted shared access to the experiences of slavery and the Middle Passage in a unique and unprecedented way. Landsberg also praised Applebaum's technique of model-ing the sculptures upon the real appearances of Detroit's children and teenagers, which "dramatically suggests that children might play a particularly important role in remembering slavery. It also suggests that people might be able, through an act of prosthesis, to take on memories of events through which they never lived."[71] Landsberg, however, did not mention the public complaints against the exhibit—a crucial omission. For these audiences, the static plaster forms fea-tured by Of the People had failed to create what Landsberg termed a "public cultural memory."

Public protests and scholarly critiques aside, more than 100,000 people visited the Museum of African American History and toured Of the People during its first three weeks after opening in 1997; museum administrators opti-mistically hoped that attendance would climb from an average of 70,000 to 500,000 in its first year. Yet paid attendance at the MAAH dropped from a high of 202,754 during its opening year to just 37,793 by 2003.[72] While Black History Month still attracted crowds, *Detroit Free Press* reporter Frank Provenzano pointed out that "every month isn't February." The collections content of the museum also came under fire, as Provenzano maintained that its exhibits were "too few, and often uninspired . . . there hasn't been a can't-miss blockbuster since the museum opened its burnished 1,000-pound doors, leaving some who drive by to wonder what, if anything, is going on inside."[73]

Demonstrators protest the Charles H. Wright Museum of African American History's decision to have a white artist, Ralph Applebaum, design a replica of a slave ship for the museum's new permanent exhibit, Of the People: The African American Experience. Photograph by Dale Rich, 1995. Courtesy of the Walter P. Reuther Library, Wayne State University, Detroit.

Faltering attendance and membership, coupled with the museum's already controversial reputation in Detroit and the city's own economic turmoil, translated to a steady funding decline for exhibits and public programs. In 2004, for example, the African American newspaper *Michigan Chronicle* reported that expenses for health care, insurance, and utilities at the museum had shot upward by nearly 80 percent since 1999, while museum staff had been reduced by 20 percent.[74] In light of these numbers, the *Chronicle* suggested that the MAAH's grand institutional vision simply could not be "matched by a sufficient amount of resources to transform that vision into a workable reality."[75] Melba Boyd, a professor of Africana studies at Detroit's Wayne State University, opined that the museum's troubles stemmed not only from its lack of financial resources but from the pervasive "anti-Detroit feeling," shared by suburbanites and Detroit residents alike, regarding their struggling city. In other words, both suburban whites *and* Detroit's black (and white) residents could not bring themselves to support the museum because they had been so overwhelmed by their negative perceptions of Detroit. On a wholly practical level, Boyd admitted that "those who need to be members of the museum just can't afford to give up any of their money."[76]

In a 2004 interview with the *Michigan Chronicle*, the museum's chief executive officer, Christy Coleman, countered the suggestion that membership had declined because audiences perceived the MAAH as "more of a place for social gatherings than one of learning and history." She disagreed, arguing that "as a community, we don't have the Black Bottoms and the Paradise Valleys where we're all concentrated in one area anymore." Precisely because African Americans lacked these formerly vibrant gathering places that had been destroyed by urban renewal, museums like the MAAH should be able to host community events like weddings and graduations.[77] Coleman's reference to the impact of Detroit's destructive urban renewal programs as justification for allowing the adaptive reuse of the MAAH skillfully deflected criticism that the museum had neglected its core mission. For Coleman, the museum offered its own African American-centered version of urban renewal—a space for celebration and remembrance—even as city boosters planned new stadiums and casinos in an effort to remind suburbanites, isolated from the city's core by miles of highways, sprawl, and fear of the city itself, about Detroit's cultural offerings. Still, she neglected to answer the question of whether declining museum membership was somehow linked to the possibility that the museum had lost touch with Detroit's African American community after this, its third and most costly, expansion.

Charles Wright had recognized in the early days of operating the International Afro-American Museum that, while sustaining the new museum meant attracting new members, people must also be able to become members regardless of their income level—hence his suggestion to sell membership shares for one cent.[78] Establishing a one-cent membership was probably not feasible for the Museum of African American History in its current 120,000-square-foot manifestation. Still, museum staff needed to consider the intent behind Wright's gesture, as well as the institution's historic connection to both the Civil Rights Movement and, especially, the Black Power Movement. Moving the museum first from a residential neighborhood to a new building in downtown Detroit, and then abandoning this building less than ten years later in order to create a third museum, may not have been the most sustainable step for a cultural institution that needed to operate in an unstable local and state economy.

Wright publicly went on record against the museum's relocation campaign during the late 1980s and early 1990s. By then in his early seventies, he was not fundamentally opposed to expanding the museum; as we know, he had supported the efforts to move the institution out of his apartment on West Grand Boulevard and into the new museum on Frederick Douglass Avenue in 1987. Yet as rumors of another, far more ambitious relocation project swirled, Wright "often felt out of the loop, seldom consulted about museum matters."[79] Specif-

ically, he began to spar with Marian Moore, who became executive director of
the museum in December I988. In a I989 memo from Wright to Moore regarding the museum's 25th anniversary celebration, Wright indicated that his participation at the banquet would be limited for several reasons—the main one being
the circumscribed role to which the museum staff proposed to relegate him:

> Another development deters, on a broader scale, my active participation in all
> future Museum events. It is the CODE OF SILENCE that is being observed by
> members of the staff and Board on the plans to sell this museum and build
> another one. As long as this practice, to exclude me from such discussions, is in
> effect, I shall not be able to speak or work in behalf of the museum, without the
> risk of misrepresenting the real facts. Moreover, I do not accept the authority of
> others to decide when and where my knowledge, experience and influence will be
> used to advance the cause of the Museum.[80]

Although Wright ultimately did attend the banquet, newspaper reports indicate that he abruptly (albeit temporarily) resigned from the museum's board of
directors at the event. The reason he resigned, according to the *Detroit News,*
stemmed from his belief that "it was folly to replace a 3-year-old museum with
a larger one that could cost an estimated $15 million when the city had an $81
million budget deficit." Wright further believed that it would be extremely difficult for the museum's small staff to operate such a massive facility, and his
"greatest fear was that the museum would move away from a dynamic and
flexible educational facility to an overly extended piece of prime real estate."[81]

The daily logs Wright kept, though brief, outline the escalating conflicts
between him, museum staff, and city administrators over the issue of museum
relocation and oversight. On December 2, I990, he reprimanded Mayor Coleman Young (and the people of Detroit) for backing a new museum even as the
city was slashing vital municipal services. Exasperated, Wright wrote that "there
seems a certainty that the new museum will be built despite the apparent oncom-
ing recession and absence of street lights, etc. The people have not been outraged
by the downslide of their city and still seem to be awaiting a miracle from their
miracle man, the mayor."[82] If the museum intended to serve Detroit's African
American community, Wright held that it should remain in its current location
on Frederick Douglass Avenue. He also wanted the MAAH to focus on those
who had originally comprised its primary audience—children: "I wanted a place
for the children to really love and appreciate everything that is Black history and
art. That's what I wanted, and I always want it to be our museum."[83]

Mayor Young, on the other hand, declared that he "did not want the museum to be the ghetto on the block. We are the 'Black city,' so we should have the best Black museum."[84] For Young, the "best" meant what was most architecturally distinctive. The building on Frederick Douglass Avenue did not forcibly suggest the strength of Detroit's black heritage, whereas the impressive new museum that opened in 1997 visually recalled African and African American cultural traditions—and sent the message that African Americans had played a powerful role in constructing the city's history, and would continue to do so in its present and future.[85] Yet Young's aversion to inhabiting a "ghetto on the block" institution overlooked how the MAAH's "humble" origins as a neighborhood museum, with its unassuming facades at both the West Grand Boulevard and the Frederick Douglass Avenue locations, may have been the most effective method of reaching Detroit's black community. The MAAH's costly construction of an expansive new museum seemed to complicate Wright's original mission, and, given Michigan's declining economy, the need for a multimillion dollar fund-raising campaign to keep the institution afloat was not necessarily sustainable over the long term.

In her 2004 interview with the *Michigan Chronicle*, Christy Coleman pointed out that Young's and Wright's visions were not mutually exclusive. Still, she admitted the challenge of maintaining staff and community momentum after the museum's opening year, which made it even more difficult to convey the relevance of the Museum of African American History to its core audience. As Coleman conceded, "You're talking about an organization that grew very quickly. It grew from a budget of a little less than $2 million, more than 80 to 90 percent of that covered by the city, to one that was over $7 million and the system and processes to manage it were simply not in place. We were relying on the expertise of individuals, (who) . . . weren't confident at . . . the level of new operations. Because of that, we experienced some very poor management issues."[86]

The MAAH's management issues, to say nothing of the earlier leadership conflicts that plagued the DuSable Museum in Chicago and the African American Museum in Philadelphia, reflected concerns expressed by the Institute of Museum and Library Services (IMLS) during their 2004 conference on "African American History and Culture in Museums: Strategic Crossroads and New Opportunities." In addition to the need for greater professional development and improvement of museum infrastructure, the IMLS cited the issue of governance as the "single most important—yet least discussed—crisis facing the African American museum community." The report noted that many black museums "were created by dynamic and strong leaders who are now retiring. Making the difficult transition from *founding director to board-led organi-*

zation requires renewed attention to educating board members so that they can effectively advance the museum's mission."[87] Charles Wright's fierce objections to the museum's continued expansion, and the other conflicts between Wright, museum staff, and Mayor Coleman Young, reaffirmed the IMLS's assessments about the intense complications that African American neighborhood museums often experienced throughout the 1980s and early 1990s. As these museums made the transition from being led by a single-minded founding director with close ties to the radical politics of the Civil Rights and Black Power Movements to being administered by a board of directors consisting of members of varied professional backgrounds, competing visions shaped—and sometimes divided—these institutions.

Reassessing Institutional Vision

National media attention increased as several major African American museums besides the DuSable and the MAAH began to falter publicly during the 1990s and early 2000s. In 2004, National Public Radio's Joel Rose interviewed African American museum directors and staff members about the difficulties facing their museums.[88] A common theme throughout the interviews concerned the trouble black museums had attracting financial support without experienced grant writers and public relations teams, which most of them (and, indeed, most mid-sized cultural organizations) lacked. Some interviewees also discussed the ongoing strife between African American museums and better-funded mainstream museums. Howard Dodson, the director of the Schomburg Center for Research in Black Culture in New York, cited a traveling exhibition about the African American artist Romare Bearden (1911–88) as one example of this conflict. The Art of Romare Bearden, which opened in September 2003 at the National Gallery of Art in Washington, D.C., traveled to New York City in 2004 and debuted, not at an African American art museum like the Studio Museum in Harlem, but at the Whitney Museum of American Art. While relations between the black community and the Whitney may have improved in the decades since the Black Emergency Cultural Coalition led their protests against the museum during the 1960s and 1970s, the Whitney's claim on the Bearden exhibit (and the Studio Museum in Harlem's failure to secure the traveling exhibit) reopened old wounds.

Whitney director Adam Weinberg maintained that the Bearden exhibition actually aided the Studio Museum in Harlem in the long run, as the Whitney's promotion of African American art would ultimately highlight the Studio Museum's collections and work. Yet Joel Rose noted the significant financial disparity that separated the Whitney from the typical African American museum: "the Whitney's annual budget is around $30 million . . . African American Museum in Philadelphia CEO Harry Harrison compares that to his annual budget of $1.7 million." A budget of $1.7 million, Harrison argued, was "just an exhibit" for larger museums.[89] Financially strapped museums like the African American Museum of Philadelphia or the Studio Museum in Harlem rarely had a chance to secure large-scale traveling exhibitions like the Bearden exhibit. Unless the National Gallery of Art loaned the Bearden exhibit to the Studio Museum in Harlem, Weinberg's statement that the Whitney would ultimately "help" the Studio Museum seems somewhat disingenuous. In the end, black museums advocates believed that one crucial distinction separated African American cultural institutions from "white establishment" museums like the Whitney. As DuSable trustee Earl Moore vividly put it: "Most [museums] in the city were endowed with money. Our institution was endowed with blood, sweat, and tears."[90]

Other commentators during the radio interview suggested possible ways to lessen the financial problems of museums designated as "African American." Much of their advice revolved around expanding their audiences. Rita Organ, a former Detroit Museum of African American History staff member, and director of exhibits and collections at the National Underground Railroad Freedom Center in Cincinnati (founded in 2004), asserted that, whereas African American museums often addressed controversial or emotionally difficult topics, they should instead create exhibits with greater mass appeal—thereby attracting broader audiences.[91] Lawrence Pijeaux, executive director of the Birmingham Civil Rights Institute in Alabama, concurred, saying that his museum's success rested partly upon the intentionally wide-ranging subject matter depicted in its exhibits. Contrary to Rita Organ's suggestion, however, the Birmingham Civil Rights Institute, which opened in 1992, did not necessarily shy away from emotionally difficult topics: "We've had exhibitions about the Holocaust. We've had exhibitions on AIDS in Africa and locally. I don't see how you can survive if you have a narrow support base and a narrow base of interest."[92] Pijeaux added that his institution ended the year with a budget surplus because, among other reasons, "30 percent of the museum's visitors are not African American."[93]

In 2011, Rick Moss, executive director of the African American Museum and Library at Oakland (AAMLO), also agreed that broadening his museum's interpretative focus could result in pulling in larger audiences. AAMLO, which is based in Oakland, California, was officially incorporated in 1965:

one year before Huey Newton and Bobby Seale founded the Black Panther Party for Self-Defense, also in Oakland. Although acknowledging AAMLO's historic ties to the Black Power Movement (as do several of the museum's permanent exhibits), Moss maintains that his vision for this combination of library, archive, and museum has necessarily moved beyond the narrative "niche" inhabited by most early African American museums and community centers—one that typically emphasized narratives of "victimization," "battle," and "survival." Instead, he intends to approach black history from the point of "cooperation and communication among and between sometimes competing ethnic groups, especially in the west and in Oakland."[94]

AAMLO's exhibitions reinforce Moss's efforts to expand beyond the narrative of confrontation between blacks and whites to one that interprets the cross-cultural exchanges among the multiple racial and ethnic groups who have historically settled in Oakland. Still, completely discarding this familiar, "reactionary" narrative may be easier for museums (such as the Birmingham Civil Rights Institute) that, unlike AAMLO, did not originate as neighborhood institutions during the black museum movement of the 1960s and 1970s. Black museum leaders, many of whom were concurrently active in the Civil Rights and Black Power Movements, founded these neighborhood museums in reaction to, among other factors, legalized segregation, discrimination, and the failure of the public school system to acknowledge or accurately interpret African American history. This set of circumstances is not necessarily shared in the same way by newer African American museums, which—perhaps ironically—may be less "burdened" by their history than museums like the Anacostia Neighborhood Museum or the DuSable. As a consequence, these new institutions may possess greater leeway in reinterpreting and reimagining their missions and identities when they are confronted with budget shortfalls and changeable audiences.

Regardless of the circumstances surrounding their origins, both new *and* older African American museums that wish to operate successfully in the twenty-first century must also be attentive to the debut of the National Museum of African American History and Culture in Washington, D.C. The opening of this museum, scheduled for 2015, will offer the leaders of local African American cultural organizations a new chance to reassert the centrality of their core missions: the preservation, interpretation, and presentation of African American history for diverse audiences.

CHAPTER 6

A MUSEUM FOR THE FUTURE

The National Museum of
African American History and Culture

In transforming the museum profession, black museum leaders embraced with creative verve the clarion call of activists such as June Jordan, Stokely Carmichael, and Malcolm X to bring the doctrines of the Black Power Movement—that is, black institutional capacity, self-sufficiency, and black pride—to museums and other sites of public history. Positioning black power as a subtext of the black museum movement reveals not only why, but how, these institutions challenged and reinterpreted the traditional model of museum as a repository for Eurocentric artifacts and narratives. African American neighborhood museum founders like John Kinard, Margaret Burroughs, and Charles Wright presented a new and public analysis of African American history and heritage, one that not only focused on black achievement but also attempted to unravel the charged interactions between African American and American history. No longer would those who refused to interrogate this relationship control the interpretation and presentation of the very American stories of slavery, Jim Crow, and discrimination.

Black museum leaders employed the cultural constructions of white society (i.e., the "museum") and the accepted artifices of these institutions (the display of "artifacts") in order to challenge and remake what a museum could be and represent. By exhibiting and interpreting nontraditional objects and creating innovative educational outreach programs, black museums delegitimized the existing narratives of African American history and culture that had been designed by the "white architects of black education."[1] These narratives had long functioned to maintain (and later, excuse or mollify) the institution of slavery, and to perpetuate the innate superiority of whiteness. For leaders of the black museum movement, African American neighborhood museums did not represent a quaint institutional outgrowth of the black freedom struggle but a critically important component in how ordinary African Americans could absorb and impart the ideals and practice of civil rights and, especially, black power.

At the same time, black museum leaders had to modify the ideals of black power in order for their museums to function. Rather than pursue an exclusively separatist agenda, black museum leaders pressured, compromised, and at times sought out white supporters and politicians, as well as members of the so-called black establishment. Their adaptation of black power ideology did not undermine the black museum movement's potential for grassroots activism. Instead, it complicated the popular image of the Black Power Movement as comprised solely of aggressively militant separatists more prone to taking up arms in self-defense and wearing stylized clothing than engaging in practical relationships with those of differing viewpoints.

Indeed, the story of the black museum movement demonstrates that black power must also be seen in the context of black institutional development among black professionals and white institutional policymakers. In order for African American museums to move from their storefront beginnings into larger structures, from obscure exhibits to more comprehensive presentations, a more practical relationship between blacks and whites had to be developed. No matter how angry about white indifference and hostility, no matter how undesired whites were within the emerging black power philosophy, African Americans still needed to form coalitions in order to get what they needed and wanted. Black museum leaders often formed these alliances reluctantly, fearing a loss of control over the content and direction of their institutions if the alliances they made with the white establishment fell out of balance. The mandate for complete separation from white America, however, simply did not mesh with the environments in which black museum leaders worked. Consequently, museum leaders applied for state and federal grants, negotiated with and pressured politicians for financial support, and appealed to "white" cultural institutions for assistance in garnering artifacts and other forms of material assistance. Successful black museum makers understood that whites could be important to the black museum movement, though not central to its vision.[2]

By the mid-1970s, the national Black Power Movement had faded, accelerated in part by the arrests, self-imposed isolation, or deaths of its charismatic leaders. Although these figures remain important touchstones in modern black political and cultural thought, the movement was left bereft without them. Yet even as the national movement declined, African American politicians began to secure greater access to political office—a direct result of the groundwork already paved by black activists. These newly minted politicians took office just as cities struggling with postindustrial transformation attempted to confront the challenges of unemployment, poverty, and industrial relocation.[3] African American neighborhood museums, located in the hearts of these increasingly "black" metropolises, felt the full effects of this crisis, as evidenced by their constant financial battles during the last three decades of the twentieth century. Black urban poverty, community displacement engendered by urban renewal, and other external economic factors affected vital areas like museum membership, leadership, and finance. As such, the apparent disengagement between Detroit's International Afro-American Museum in 1965 and the new Charles H. Wright Museum of African American History in 1997—and, indeed, the distance between all of the museums in this study from their original manifestations in the 1960s and 1970s—was not simply a consequence of the passage of time or architectural transformation, but also a reflection of the ideological changes that encompassed and transformed the black freedom struggle in the late twentieth and early twenty-first centuries.

Despite their troubles, African American neighborhood museums set a precedent that prominent public history sites could not continue to blithely ignore without being prepared to justify such practices. Renowned museums such as the Metropolitan Museum of Art and the Smithsonian Institution began to respond—however tentatively and reluctantly at first—to this call for transformation by incorporating elements of African American history and culture once excluded from their own exhibits and programs.[4] Many other mainstream museums and public history sites, even those once wholly devoted to the Anglo experience (such as Colonial Williamsburg), followed their lead during the last two decades of the twentieth century. By the time the Smithsonian Institution's Board of Regents designated a final building site for the construction of the National Museum of African American History and Culture (NMAAHC) in Washington, D.C., in 2006, one could consider the black museum movement a success—even if that success had been tempered by knowledge of the numerous, and often divisive, external and internal difficulties that continued to challenge the movement's longevity. Although most African American museums remained at a distinct financial disadvantage compared to mainstream institutions like the Smithsonian, as well as smaller regional museums (with which they are more comparable), they nonetheless had exploded tradition-bound conceptions of what a "museum" can be and the audiences a museum may serve. While black neighborhood museums have evolved in mission and physical form since their inception, the grassroots applications of the Black Power Movement—those which call for knowledge and pride in one's heritage—persevere in their daily work.

The construction of the NMAAHC arguably brings the black museum movement into its most public and emblematic manifestation. Technically, of course, the NMAAHC does not represent the first, nor the only, African American museum to operate as a "national" institution.[5] For example, the National Underground Railroad Freedom Center, which is an affiliate of the Smithsonian, opened in Cincinnati, Ohio, in 2004. The museum is positioned within a city and landscape that had been vital to the Underground Railroad's operations. Yet the Freedom Center's designation as a national museum, further reinforced by its relationship with the Smithsonian, does not necessarily command the same prominence as a museum situated on the National Mall. Indeed, it is possible that its "second-tier" national status might have contributed, at least in part, to the organization's ongoing turmoil regarding its identity and finances.[6]

The NMAAHC's supporters believe that the museum's location on the National Mall presents, both figuratively and literally, a monumental statement about the integral place of African Americans in the national landscape. Situating a national African American museum in Washington, D.C., is a natural fit, argues Alison Landsberg, because of the historic symbolism associated with the city. "If mass cultural sites do in fact have this pedagogical potential," Landsberg posits, "should not such a museum be located in Washington D.C., the nation's political and symbolic capital? . . . an African American history museum might make it possible for visitors of all backgrounds to take on the painful memories of racial oppression and, in so doing, challenge their own assumptions and ideologies."[7] Yet the existence of the NMAAHC may also constitute a step beyond the founding goals of the black museum movement, in that the museum, asserts Executive Director Lonnie Bunch, is "not being built as a museum by African-Americans for African-Americans. . . . The notion that is so important here is that African-American culture is used as a lens to understand what it means to be American."[8]

Bunch's extraordinary statement in some ways breaks with the impetus that drove pioneers like Margaret Burroughs and Charles Wright, who transformed the postwar cultural landscape by building institutions responsive to the needs and interests of African Americans—"for us, by us." The apparent disjuncture between these two ideals underlies the often difficult relationship that has historically existed between national museum advocates and leaders of black neighborhood museums. As such, in order to understand the challenges and opportunities presented by the NMAAHC, we must also recognize its historic and contested bond with local African American museums.

"A Matter That Must Be Controlled By Black People Who Think Black"

The drive to establish a national museum of African American history began in the early twentieth century, when a group of African American Civil War veterans and their descendants pushed for the authorization of a federal memorial building that paid "tribute to the Negro's contributions to the achievements of America."[9] Though their campaign was unsuccessful, calls for a national African American museum picked up speed during the 1960s. Yet within the black museum community, support for a federally sponsored African American museum was by no means unanimous. Several black museum leaders objected vehemently to the construction of a national museum, with the dispute reaching fractious heights during the 1960s and again during the 1980s. Indeed, during the mid-1960s, International Afro-American Museum founder Dr. Charles Wright campaigned to prevent the federal government from passing a national museum proposal, arguing that the government, as well as members of the "Black Establishment" who supported such a project, would inevitably compromise the integrity of the stories that a national African American museum must tell.

In 1965 Representative James Scheuer (D-NY) introduced federal bill H.R. 10638 to the House of Representatives, proposing an exploratory "Commission on Negro History and Culture" that would research the feasibility of establishing a "national Negro museum." Suspicious of the bill's implications, Wright called an emergency meeting of the International Afro-American Museum planning committee on September 26, 1965. Wright informed the committee that while Scheuer, who was white, may have introduced the bill because of a "desire to 'do something'" for blacks, nevertheless the Congressman "did not ask the help of any Negroes in framing the bill . . . it might be better for Negroes themselves to supply the initiative for such a bill."[10] The committee agreed that black museum advocates should author another bill and introduce it to both the House and Senate in order to "supersede" Scheuer's proposal.

Prior to founding the International Afro-American Museum in Detroit, Wright had supported the idea of creating a national black history museum, whether in Detroit or in another city, such as Washington, D.C. Securing a national charter for the IAM, Wright argued, would "give the project the sort of status that would attract the support of the whole country."[11] Although Wright agreed that "everybody wants it in his own city," Detroit Institute of Arts director Willis F. Woods, who served on the IAM planning committee, maintained that New York City or Washington, D.C., offered the best possible locations for a national museum. In the end, the group combined their interest in creating a national African American museum with their dedication to the local. The committee unanimously passed Wright's proposal that "the people of Detroit will participate in it [the creation of a national black museum] and represent Michigan in whatever national effort there is" and then continued with their plans to build an African American museum in Detroit.[12]

Wright's opposition to the bill thus did not stem from a total rejection of the concept of a national African American museum. Rather, he repeatedly stressed that the historical incompetence and bias shown by the federal government toward African American issues necessitated that such a bill—authored by a white politician, rather than by himself or other African American museum leaders—must not pass. Wright maintained that federal oversight of such a project removed control from the very people the museum purported to represent. In a letter to African American journalist Carl Rowan in March 1966, Wright explained: "You may know that there was a bill introduced in Congress, last August, for the Federal Government to set up a Negro History Commission. . . . We opposed such a bill, because we feel that the Negro, himself, must be a positive, creative force in such a project if it is to create for him the identification that is so vitally needed."[13] Despite Wright's public crusade, however, support for a national African American museum gained momentum in Congress and among some African American cultural organizations, including the Association for the Study of Negro Life and History.

Although Congressman Scheuer's original proposal for a national African American museum failed to pass, he renewed the bill in 1968. Scheuer explained his persistence in a letter to Congress. Pointing to the "almost complete submergence of the American Negro's historical and culture heritage," he proposed to remedy this "significant loss" by establishing a presidentially appointed Commission on Negro History and Culture. The commission would examine "all aspects of the problem of preserving, collecting, and ultimately integrating evidence of the Negro past into the mainstream of American history. To highlight the importance of this effort, the Association for the Study of Negro Life and History and I are co-sponsoring a one-day conference on February 15, scheduled to coincide with National Negro History Week. . . ."[14] The conference program for the conference featured panels on topics such as "What should be collected and why?" "Where should materials be placed—in a national museum/library, or in regional museums and libraries?" Conference attendees also debated issues such as "How can we get Negro history integrated into American history and our educational systems?" "Do TV, radio, and films adequately treat Negro history? If not, what can be done?"[15]

Notwithstanding the conference's focus on issues deeply important to Wright, he and the staff of the International Afro-American Museum continued to object to the revived national museum proposal. In a letter to the editor of the *Christian Science Monitor*, IAM treasurer Oretta Todd declared that the government "must not play its habitual ugly-American role, giving to the black man what government thinks the black man needs."[16] Likewise, in a March 1968 letter to the Select Sub-Committee on Education, Wright emphasized that "whether or not such a monument—a museum of Negro History—is constructed should depend on the Negroes themselves. The impetus must come from within the Negro community, not from outside it."[17] Pointing to the existence of museums like the IAM and the DuSable, Wright argued that the black community clearly possessed the ability and momentum to create such a museum. Indeed, the passage of the Scheuer bill might ultimately detract from the success of these grassroots institutions, for, as Wright mentioned, "some are raising the question as to the wisdom of supporting a private organization if the federal government is going to do it for us."[18]

If the government truly wanted to promote African American history, contended Wright, it should follow the three recommendations he presented during the Congressional hearings on the Scheuer Bill on March 18, 1968:

1. Assist in the immediate preparation of 100 Mobile Exhibits (similar to the IAM Exhibit). They would travel throughout the country, telling the story of Afro-Americans.
2. Assist in the establishment of a nation-wide system of Oral History committees to record for posterity the wealth of stories that elderly

Afro-Americans have to tell and, at the same time, seek out the many documents, artifacts, and so forth that are so necessary to tell our story.

3. Encourage and support grass-roots organizations that are already involved in Afro-American history. Some of these include: The Chicago African American Museum of History and Art; The American Negro History in Beacon Hill, Boston; and our International Afro-American Museum, Inc., Detroit.[19]

While Wright thus believed that federal moneys should be made available to assist local African American museums, none of the steps he proposed involved the government's taking control from community organizations already engaged in remembering and interpreting African American history and culture. Although Wright supported the construction of a "monument to the Afro-American's struggle for freedom," he reiterated that the historically conservative nature of the Smithsonian Institution mandated that such an organization could never be in charge of a national African American museum. "One of the early architects of this bill was asked," Wright reported, "'can you assure us that a federally-sponsored museum project would deal fairly with DuBois, Garvey, Robeson and Malcolm X?' Of course not. The Smithsonian Institute, to name just one example, has been more concerned with reptiles and birds than with Black Americans."[20]

Wright's selection of past and present advocates of black power—Marcus Garvey, Paul Robeson, W. E. B. Du Bois, and Malcolm X—is significant. These architects of twentieth-century black intellectual thought and activism shaped Wright's creation of the International Afro-American Museum far more than the "black establishment" leaders that he consistently challenged during his tenure at the museum.[21] Wright mistrusted the government's ability to fairly address and incorporate the work of controversial black radicals into a national museum. For him, creating a national African American museum remained a "matter that must be controlled by black people who think black."[22]

Wright's clash with the black establishment further unfolded in the numerous letters he composed against the national museum bill. In a June 1968 letter addressed to National Urban League executive director Whitney Young, African American social scientist and federal adviser Kenneth Clark, and NAACP executive director Roy Wilkins, Wright beseeched them to reconsider their support of the Scheuer bill. Citing the roadblocks the IAM and other black neighborhood museums faced, Wright maintained:

Our attempts to gain the interest and support of the black establishment throughout the country [have] failed. Yet many of these whom we have approached have
given their support to Congressman Scheuer to gain passage of his bill, H.R.
12962. We, along with other organizations similar to ours in Chicago, Boston,
and California, are opposed to this bill. . . . The bill, if passed, will duplicate
the work of black controlled organizations that represent the will of the people.
. . . It seems strange to us that Mr. Scheuer has been able to rally so many black
people behind his bid for immortality behind an unnecessary bill that will cost
the tax payers at least a half-million dollars, while the black sponsored project
to get $50,000 to restore Frederick Douglass's other house in Washington has
failed miserably. . . .[23]

One year later, Kinard wrote to Henry Moon, editor of *Crisis* magazine, to com-
plain about Wilkins's continued failure to speak out against the Scheuer bill, as
well as the NAACP's lack of public support for the IAM. Wright wrote that an
article Wilkins had published in *Crisis*, "Negro History or Mythology," repeated
the "continuing complaint . . . about how the poor blacks fare at the hands of the
white power structure. Yet they, the black leadership, frequently fail to assist black
organizations that would make such complaints unnecessary. For four years we
have tried to interest Mr. Wilkins and the NAACP in just a token of recognition
of our efforts in the field of Negro history, without success."[24]

    Wilkins and his "establishment" colleagues likely supported the bill proposed
by Scheuer because the construction of a national African American museum
would undoubtedly bring a degree of prominence to black history and culture
that small, regional museums like the IAM could not begin to match. Furthermore, although Wright's objections to the Scheuer bill revolved around his aversion to federal oversight of the interpretation of black history, he also realized
that his museum would inevitably have to compete with a national museum for
financial resources, artifacts, and public attention. In other words, he feared a loss
of local power should a national museum be established. In many ways, Wright's
conflict with national museum advocates paralleled the numerous clashes between
the Anacostia Neighborhood Museum and the Smithsonian Institution, or the
DuSable and the Chicago Historical Society during their battle over the Doug-
las/Grand Boulevard exhibit in the 1990s. This time, however, the conflict was
writ large, on a national scale, resonating between a black-owned institution
devoted to African American history and a nationally conceived museum that
(presumably) touted the same goals, but with markedly different constituents.

By early April 1968, support for the revised Scheuer bill had progressed to the extent that Congressman Clarence Brown, Jr. (R-OH), introduced a new bill proposing that a national African American museum be located in Wilberforce, Ohio.[25] While the city of Wilberforce might not automatically connote a "national" status in the way that a Washington, D.C., location would, Brown argued that it was an appropriate site because both Central State University and Wilberforce University ("the first Negro institution of higher learning in the United States") were located there. In addition, the city had historically served as a hub for the Underground Railroad. In a letter to his congressional colleagues, Brown reasoned that a national African American museum in Wilberforce not only would function as a repository for artifacts and learning but would also "improve the Negro's sense of pride and place as a responsible citizen in America. At a time when the Negro is reputedly becoming more and more alienated from our culture, I think that Congress should take a more affirmative role to emphasize the Negro's participation in and influence on our Nation. Perhaps, this would help reduce the trend toward action outside our society."[26] Although it is unclear just when, exactly, Brown composed this letter, he distributed it on April 4, 1968. On this same day, James Earl Ray assassinated Martin Luther King on the balcony of the Lorraine Motel in Memphis, Tennessee. Cities across the nation, including Washington, D.C., subsequently faced the violent and grief-stricken reaction to King's murder.

The tenor of Brown's proposal insinuates that no other museums dedicated to black history and culture had yet been established, when in fact not far from the U.S. Capitol Building the Anacostia Neighborhood Museum—itself a federally funded museum—had recently opened its doors. Charles Wright, then, had correctly assumed that the achievements of local African American museums went relatively unnoticed by prominent national museum advocates. Congressman Brown's contention that a national black history museum would reduce "action outside our society" also meshed with the ways in which politicians applied the containment discourse of the Cold War as a way of understanding the motivations that ignited urban unrest; some believed that Communist-inspired "subversives" or "outside agitators" fueled the riots. If Brown did not specifically identify these elements in his letter, however, he did imply that those who expressed "alienation from our culture" (in this case, "our" should be read as "white") operated against social norms. In this role, they were more likely to participate in "outsider" movements like black power. Brown assumed that creating a national African American museum would counter these outsider tendencies by reinforcing responsible citizenship: the physical presence of a national African American museum would encourage black men to identify, and claim, a properly defined sense of place within American society. That Brown believed a national African American museum could begin to ameliorate such problems speaks to the rather remarkable power that he and his supporters were ready to confer upon a government-sanctioned cultural institution.

In September 1968, John Conyers (D-MI), an African American member of the House of Representatives who opposed the Scheuer bill, informed Charles Wright that the proposal to establish a Commission on Negro History and Culture (H.R. 12962) had passed the House by a "record vote of 263 yeas to 45 nays."[27] Yet though the House approved the proposal, a significant delay lapsed between the introduction of Brown's legislation and the actual establishment of a national African American history museum in Wilberforce. Indeed, the Wilberforce National Afro-American Museum and Cultural Center only opened its doors in 1987 after a series of financial and administrative difficulties. Primarily funded by the Ohio Historical Society and private donations, the museum's exhibits and archives focus on the broad expanse of African American history, with a permanent exhibition titled From Victory to Freedom: Afro-American Life in the Fifties, as well as a smaller exhibition on Wilberforce's role in the Underground Railroad.[28]

As the Wilberforce museum began its operations, support resumed for the creation of a federally funded African American museum located at a site that automatically communicated a national significance and prominence: Washington, D.C. Members of the African American Museums Association continued to express their misgivings about the plan, however. At a 1988 association meeting, John Kinard took up Charles Wright's earlier fight, contending that neighborhood African American museums would suffer, not only financially but also in terms of their ability to secure exhibitions and artifacts, if a national museum was established.[29] As did several other members of the association, including Margaret Burroughs, Kinard proposed that any congressional resolution to create a national museum must also contain a provision to establish a $50 million endowment, which would be divided among local African American neighborhood museums.[30]

Kinard's long-standing unease about the Anacostia Neighborhood Museum's position within the Smithsonian community of museums fueled his objections. Like Charles Wright, Kinard remained skeptical about the implications of federal control; he also believed that the ANM's identity and independence in relation to the Smithsonian Institution continued to be precarious even twenty years after its founding. If a national African American museum finally took shape in Washington, D.C., rather than Wilberforce or other distant locales, the ANM's independence and status might slip further. Media reports regarding the unsteady position of the ANM reinforced Kinard's fears. A 1980 Smithsonian committee report questioned the Anacostia Museum's ability to achieve national status and recommended instead that the museum remain neighborhood focused. Likewise, a 1984 *Washington Post* article reaffirmed the Smithsonian's perception of the ANM as lacking in national potential, despite the museum's groundbreaking work and the international attention it had received: "the political forces prevailing in the Smithsonian Institution and in Congress seemed to favor a more traditional national museum of African American history on the National Mall, with a small community museum remaining in Anacostia."[31]

To counteract the official pigeonholing of the ANM as an exclusively "neighborhood" institution, Kinard began to institute sweeping changes that appeared to shatter his original vision of the ANM as a community-focused museum. In addition to moving out of the former Carver Theater and constructing a new museum, Kinard approved a significant name change: the locally focused "Anacostia Neighborhood Museum" became the much broader "Anacostia Museum and Center for African American History and Culture." In keeping with the name change, exhibitions once formerly devoted to immediately local concerns, such as The Rat: Man's Invited Affliction (1968), became increasingly outnumbered by exhibitions that featured less local themes. Although Kinard continued to emphasize the museum's ties to the community, ANM historian Portia James indicates that as early as 1982 the exhibition calendar featured just ten exhibits out of thirty-four that referenced subjects pertinent to the immediate neighborhood.[32]

Kinard's ability to follow through on the sweeping institutional changes he envisioned was short-lived. In 1989, at the age of fifty-three, he died of myelofibrosis. Museum staff and the community of Anacostia, bereft, prepared for a new decade without his visionary leadership, even as official movement toward creating a national African American museum in Washington, D.C., continued.

Locating the NMAAHC

Congressman James Scheuer's proposal to launch an independent yet federally controlled African American museum had clashed with the views of some museum professionals during the 1960s, who argued that black history must be integrated into existing museums in order to demonstrate how vital these narratives were in understanding American history. Even during the 1990s, the National Museum of American History director Roger Kennedy recommended that creating a black history wing within the NMAH was a better solution than building an entirely separate museum—a tactic he feared would ultimately "ghettoize" black history.[33] Yet despite voices of opposition from people like Wright, Kinard, and Kennedy, by the 1990s many national black museum advocates increasingly maintained that creating an independent African American museum (albeit one overseen by the Smithsonian) would guarantee a degree of autonomy—indeed, black autonomy—that integration within an existing Smithsonian museum would not.

In 1991, the Smithsonian-appointed African American Institutional Study Advisory Committee published a report advocating the establishment of a national African American museum on the Mall overseen by the Smithsonian Institution. The committee, chaired by the former Studio Museum in Harlem director Mary Schmidt Campbell, did not fully agree on supporting the late John Kinard's idea of a "national trust" for existing African American museums. Their ambivalence distressed members of the African American Museums Association, who, upon reviewing the report, objected to the advisory committee's "profoundly disappointing" conclusions regarding the place and worth of local African American museums.[34] As Charles Wright had repeatedly stressed during his battle against the national museum proposal in the 1960s, the AAMA contended that the advisory committee both diminished the work of local black museums and "appropriate[d] to the proposed [national] museum roles which should be shared nationally by many Black museums or which have already been assumed by the AAMA."[35] In order for the AAMA to publicly support the national museum, the organization argued that local African American museums must be ensured guaranteed access to an endowment.

Their insistent call for a multimillion dollar endowment accessible to local African American museums came during a particularly traumatic period for many cultural organizations, both public and private. During the late 1980s and early 1990s, Congress slashed federal funding to the NEA and the NEH. Increasingly vitriolic "culture wars" encompassed public dialogue about any form of federal funding for museums and other cultural institutions, as conservative politicians spoke out against multicultural narratives that they decried as revisionist at best and potentially treasonous at worst. Senator Jesse Helms

(R-NC), who vehemently opposed the 1989 congressional act to establish the National Museum of the American Indian, purposefully delayed Senate discussion on a national African American museum proposal introduced by Senator Paul Simon (D-IL).[36] Helms pondered the slippery slope he believed might result if a national African America museum were established: "Once Congress gives the go ahead for African-Americans . . . how can Congress then say no to Hispanics, and the next group, and the next group after that?"[37] Helms did not perceive multiculturalism as a unifying force but a divisive one. Congress, he claimed, should not tolerate what he saw as the cultural and national fragmentation being demanded by "the next group, and the next group after that." In light of such fervent objections pouring forth from Congress and conservative commentators, to many advocates of the national African American museum it seemed highly unlikely that the federal government would both approve such a museum and grant millions of dollars to already existing African American community museums.

It is perhaps not surprising, then, that in this contentious climate the national African American museum proposal languished. Disagreements regarding management and finances divided supporters, with some advocates continuing to support Smithsonian oversight while others insisted that a private, African American-controlled foundation should fund the museum.[38] In 2001, a surge of renewed activism, led by veteran civil rights leader and Congressman John Lewis (D-GA) in 2001, enabled the passage of H.R. 3442, the National Museum of African American History and Culture Plan for Action Presidential Commission Act. The law, which authorized the commission to develop a plan to create a national museum in Washington, D.C., ultimately recommended that the Smithsonian Institution oversee the museum's implementation. On January 30, 2006, after nearly a century of debate and setbacks, the Smithsonian's Board of Regents chose a five-acre parcel of vacant land on 14th Street and Constitution Avenue, just northeast of the Washington Monument and adjacent to the National Museum of American History, as the final museum site.[39] The museum, financed with a $250 million appropriation from Congress, and with $250 million being raised in private funds, began construction in 2012, with a targeted public opening in 2015.[40]

Not surprisingly, choosing an appropriate site to build the national museum proved to be a difficult task fraught with questions about visibility, public access, and the symbolic import of the museum's physical location in Washington. Initially, in 2003, the National Museum of African American History and Culture

Plan for Action Presidential Commission recommended a "trapezoidal slice of land at the foot of the Senate side of the Capitol" for the museum's construction, which museum advocates also approved.[41] The symbolism of building a national African American museum within sight of the building where lawmakers had authorized the slave trade and reinforced Jim Crow policies was not lost on museum advocates—nor upon those who opposed the museum's construction.[42] As in the case of the African American Museum of Philadelphia, whose supporters lost their battle to build in Society Hill, strident vocal opposition to building a national African American museum on or near the grounds of the U.S. Capitol forced museum advocates to consider other sites.

Supporters of the national museum subsequently debated four other possible locales, including the Smithsonian's Arts and Industries Building, which opened in 1881. Although the Arts and Industries Building is located on the Mall, its Victorian architecture and small rooms did not bode well for the development of a modern museum. The most promising site that remained, then, was located at 14th Street and Constitution Avenue. According to Executive Director Lonnie Bunch, this site represented "a place that will make sure most Americans have access to the rich story of African American culture. . . . And frankly, the visibility helps us with fundraising."[43] By literally positioning the NMAAHC next to the monuments and memorials on the National Mall, museum advocates hoped to bypass the spatial confinements historically experienced by many African American neighborhood museums, as their leaders strove to balance the restrictions of neighborhood boundaries, design guidelines, and, sometimes, local prejudices. Yet this site also presented limitations. By virtue of its designation as a branch of the Smithsonian Institution, coupled with its highly visible position on the National Mall, museum leaders had to parley between federal and private expectations. Negotiating this balance might result in conflicts of interest—a possibility realized by those, like John Kinard and Dr. Charles Wright, who opposed the national museum's construction.

The NMAAHC Takes (Virtual) Shape

The NMAAHC's public programming and temporary exhibitions began even before ground was broken for the building. For example, its "Save Our African American Treasures: A National Collections Initiative of Discovery and Preservation" program featured multicity workshops on topics such as local heritage, clothing and textile preservation, and digital history instruction. A June

2011 session held in Dallas on "Building a National Collection" featured the curator of collections, Michele Gates Moresi, who discussed how the museum differed from other Smithsonian museums "in that it does not begin with a collection. Developing and caring for a collection of materials that reflects the diversity of the African American experience provides the Museum with an array of challenges and opportunities."[44]

Those who could not attend these sessions in person had the option of contributing to the nascent museum–community partnership through the NMAAHC's digital "Memory Book," which requested that users register and post their memories about their heritage, or about African American history and issues in general, as well as their reflections upon the NMAAHC.[45] From 2007 to 2011, users submitted around one hundred personal stories, which ranged from memories of growing up in Atlanta during the 1950s to participating in the 2011 Million Woman March in Philadelphia. Museum staff then tagged each entry with key words, such as "activism" or "fashion," allowing readers to click on the tag that would take them to additional stories with similar foci. A visual map of these tags further illustrated the connections between seemingly disparate stories.[46] The success of this digital project was so great that the museum had to take down the site in early 2012 with plans to reopen it on a much larger software platform. With initiatives like "Memory Book," the NMAAHC shares historical authority with their audiences, a tradition begun decades earlier by African American and ethnic neighborhood museums. Indeed, it is only relatively recently that mainstream museums and other public history sites have begun to consider this paradigm shift in conceptualizing their relationships with audiences.[47]

While the digital realm emphasizes the NMAAHC's intent to connect with African American communities throughout the United States, its architectural design clearly showcases a significantly different facade from that of most African American neighborhood museums—institutions whose physical characteristics and institutional missions were, at least initially, often informed by the circumstances of their immediate surroundings in working-class and middle-class African American neighborhoods. The NMAAHC comprises approximately 315,000 square feet; during the design process, the lead architect, David Adjaye of the Freelon Adjaye Bond/SmithGroup, proposed large skylights, green space, a wraparound porch, and a walking bridge meant to symbolize the Middle Passage. According to National Planning Capital Commission member Ken Walton, the porch represents a crucial design element, in that it links the grand, symbolic space of the National Mall with the intimacy of the African American vernacular: "the porch is seen as an iconic element in African American culture. . . . It's a welcoming and gathering space."[48]

The dominant feature of the building initially consisted of three bronze "coronas" that invoked a crown motif derived from Yoruban sculpture; the motif would envelop the entire museum.[49] When Adjaye unveiled the architectural plans, however, concerns regarding the building's height, setback, and sight lines resulted in the reduction of the three coronas to a more streamlined two. Adjaye also downsized the museum by 17 percent of its originally proposed size.[50] The building's interior design, divided into thirds, will feature exhibits on slavery, sports, music, and visual arts. Interestingly, a significant portion of the interior will re-create sites from historically important local black communities across the nation, such as a fugitive slave settlement in the Great Dismal Swamps, and Moton Field in Tuskegee, Alabama, where black pilots trained during World War II.[51] The museum's interior layout is meant to encompass a sweeping representation of African American history and culture, while still paying heed to regionally specific history that might normally be overlooked in a national museum.

The methods by which the NMAAHC physically presents itself and the narratives that it communicates are inseparable. As such, criticism of the content of another Smithsonian Institution museum located on the National Mall—the National Museum of the American Indian—may prove instructive for NMAAHC staff as they forge an identity among the community of national museums in Washington. Among other faults, critics took the National Museum of the American Indian (NMAI), which opened in 2004, to task for the absence of explanatory text accompanying artifacts, as well as for the limited number of neatly packaged didactic lessons and linear narratives that typically comprise museum exhibits—particularly those on display in national museums. For some, the museum's exhibitions failed in that they did not require visitors to think critically, but instead embodied what critic Tiffany Jenkins has characterized as the "cringe-making, sentimentalised exhibitions that are driven, not by knowledge, but by the identity-affirming imperatives of cultural politics."[52] Yet Amanda Cobb, editor of the *American Indian Quarterly* and former administrator of the Chickasaw Nation Division of History and Culture, has argued that it is unfair to portray the museum as a failure simply because it did not conform to "long-standing Western museological standards." Indeed, Cobb asserts that "it does not seem to matter to these critics that those museological standards have exploited and objectified Native Americans in very specific ways."[53] In other words, while the NMAI may not present conventional narratives and displays, this was a conscious decision meant to counter centuries of skewed interpretations applied by outsiders to Native American cultures.

Should the NMAAHC's design and exhibits veer too far into what is deemed to be "nontraditional" for a museum on the National Mall, and if its curators dare to overemphasize the "sentimental" insistence on "identity affirmation," the museum will likely be subjected to the same sort of intense disapproval as that leveled at the NMAI. NMAAHC director Lonnie Bunch is keenly aware of such criticisms—e.g., that the NMAI's exhibits are overly romanticized, and that its staff eschewed scholarly input from those of non-native heritage. Bunch has publicly countered this particularly contentious point by asserting that the NMAAHC will "reflect the best scholarship on black history, no matter who wrote it, and . . . tell a sweeping narrative from slavery to the present."[54]

Yet while Bunch may rightfully take a cautious approach in planning how the national museum will interpret and present African American history to mass audiences, the NMAAHC should not hesitate to build upon, and create, "nonmainstream" models for museum form and function—much as the NMAI's curators and educators intended with their own institution. In doing so, Bunch and museum staff will pay homage to the radical work initiated by their neighborhood museum predecessors during the 1960s and 1970s. By rejecting or subverting traditional methods of interpretation and design, the NMAAHC could forge an image as a twenty-first-century museum that operates in multiple spaces and among multiple audiences: local, international, and imagined, or "prosthetic." Although the museum must function within a national setting that is at once expansive and potentially limiting, its ability to connect with the intimacy of African American local histories may allow it to maneuver around such constrictions.

Negotiating Tensions between Local and National

To date, the broader African American museum community has largely embraced the NMAAHC. Nevertheless, the potential remains for tension over issues such as the distribution of finances and accesses to collections—in short, many of the same concerns that motivated Dr. Charles Wright's objections to the national museum campaign during the 1960s. A photograph that subtly (if unintentionally) highlighted this possibility of lingering conflict was prominently framed in a January 2011 *New York Times* article on the history of the national African American museum. In the photograph, a woman named Katricia Gray is shown conversing with a researcher for the NMAAHC. Gray, who resides in Detroit, brought an African sculpture to be appraised as a possible donation to the NMAAHC. The reasons behind her decision to bring the artifact to this event, rather than donating it to the Charles H. Wright Museum of African American History in Detroit, were not provided in the article nor was the often contested historic relationship between the NMAAHC and the MAAH mentioned.[55]

Lonnie Bunch has downplayed any residual conflict between local African American museums and the NMAAHC, contending that the stories the national museum will interpret are national in scope in a way that other museums, both African American and traditional, are unable to access. "We will be able to tell the full sweep of the African American experience," Bunch assures audiences. "Whether it's about slavery or civil rights or the migration of blacks form the South to the North, we can tie the story together in a way that other museums cannot."[56] The results of the 2003 survey of African American museums conducted by the Plan for Presidential Action Commission reinforced Bunch's optimism, as the statistics indicated that 87 percent of respondents supported a national museum, while just 12.5 percent of respondents "expressed concern that a National Museum would compete for visitors, collections and/or funding." Most respondents also conveyed interest in forming a collaborative relationship with a national museum, whether by sending staff to the NMAAHC for training (68 percent of respondents) or by housing temporary exhibitions produced by the national museum (65 percent).[57]

Still, despite the overwhelmingly positive response toward the NMAAHC, the survey results also produced a few handwritten comments that expressed reservations. For example, one stated, "I do not support a concept that a national . . . museum would be a centralized control center for [African American] museums as advanced by one of your spokespersons." Another respondent admitted fears regarding funding. Their institution had received "over $1 million from the [government] over the last 3 years and [we] are scared the [national] museum may cause this funding to end." Given the economic downturn of the late 2000s, these fears were not unreasonable.[58]

Rick Moss, director of The African American Museum and Library of Oakland, California, does not believe that the NMAAHC's public programs and exhibits will conflict with the work, financial strength, and identity of local

African American museums. Rather, Moss perceives the national museum as representative of the "ultimate in the evolution that started in the 1960s with public history and social history." Furthermore, the national museum will act as the "hub of a wheel in which there is more cooperation, maybe the development of more regional associations among African American museums."[59] Individual African American neighborhood museums, libraries, and historical societies will serve as the vital spokes that turn and balance this national "hub." In order to maintain this mutually beneficial balance between local and national, Moss suggests that it is crucial to form regional associations of African American museums. As he argues, "Getting back to the subject of survival, I think that's what we're going to have to do. There's going to have to be regional associations of [African American] museums so we can share the burden of our financial responsibilities, share in exhibition development and traveling shows, share in public programming."

Moss also maintains that the Smithsonian Institution has succeeded in eliminating fears that a national African American museum intends to "rob your neighborhoods and your communities of all your artifacts and take them back, because we [the NMAAHC] have more than we can handle." Instead, Moss states that the national museum wants to "share them [the artifacts] with you."[60] Moss's point about the NMAAHC possessing "more artifacts than we can handle" is interesting, however, in that as of 2011 the national museum was in the active process of acquiring an additional twenty thousand artifacts to add to its existing collection of eleven thousand.[61] As a result of this acquisition process, even some museums within the Smithsonian system, let alone smaller independent black museums, have hesitated to loan significant objects to the NMAAHC. For example, the National Museum of American History owns a large segment of the Woolworth's lunch counter from the landmark 1960 Greensboro, North Carolina, sit-in movement. If this lunch counter were removed and donated to the NMAAHC, as some have expressed interest in doing, curators at the NMAH maintain that the museum's ability to tell the full story of this crucial moment in the Civil Rights Movement would be compromised. Even more troublesome, according to Smithsonian Institution spokesperson Linda St. Thomas, removing the Woolworth's lunch counter and "stripping the American history museum of its African-American material would leave [the NMAH] as the 'white museum.'"[62]

While this is a valid concern, until very recently the Smithsonian Institution promoted a version of American history that, whether intentionally or not, marginalized and excluded African American narratives. Only with the implicit and explicit pressures applied by black neighborhood museums, along with the revolution in new social history, did the Smithsonian begin to reconsider its narrow focus. Although the theoretical absence of the Woolworth's lunch counter would certainly represent a loss for the National Museum of American History and its audiences, recasting their other exhibits to tell a fuller story of "nonwhite" history might alleviate the artifact's absence.

Jostling for Space on the National Mall

As the NMAAHC took shape in blueprints and in the digital realm, questions (and concerns) arose about whether this institution would truly be the "last" museum on the National Mall. In 2003, formal congressional hearings regarding the initiation of the National Museum of the American Latino (NMAL) began; in 2008, Congress authorized the creation of the Commission to Study the Potential Creation of a National Museum of the American Latino.[63] The discourse surrounding the proposed museum shares many similarities with the historical debates around the establishment of the NMAAHC. For example, while largely supportive of the concept of a national Latino museum, Tey Marianna Nunn, the director and chief curator of visual arts at the National Hispanic Cultural Center in Albuquerque, New Mexico, questioned whether such a museum might not compress Latino history into a narrative that skims over complicated history in an effort to attract audiences and funding. Nunn admitted, "I am concerned that because of political pressure from multiple entities, a national Latino museum might commodify and ghettoize (or should I say barrio-ize?) the Latino experience into a vibrant, colorful, worry-free 'fiesta' in order to begin to teach a general museum visitor about Latino culture."[64] Like Charles Wright and John Kinard, Nunn also wondered whether, and how, a national Latino museum would recognize and build upon the years of pathbreaking work already conducted by local Latino museums and *centros,* many of which struggle to access funding and political support.

On the one hand, Nunn's concern that the future NMAL might detract from existing Latino cultural institutions, and potentially "barrio-ize" the Latino experience, might be alleviated if its leaders concurred with Lonnie Bunch's insistence that a national museum can avoid such "ghettoization." Bunch intends that the NMAAHC function, not as an intensely specialized, compartmentalized examination of black history and culture, but rather as a "lens to understand what it means to be American." If the leaders of the National Museum of the American Latino were to draw from Bunch's approach, their institution would not marginalize the Latino experience, but rather contextualize it within the broader narrative of American history.

Another branch of the debate surrounding the "ghettoization" of racial and ethnic history, however, posits that building a separate African American or Latino museum will detract from the linear narrative of American history found in more general-purpose national museums, such as the National Museum of American History. In May 2011, for instance, Representative James Moran (D-VA) expressed anxiety "about the direction we are taking at the Smithsonian" and worried that, by establishing both the NMAAHC and the National Museum of the American Latino, "we are breaking up the American narrative."[65] While asserting that "every indigenous immigrant community" has a right to tell its story, separating these stories into museums based on race or ethnicity created a dilemma. Indeed, Moran speculated that, "as much as we would like to think that all Americans are going to go to the African American Museum, I'm afraid it's not going to happen. . . . The Museum of American History is where all the white folks are going to go, and the American Indian Museum is where Indians are going to feel at home. And African Americans are going to go to their own museum. And Latinos are going to go their own museum. And that's not what America is all about."[66]

Despite his differing political affiliation, Moran's concerns were not so far removed from the more vehement sentiments expressed by the late Senator Jesse Helms during the culture wars of the 1990s. According to both Helms and Moran, if Congress continued to allow the creation of federally funded museums focusing on different ethnicities and races, the national story might irreparably fragment. Faced with a multitude of potentially competing narratives, those audiences visiting Washington, D.C., would be left unsure of the "correct" version of American history, and their role in shaping this story.[67]

In rebuttal to these fears, however, critics like Moran would do well to examine the historic work and achievements of local neighborhood museums like the International Afro-American Museum and the Anacostia Neighborhood Museum. Rather than acting as divisive forces intent on rupturing a sense of community, these institutions have long attracted those who felt alienated from traditional interpretations of American history and the physical representations of those narratives. In short, black neighborhood museums have reinforced and cultivated a sense of citizenship and inclusion among those often desperately searching for this measure of belonging, even as museum leaders deftly probed and dismantled outmoded and exclusionary stereotypes.

A well-conceived national museum of African American history or Latino

history would, ideally, function in much the same fashion. Rather than disman-
tling a sense of community and the collective memory of a single "American
story," such institutions aim to draw audiences together in appreciation of the
historical multiplicity of American stories and memories, and to reclaim the
ways in which these memories interweave throughout the diaspora. It is also
probable that museums like the National Museum of African American History and Culture and, potentially, the National Museum of the American
Latino will not be able to consistently interpret the regionally specific minutiae
of African American and Latino histories in same fashion as local museums
can. Because of this, community museums possess a unique opportunity to
emphasize their neighborhood-centered identities and revitalize their missions.
In some cases, though, their connection with the local and their dedication to
social change must be rediscovered.

THE TIES THAT BIND

Museums as Community Agents

I n the 1972 issue of *Museum News*, Anacostia Neighborhood Museum founder John Kinard spoke plainly about what he believed to be the responsibility of the museum profession toward underserved audiences: "The day when established institutions can deny their responsibilities and cheat the masses is swiftly coming to an end. If museum people do not realize this, they only demonstrate their blindness and lack of concern for humanity."[1] Three decades later, John Fleming, vice president of the Cincinnati Museum Center, expressed a similar sentiment, arguing that the crucial question museum administrators need to ask is "whether the museum is relevant to the issues facing the community it serves."[2] The ties that bind these two very different museums—one rooted in the culture, history, and politics of an African American neighborhood, and one that serves as an umbrella organization for multiple cultural institutions in Cincinnati, Ohio—testify to the profound impact black neighborhood museums have had upon the museum profession and its methodology.

While not all leaders of African American museums believed that their institutions had to function as instigators of social change within their communities, the core identity of the black museum movement centered upon this conviction. Yet the imperative to address and embrace this challenge (or, as Oakland Museum founder J. S. Holliday termed it, "tyranny") of community relevance has not always been accepted by museums—even those institutions designated as "African American." During the charged debates that took place throughout the 1970s about whether the Studio Museum in Harlem should relocate, Richard Clarke, chair of the museum's board, offered a startling rebuttal to Executive Director Courtney Callendar's sense of obligation to the people of Harlem. Clarke contended that the Studio Museum must now concentrate solely on art rather than function as a "social service organization for the neighborhood."[3] He thus questioned the museum's supposed *obligation* to address the needs of the local black community at the expense of fully developing its status and identity as a cultural institution that, ideally, was separate from, and even above, such mundane issues.

Richard Clarke's rejection of the Studio Museum as beholden to the African American community in Harlem clearly broke with the mission that had once fundamentally distinguished African American neighborhood museums from their mainstream counterparts. During the 1980s and 1990s, however, this reassessment of a museum's community obligations also took place at other African American and ethnic museums. For instance, in 1994 board members of New York City's El Museo del Barrio, originally conceived as a neighborhood museum devoted to Puerto Rican culture, introduced the term "Latin American" into the organization's mission statement.[4] The revised statement subsequently read: "El Museo del Barrio's mission is to establish a forum that will preserve and project the dynamic cultural heritage of Puerto Ricans and all Latin Americans in the United States."[5] As did the Studio Museum in Harlem and, for a time, the Anacostia Neighborhood Museum, El Museo's board hoped to expand the museum's focus from local to global. By inserting the broad designation "Latin American" into its mission statement, El Museo del Barrio could significantly increase its collections and feature artists from throughout Latin America rather than limiting itself to those from Puerto Rico or those of Puerto Rican descent living in New York. Exhibitions featuring well-known Latin American artists such as Frida Kahlo or Diego Rivera were likely to draw more crowds—and thereby more funding.[6]

The board went one step further in 1996 by completely removing "Puerto Ricans" from the museum's mission statement: "El Museo del Barrio will collect, preserve, exhibit, interpret and promote the artistic heritage of Latin Americans, primarily in the United States." For some critics, this deletion constituted a betrayal of the museum's original constituency. As one community member charged, "how can you change the mission of an institution without communicating to the community that created that institution?"[7] Ceding to pressure in 2000, the board reinserted the denomination: "The mission of El

Museo del Barrio is to present and preserve the art and culture of Puerto Ricans and all Latin Americans in the United States."[8]

Despite El Museo del Barrio's nominal reclamation of its original obligation to the Puerto Rican community, the breach between the museum and the people widened. In 2002, El Museo discarded its early exhibition catalogues in a dumpster behind the museum, which were later discovered by an outraged community member.[9] This maneuver suggested to critics that El Museo had completely rejected its own history, for the exhibition catalogues contained vital information about the museum's early years. In response, a museum watch group named "We Are Watching You" formed, claiming to represent the Puerto Rican community that El Museo had seemingly forgotten.[10]

As Kevin Moore has argued, museums' constant self-promotion as community leaders can mask the insidious fact that these same organizations may do little to effect actual change within the community.[11] Thus, a presumed "museum for the people" may conceivably adopt the expansive identity of a "community museum," even though its actual engagement with the community falls short of the community's expectations. The outraged citizens who formed We Are Watching You sensed that the changes to El Museo del Barrio's mission statement reflected this shallow understanding of the term "community."

On the other hand, to what extent can institutions like El Museo del Barrio consistently represent community interests? How should a museum respond if the original community surrounding the institution has changed or been displaced, as can occur through processes such as urban renewal, immigration, and gentrification? Creating "a museum for the community" is an inherently difficult enterprise, argues Arlene Davila, for "community institutions are consistently valued on imposed standards, never on their own terms."[12] To claim the label of "community" museum and fulfill what may be, to some extent, the externally imposed obligations of the term demands a delicate balancing act. True, El Museo's disposal of their archival records constituted a heinous breach of community trust. Failing to consult any community members regarding proposed mission statement changes contradicted the fundamental principles upon which this museum was founded. Yet to insist that a museum established in 1969 must still function, in terms of mission and identity, in the same manner ten or twenty years later is also problematic and may serve to strangle the institution's creative capacity. To reject institutional change for the sake of holding onto—or placating—a museum's original audience deprives it of the capacity to adapt, reinterpret, and challenge the institution.[13]

What Richard Clarke also perhaps failed to consider when he rejected the Studio Museum of Harlem's social obligations was that to fully separate museums from community concerns while simultaneously ensuring that these institutions remain financially solvent, contextually groundbreaking, and favorably perceived, may be impossible. Because public history sites communicate distinct narratives about culture and society through their exhibits and programs, they are bound to promote certain perceptions about different groups of people.[14] If one cannot separate museums from these dynamics, then by that reasoning museums cannot function as purist, isolated institutions. They must inevitably serve as active (or inactive) forces within the community, whether one defines the community geographically, or as the community of people constituting the museum's audience, or even as communities of which the museum is not yet aware. Therefore, a museum always possesses the intrinsic ability—*if not the mandate*—to positively affect the "lives of disadvantaged or marginalized *individuals*, act as a catalyst for social regeneration and as a vehicle for empowerment with specific *communities* and also contribute towards the creation of more equitable *societies*."[15] The question, of course, is whether and to what extent museums and other public history sites recognize and act upon their innate capacities for activism.

Toward a New Century of African American Museums

Continual reinvention does not necessarily produce effective results for struggling museums or for public history sites in general. Indeed, African American museums that have constantly reinterpreted their approaches to conveying public history to a mass audience without surveying that audience about its needs and interests may have caused the connection between the grassroots spirit of the black museum movement and its modern embodiment to falter and widen.

As we have seen, one of the primary ways in which the black museum movement appeared to lose strength both publicly and privately stemmed from problems surrounding the intense relocation and expansion campaigns staged by many leaders of African American museums throughout the 1970s and 1990s. Chicago's DuSable Museum, the Studio Museum in Harlem, Detroit's Museum of African American History, and the Anacostia Neighborhood Museum expanded and relocated in an effort to attract new audiences, funding, and status. In conjunction with these efforts, these museums (as well as the African American Museum of Philadelphia, which has remained at its original site) staged prominent fund-raising galas and underwent numerous shifts in admin-istration. These types of public changes occasionally met with significant com-munity resistance, even on the part of some museum staff members, who feared the disintegration of the grassroots spirit of their organizations. The physical manifestation of this grassroots spirit was embodied in the ordinariness of the very buildings and landscapes in which many of these museums were first housed—former movie theaters, modest apartment buildings, and clubhouses that historically catered to African Americans.[16] Once museum leaders vacated their original buildings and began to alter mission statements, programs, and occasionally even the names of their organizations, their museums (some to a greater degree than others) experienced more problems connecting with audi-ences and maintaining financial solvency.

The decision to build new and costly museums to meet perceived audience demand contributed to the difficulties experienced by certain African American museums. In retrospect, reconsideration of the potential of a museum's existing location may have offered a better solution for museum leaders seeking to retain and attract audiences. For example, the Charles H. Wright Museum of African American History in Detroit (MAAH) could have remained at its second loca-tion on Frederick Douglass Avenue during the 1980s and undergone the expan-sion and remodeling necessary to improve the space. Instead, the Douglass Avenue site barely had a chance to register with most Detroit residents before it was abandoned just a few short years later for the third, far more impressive (and expensive) incarnation of the museum.

It is also important to note that the successful expansion of African Amer-ican neighborhood museums in their original locations is not without prece-dent. For instance, The National Great Blacks in Wax Museum in Baltimore, Maryland, founded in 1983, experienced increased attendance during the 1990s and 2000s despite the downward trend in attendance at other African American museums. Rather than pursue relocation to Baltimore's Inner Harbor District, which had become a thriving tourist destination, the museum contin-ues to inhabit an "East Baltimore street corner across from a boarded-up shop-ping center" embedded in one of Baltimore's historically African American neighborhoods. In 1995 annual attendance at the 15,000-square-foot museum had reached 100,000; by 2004 it had doubled to more than 200,000. Based on the strength of these numbers, founder Joanne Martin is presently engaged in a $75-million-dollar capital campaign to increase the museum's size to 120,000 square feet (comparable with the dimensions of Detroit's Museum of African

American History) and to expand the existing museum to encompass an entire city block.[17]

When faced with declining attendance and budgets, museums often launch vigorous public outreach campaigns. Rather than focusing only on attracting audiences *to the museum,* African American museums that also work to bring their institution *to the people* have come full circle, back to the mobile exhibitions that galvanized institutions like the International Afro-American Museum during the 1960s. In the case of the IAM's descendant, the Charles H. Wright Museum of African American History, most visitors are recruited to visit the museum in person or to virtually peruse their digital archives and online exhibits. Other than the use of traveling exhibits, which typically end up in other museums or more restricted spaces such as universities, airports, and libraries, physically bringing the MAAH into the working-class (and underclass) neighborhoods of Detroit does not appear to be a high priority. Consequently, Detroit residents may have little reason to care that the museum was created for and by them. Any lingering fissures between the MAAH and Detroit residents, however, might be bridged through the reinstallation of their innovative mobile exhibit van, thus continuing the spirit and practice of Charles Wright's original museum.[18] The Black History 101 Mobile Museum, a popular traveling museum that Detroit schoolteacher Khalid el-Hakim created in 1991, might provide the MAAH with a unique model or potential collaborative partner to reach those seeking access to African American history—but not necessarily in the form of a "traditional" museum (even one that has been as consistently groundbreaking as the MAAH).[19]

Faced with the cumulative effects of decades of financial upheaval and, at times, uncertainty regarding their mission and relationship with the local community, several of the museums in this study, including the MAAH, have begun to implement important changes to exhibits, programs, and the physical structure of the buildings themselves. In 2011, for example, Chicago's DuSable Museum addressed this problem of disconnect between the museum and underserved audiences by initiating a mobile exhibition titled Taking It to the Streets! The exhibit featured interactive displays on the life of Jean Baptiste Pointe DuSable, together with related educational programs.[20] In addition to creating a new mobile exhibit, the DuSable Museum underwent structural renovations focused on improving its archival and collections capacity—steps recommended by the 2004 Institute of Museum and Library Services report, which concluded that the infrastructure of African American museums was in dire condition.[21]

The MAAH has also taken important steps to improve its approach and reception in the community. For example, after an emergency financial bailout from the city of Detroit in 2004, MAAH staff removed the exhibit Of the People: The African American Experience, which had been criticized for its reinforcement of African Americans as victims and its lack of vitality. In its place, curators began planning a permanent installation titled And Still We Rise: Our Journey through African American History and Culture. The well-received exhibit, which opened in November 2004, highlights the museum's local roots through its examination and re-creation of sites historically significant to Detroit's African American community, such as the Black Bottom neighborhood, the Paradise Valley business district, and the Ford Rouge Plant foundry.[22] The museum also received a $2.5 million Kresge Foundation challenge grant in September 2006. Under the terms of the challenge, the MAAH was required to attract seventy thousand paid admissions and increase their membership to twenty thousand. The overwhelming response of Detroit's residents and local African American business owners, who contributed $1 million during this process, helped the museum meet the Kresge Foundation's requirements and thereby lessen their dependence, at least for a short time, upon city funding.[23] Although the organization, like the city itself, continues to face significant financial challenges, this example of positive response from Detroit residents and museum supporters attests to the reservoir of goodwill the MAAH has accrued.

Even without the receipt of grants or other substantial funds, institutional change and acknowledgment of community needs may be achieved through the smallest measures, as the past and current histories of the black museum movement indicate. The symbiotic relationship between museum and community guided John Kinard during the Anacostia Neighborhood Museum's early years as he produced renowned programs and exhibits, such as The Rat and Evolution of a Community. Kinard veered away from local themes during the 1980s due to concerns about the museum's inferior status in relation to the rest of the Smithsonian system. In 2007, however, staff renewed the museum's community focus by presenting East of the River: Continuity and Change (September 2007–November 2008), which explored the histories of neighborhoods east of the Anacostia River. Subsequent exhibitions also struck a more even balance between local, national, and international themes. Finally, in July 2006, the Anacostia Museum and Center for African American History and Culture (formerly the Anacostia Neighborhood Museum) changed its name to the Anacostia Community Museum. The museum's director, Camille Giraud Akeju, instigated this important shift toward (re)acknowledging the vital interaction between the museum and the community.[24] The Anacostia Community Museum's reclamation of its community identity may help it to redefine and secure its status as a vital African American cultural institution in Washington, D.C., even as a far grander museum of African American history carves out a space on the National Mall.[25]

African American community museums founded during the 1960s and 1970s must also function in the midst of the second, ongoing phase of black public history, as sites of historical importance in modern African American history (such as the Lorraine Hotel in Memphis, Tennessee, or the historic highway leading from Selma to Montgomery) are converted into museums or otherwise officially commemorated.[26] Historian Bernard Armada has raised several critical questions regarding the design and function of these new African American museums and historic sites, arguing that organizations such as the National Civil Rights Museum in Memphis (NCRM) place too much emphasis on the audience's sensory experiences and prioritize entertainment through consumption—in this case, the museum gift shop. Such comments are not unusual in the scholarly assessments of many modern museums, as critics have long accused these institutions, whether deservedly or not, of "dumbing down" their exhibits and programs in order to appeal to broader audiences. Indeed, this critique surfaced as early as the Metropolitan Museum of Art's media-centric presentation of Harlem on My Mind in 1969.[27] These perceived weaknesses detract from museums' potential to act as effective agents of community change and, in the case of the NCRM, lessen their status as national sites of remembrance. Armada further maintains that, as a result of its design limitations, the NCRM "inadvertently has compromised the resistive and more radical edge that seems necessary for significant political progress for black civil rights." In moving to the commodified center, the NCRM has fallen from the "peripheral edge"—an edge necessary to maintain and cultivate the grassroots energy that lies at the core of the black museum movement.[28]

To achieve success comparable to that of early African American neighborhood museums—success not necessarily measured by monumental architecture or elaborate fund-raising galas, but rather by audience response and appreciation—all African American museums and public history sites must recognize this "peripheral edge" that pushed black museum movement leaders to challenge and refashion the staid conceptions of how a museum must function. The cultivation of this peripheral edge, engendered by their activism and adaptation of the ideals of the Civil Rights Movement and, especially, the Black Power Movement, allowed leaders like John Kinard to present the grim narrative of The Rat and helped International Afro-American Museum volunteers to traverse the scarred landscapes of Detroit in their "museum on wheels." The peripheral edge also shaped the Studio Museum in Harlem as its artists and leaders challenged tradition-bound institutions like the Metropolitan Museum of Art and the Whitney Museum of American Art. Likewise, Margaret Burroughs's long history of grassroots activism and willingness to subvert political dogma during her years as a teacher in Chicago's public schools inspired the DuSable's creation of groundbreaking educational outreach programs and its connection to international freedom movements. The advocates of the African American Museum of Philadelphia also stood on the peripheral edge when they forced city officials to acknowledge that they refused to tolerate a sanitized version of the Bicentennial that excluded discussion of African American history and culture.

In both design and operation, the National Museum of African American History and Culture intends to combine the grandeur of the iconic with the immediacy of the vernacular. Whether this museum can both match and reinvigorate the activist energy of the original African American neighborhood museums will serve as the next major test for the black museum movement. Under the protective mantle of the Smithsonian Institution and within the contested space of the National Mall, the NMAAHC cannot serve solely as a triumphant monument to African American history and culture, nor can it veer in the opposite direction and reinforce the sense that African Americans have been the perpetual victims of history. Instead, the museum should critically provoke diverse audiences to realize that the work begun by generations of black museum leaders and civil rights activists is not yet finished. In doing so, the museum must not hesitate to tackle what some deem to be controversial subjects. As NMAAHC director Lonnie Bunch himself has argued, "rather than champion limits on controversy and debate within exhibits, museums and curators must have the courage to embrace controversy."[29]

The construction and debut of the national African American museum will no doubt ignite a potentially competitive spark; local African American museums that have become detached from their community origins and prone to bureaucratic stagnation may once again be reinvigorated. In turn, leaders of the NMAAHC, ideally, will remember and acknowledge the historically contested origins of their institution and work to build equitable partnerships with local museums that, through both their support *and* their dissent, helped to ensure the creation of this national monument to black history. Many will scrutinize the ways in which the National Museum of African American History and Culture chooses to address the challenge of maintaining the historically community-based mission of African American neighborhood museums while simultaneously creating a national and international symbol of African American heritage. Among those watching will be those who began the black museum movement with little more than a space in which to display a few artifacts, together with a deep-rooted conviction about the vital importance of exhibiting and interpreting the hidden stories of African American—and American—history.

NOTES

Introduction

1. Emily Dennis Harvey and Bernard Friedberg, eds., *A Museum for the People: A Report of Proceedings at the Seminar on Neighborhood Museums, held November 20, 21, and 22, 1969, at MUSE, the Bedford Lincoln Neighborhood Museum in Brooklyn, New York* (New York: Arno Press, 1971), ix. The Museums Collaborative was a "cooperative program of eighteen New York City museums working jointly on the development of decentralized museum services for the city's schools and communities," ("About the Editors," n.p.). The Brooklyn Children's Museum, which was in the midst of constructing a new building, opened the Bedford Lincoln Neighborhood Museum as a temporary museum. The site was deliberately modeled after the Anacostia Neighborhood Museum. Brooklyn Children's Museum, "Who We Are: History," www .brooklynkids.org/index.php/whoweare/history.

2. Harvey and Friedberg, *A Museum for the People*, ix.

3. Ibid., xi.

4. Ibid., ix. Anacostia Neighborhood Museum director John Kinard and Studio Museum in Harlem director Edward Spriggs also attended the conference, as did representatives from a few traditional museums, including the Whitney Museum of American Art. Grassroots arts and community organizations, such as the NYC Art Workers Coalition, also participated, along with intellectuals from the newly emerging field of Black Studies.

5. Benedict Anderson, *Imagined Communities: Reflections on the Origin and Spread of Nationalism* (New York: Verso, 1991).

6. Harvey and Friedberg, *A Museum for the People*, 34. For additional information on Carew's establishment of the New Thing Art and Architecture Center in 1967, see "Overcoming Cultural Racism: Profile of a Black Community Arts Center," *Music Educators Journal* 58, no. 3 (November 1971): 42–45.

7. Harry Robinson, president of the AAMA from 1986 to 1988, and Joy Ford Austin, then executive director of the AAMA, argued that the "Black museum movement emerged in the 1950s and 1960s to preserve the heritage of the Black experience and to ensure its proper interpretation in American history. In this way, Black museums instill a sense of achievement within Black communities and encourage cooperation between those communities and the broader public." African American Museums Association, *Profile of Black Museums* (Washington, D.C.: African American Museums Association; Nashville, Tenn.: American Association for State and Local History, 1988), ix.

8. Arlene Davila, "El Barrio's 'We Are Watching You' Campaign: On the Politics of Inclusion in a Latinized Museum," *Aztlan* 30, no. 1 (Spring 2005): 159. Also see Karen Mary

Davalos, "Exhibiting Mestizaje: The Poetics and Experience of the Mexican Fine Arts Center Museum," in *Latinos in Museums: A Heritage Reclaimed*, ed. Antonio Ríos-Bustamante and Christine Marin (Malabar, Fla.: Krieger, 1998), 39–66.

9. African American Museums Association, *Profile of Black Museums*, 4.

10. For a comparative study of South African museums and African American museums, see Robyn Kimberley Autry, "Desegregating the Past: The Transformation of Public Imagination at South African and American Museums" (PhD diss., University of Wisconsin-Madison, 2008).

11. Harry C. Boyte and Sara M. Evans, *Free Spaces: The Sources of Democratic Change in America* (New York: Harper and Row, 1986), 17–18.

12. Ibid., x.

13. The black museum movement also may be contextualized within what Joseph Rhea has identified as the much broader "Race Pride Movement" of the 1950s–1970s. According to Rhea, those who subscribed to the Race Pride Movement did not necessarily belong to one specific ethnicity, race, or organization. Yet the goal of those who participated in this movement was shared: the achievement of "national cultural recognition." As Rhea states, "the net result of their efforts was the cultural transformation of a nation that had already experienced a major legal revolution [i.e., the Civil Rights Movement]." Joseph Rhea, *Race Pride and the American Identity* (Cambridge, Mass.: Harvard University Press, 1997), 4.

14. Stokely Carmichael and Charles Hamilton, *Black Power: The Politics of Liberation in America* (New York: Vintage Books, 1967), 38.

15. James Del Rio, "The Conspiracy," 1963, folder 2, box 16, Series II, Detroit Commission on Community Relations—Human Rights Department Collection, Walter P. Reuther Library (hereafter WPR), Wayne State University, Detroit, 9.

16. Carmichael and Hamilton, *Black Power*, 34–35, 42.

17. Peniel Joseph, *Waiting 'til the Midnight Hour: A Narrative History of Black Power in America* (New York: Henry Holt, 2006), xiv.

18. With Carmichael's use of the term "black power" at a march honoring James Meredith in 1966, a new movement centered on black empowerment and retaliation is said to have officially begun, just as the mainstream Civil Rights Movement, with its major legislative victories (the Civil Rights Act of 1964 and the Voting Rights Act of 1965) began to decline. Yet this narrative restricts the Black Power Movement to a post-1965 birth, even though the ideas and practice of black power were reverberating well before the term was ever uttered. Indeed, prior to Carmichael's proclamation of black power, the informal practice of what Tim Tyson has termed this "ambiguous slogan" had already begun, particularly in the South, where African Americans resisted the oppression of Jim Crow through means both subtle and outwardly defiant. In recent years, numerous historians have expanded this restricted chronology beyond its usual parameters, thus ensuring that Dr. Martin Luther King's post-1963 critique of American foreign policy and capitalism—ideas that moved him closer to black power's platform—is not overlooked, and the "complex prehistory" of the Black Power Movement emerges, not from a single political rally, but on the ground in cities and neighborhoods throughout the United States, as well as abroad, in the postwar era. See Timothy Tyson, *Radio Free Dixie: Robert F. Williams and the Roots of Black Power* (Chapel Hill: University of North Carolina Press, 1999), 291; Nikhil Pal Singh, *Black Is a Country: Race and the Unfinished Struggle for Democracy* (Cambridge, Mass.: Harvard University Press, 2004), 5; Rhea, *Race Pride and the American Identity*, 3.

19. Joseph, *Waiting 'til the Midnight Hour*, 289.

20. Keith Mayes points to the creation and ongoing celebration of Kwanzaa as illustrative of the Black Power Movement's resonance in modern black cultural and political thought. As he argues, to label the movement as "dead" by the mid-1970s "is to understand Black Power only in its national dimension. . . . It can be argued that the Black Power movement survived because its cultural offspring, Kwanzaa, evolved and matured, becoming an independent entity whose charge was to educate a community about the African roots of black American culture." See Keith Mayes, "A Holiday of Our Own: Kwanzaa, Cultural Nationalism, and the Promotion of a Black Power Holiday, 1966–1985," in *The Black Power Movement: Re-thinking the Civil Rights–Black Power Era*, ed. Peniel Joseph (New York: Routledge, 2006), 248. Also see Keith Mayes, *Kwanzaa: Black Power and the Making of the African-American Holiday Tradition* (New York: Routledge, 2009).

21. African American museums, including all of those discussed in this study, created specific programs to promote and celebrate Kwanzaa during the late 1960s and 1970s. Interestingly, Karenga's conceptualization of "black history" was not necessarily compatible with the mind-set of those who initiated the black museum movement. For example, Karenga argued in 1966 that "In terms of history, all we need at this point is heroic images, the white boy got enough dates for everybody" (quoted in Rhea, *Race Pride and the American Identity*, 107–108). While African American museum leaders certainly employed "heroic images" in their exhibits, they also believed that dates were important—as well as the need to rewrite the history textbooks. The use of Afrocentric symbols and the reliance upon a "heroic African past" at the expense of an accurate revision of American history was not an option for most black museum leaders.

22. Jeffrey C. Stewart and Fath Davis Ruffins, "A Faithful Witness: Afro-American History in Historical Perspective, 1828–1994," in *Presenting the Past: Essays on History and the Public*, ed. Susan Porter Benson, Stephen Brier, and Roy Rosenzweig (Philadelphia: Temple University Press, 1986), 308.

23. Fath Davis Ruffins and Paul Ruffins, "Recovering Yesterday: An Overview of the Collection and Preservation of Black History," *Black Issues in Higher Education* 13, no. 25 (February 6, 1997): 16.

24. Ibid. For additional information on black bibliophiles, see *Black Bibliophiles and Collectors: Preservers of Black History*, ed. Elinor Des Verney Sinnette, W. Paul Coates, and Thomas C. Battle (Washington, D.C.: Howard University Press, 1990).

25. Hampton University Museum, "Collections," museum.hamptonu.edu/collections.cfm.

26. Michele Gates Moresi, "Exhibiting Race, Creating Nation: Representations of Black History and Culture at the Smithsonian Institution, 1895–1976" (PhD diss., George Washington University, 2003), 24.

27. Stewart and Ruffins, "A Faithful Witness," 309.

28. Ibid., 311. See also Amina Jill Dickerson, "The History and Institutional Development of African American Museums" (MA thesis, American University, 1988), 22.

29. Pero Gaglo Dagbovie, "Making Black History Practical and Popular: Carter G. Woodson, the Proto Black Studies Movement and the Struggle for Black Liberation," *Western Journal of Black Studies* 27, no. 4 (Winter 2003): 264.

30. The black museum movement that began after World War II should be considered distinct from Du Bois's and Woodson's achievements, even though its leaders certainly borrowed from their approach. Unlike the more amorphously defined "association," or celebratory "week," African American museums constituted brick-and-mortar institutions with

their own unique methodologies and were rooted in one city. Their audiences, at least initially, were predominantly local, as opposed to the national (and international) reach sought by Woodson and Du Bois. Woodson's ASNLH headquarters in Washington, D.C., did serve as an informal community museum that held his collection of artifacts and historical documents. Nevertheless, the primary function of the ASNLH building was not as a typical museum, but rather as the headquarters for a national organization. See Pero Gaglo Dagbovie, "'Most Honorable Mention . . . Belongs to Washington, DC': The Carter G. Woodson Home and the Early Black History Movement in the Nation's Capital," *Journal of African American History* 96, no. 3 (Summer 2011): 311.

31. Thomas J. Davis, "'They, Too, Were Here': The Afro-American Experience and History Museums," *American Quarterly* 41, no. 2 (June 1989): 329. Also see V. P . Franklin and Bettye Collier-Thomas, "Biography, Race Vindication, and African American Intellectuals," *Journal of African American History* 87 (Winter 2003): 160.

32. Numerous secondary sources clearly indicate the ways in which mainstream museums acknowledged and responded to the pressures levied by the black museum movement (as well as the work of other ethnic museums). However, an examination of the revolutionary museums that *initiated* this challenge is, for the most part, absent in the existing scholarship. For example, Michele Gates Moresi, Curator of Collections at the National Museum of African American History and Culture, documented some interaction between the Anacostia Neighborhood Museum and the Smithsonian Institution—most notably in the Smithsonian's and the Anacostia museum's response to the nation's Bicentennial. Yet her dissertation primarily focuses on how the Smithsonian as a whole evolved with regard to its treatment of race and African American history, rather than examining how the Anacostia Neighborhood Museum applied sustained pressure on the Smithsonian to change its policies. Portia James, a former historian for the museum, focused her the attention on the Anacostia Neighborhood Museum more thoroughly, arguing for its groundbreaking work as an instigator of community change; see Michele Gates Moresi, "Exhibiting Race, Creating Nation"; Portia James, "Building a Community-Based Identity at Anacostia Museum," in *Heritage, Museums, and Galleries: An Introductory Reader,* ed. Gerard Corsane (London: Routledge, 2005), 339–356. Similarly, although the Chicago Historical Society's extensive records allowed researchers such as Katherine Lewis to explore the organization's attempts to incorporate African American history during the 1980s, and the DuSable Museum's confrontation with the Society during this process, a more focused examination of the DuSable's history and work *outside* of its relationship to the Chicago Historical Society is absent. Katherine Lewis, *The Changing Face of Public History: The Chicago Historical Society and the Transformation of an American Museum* (DeKalb: Northern Illinois University Press, 2005).

33. African American Museums Association, *Profile of Black Museums,* xiii. The AAMA sent the survey to its 99 institutional members; 52 responded.

34. Ardali's survey targeted black museums that focused specifically on art, as well as museums that combined an art, culture, and history focus. Seventeen of the museums surveyed were specifically "African American," while two museums combined an African American and Hispanic focus. See Azade Ardali, *Black and Hispanic Art Museums: A Vibrant Cultural Resource* (New York: Ford Foundation, 1989), 7–8.

35. Joy Ford Austin, *National Survey of African American Museums: Prepared for the National Museum of African American History and Culture Plan for Action Presidential Commission* (Washington, D.C.: National Museum of African American History and Culture Plan for Action Presidential Commission, 2003), iv, 43–46.

36. For information on African American emigration to Canada during the eighteenth and nineteenth centuries, see George Hendrick and Willene Hendrick, *Black Refugees in Canada: Accounts of Escape during the Era of Slavery* (Jefferson, N.C.: McFarland, 2010). Discussion of the comparative research potential between black public history in Canada and the United States took center stage at the "Remembering Africa and Its Diasporas" conference. I wish to extend my thanks to its participants—in particular, Robyn Autry and Audra Diptee—for their comments on my work. Carleton University, Conference Proceedings, "Remembering Africa and Its Diasporas," Ottawa, Ontario, Canada, October 6–8, 2010.

37. Fath Davis Ruffins, "Culture Wars Won and Lost, Part II: The National African-American Museum Project," *Radical History Review* 70 (Winter 1998): 89.

38. The AAMP was formerly known as the Afro-American Historical and Cultural Museum. In the interest of clarity, I refer to the museum as the African American Museum in Philadelphia (its current name), or AAMP, unless otherwise noted. There are few accessible institutional papers associated with the AAMP. Because of these limitations, the voluminous records stemming from the city's Bicentennial programs significantly complement the researcher's understanding of this museum's creation and struggles. Records from neighborhood associations that attempted to block the construction of the African American Museum of Philadelphia also offer another vital perspective on the contested history of this institution. In the realm of secondary sources, Andrew Feffer's exploration of Philadelphia's Bicentennial celebration, "Show Down in Center City: Staging Redevelopment and Citizenship in Bicentennial Philadelphia, 1974–1977," *Journal of Urban History* 30, no. 6 (September 2004): 791–825, briefly engages with the fight that supporters of the African American Museum of Philadelphia waged to establish the museum in Philadelphia's rapidly gentrifying Society Hill neighborhood. Matthew Countryman's study of Philadelphia's black power movement in *Up South: Civil Rights and Black Power in Philadelphia* (2005) reveals how the movement created significant opportunities for African Americans to hold political office in Philadelphia during the 1970s; the emergence of the African American Museum of Philadelphia must be framed in this context.

The contentious (re)interpretation of the Liberty Bell during the early 2000s also demonstrates how Philadelphia's battles over the tenuous intersections of memory, race, and identity were as heated in the early twenty-first century, as they were when black museum advocates demanded representation during the Bicentennial celebration. Historian Gary Nash, who participated in the protests against the National Park Service and the Independence Hall Historical Planners, documented this landmark event in African American public history. Nash, however, does not reference the AAMP's earlier battles during the Bicentennial. See Feffer, "Show Down in Center City"; Matthew Countryman, *Up South: Civil Rights and Black Power in Philadelphia* (Philadelphia: University of Pennsylvania Press, 2005); Gary B. Nash, "For Whom Will the Liberty Bell Toll? From Controversy to Cooperation," in *Slavery and Public History: The Tough Stuff of American Memory*, ed. James Oliver Horton and Lois E. Horton (New York: The New Press, 2006), 75–101.

39. John Bodnar, *Remaking America: Public Memory, Commemoration, and Patriotism in the Twentieth Century* (Princeton, N.J.: Princeton University Press, 1992), 226.

40. Lisa Markowitz and Karen Tice discuss the impact of the women's movement's evolution from organizations "on the street" to political institutionalization. Although the professionalization of women's social organizations has brought their cause into the political mainstream, at the same time "such institutionalization has frequently contributed to the persistence or creation of social hierarchies within and between women's organizations, as well

as to shifts in their social change agendas and action strategies"; Markowitz and Tice, "Paradoxes of Professionalization: Parallel Dilemmas in Women's Organizations in the Americas," *Gender & Society* 16, no. 6 (December 2002): 941–58. African American social movements may also be subject to the same trends. Also see María-José Moreno, "Art Museums and Socioeconomic Forces: The Case of a Community Museum," *Review of Radical Political Economics* 36, no. 4 (Fall 2004): 506–27.

41. Eric Gable, "Maintaining Boundaries, or 'Mainstreaming' Black History in a White Museum," in *Theorizing Museums: Representing Identity and Diversity in a Changing World*, ed. Sharon Macdonald and Gordon Fyfe (Cambridge, Mass.: Blackwell, 1996), 181.

42. The modern incarnation of Dr. Charles Wright's International Afro-American Museum (IAM) in Detroit has attracted extensive academic interest, corresponding with the wealth of scholarship regarding Detroit's transformation from a "Model City" to one often characterized by its deteriorating postindustrial landscape and racial tensions. See, for example, the extensive body of literature on Detroit in the postwar era, including Thomas Sugrue's *The Origins of the Urban Crisis: Race and Inequality in Postwar Detroit* (Princeton, N.J.: Princeton University Press, 1996); Heather Thompson, *Whose Detroit? Politics, Labor, and Race in a Modern American City* (Ithaca, N.Y.: Cornell University Press, 2001); Suzanne Smith, *Dancing in the Street: Motown and the Cultural Politics of Detroit* (Cambridge, Mass.: Harvard University Press, 1999). The contested relationship between the Museum of African American History (MAAH) and the Detroit Institute of Arts, as well as the MAAH's ties to Detroit's Mayor Coleman A. Young, has also received significant attention from historians. For discussion of the MAAH and its relationship with the Detroit Institute of Arts, see Jeffrey Abt, *A Museum on the Verge: A Socioeconomic History of the Detroit Institute of Arts, 1882–2000* (Detroit: Wayne State University Press, 2001); Karen Miller, "Whose History, Whose Culture? The Museum of African American History, The Detroit Institute of Arts, and Urban Politics at the End of the Twentieth Century," *Michigan Quarterly Review* 41, no. 1 (Winter 2002): 136–154; Alison Landsberg, *Prosthetic Memory: The Transformation of American Remembrance in the Age of Mass Culture* (New York: Columbia University Press, 2004). These historians, however, do not ground their analyses of the MAAH by exploring how the International Afro-American Museum *became* the MAAH. Indeed, the origins of the IAM have received little, if any, attention from scholars, despite its pioneering work in implementing a "mobile museum" and Charles Wright's advocacy for a distinct ethos of black power—a notion that energized other African American neighborhood museums across the country.

1. When "Civil Rights Are Not Enough": Building the Black Museum Movement

1. Ray Arsenault and John Hope Franklin, "The Sage of Freedom: An Interview with John Hope Franklin," *Public Historian* 29, no. 2 (Spring 2007): 49. Also see John E. Fleming and Margaret T. Burroughs, "Dr. Margaret T. Burroughs: Artist, Teacher, Administrator, Writer, Political Activist, and Museum Founder," *Public Historian* 21, no. 1 (Winter 1999): 31–55. In 1968, the museum changed its name from the "Museum of Negro History and Art" (formerly the Ebony Museum of History and Art) to the DuSable Museum, in honor of Haitian trader Jean Baptist Pointe DuSable. In the interest of clarity, I will refer to the museum as the "DuSable" unless otherwise noted.

2. Jeffrey C. Stewart and Fath Davis Ruffins, "A Faithful Witness: Afro-American History in Historical Perspective, 1828–1994," in *Presenting the Past: Essays on History and the Public*, ed. Susan Porter Benson, Stephen Brier, and Roy Rosenzweig (Philadelphia: Temple University Press, 1986), 329.

3. John R. Kinard and Esther Nighbert, "The Anacostia Neighborhood Museum," *Museum* 24, no. 2 (1972): 103.

4. Suzanne Smith, *Dancing in the Street: Motown and the Cultural Politics of Detroit* (Cambridge, Mass.: Harvard University Press, 1999), 11.

5. Examples of Philadelphia's African American cultural organizations include the Philadelphia Library Company of Colored Persons (founded 1835); the Banneker Institute (1854); the Pyramid Club (mid-1930s), and Heritage House (1949). The Philadelphia Society for Negro Records and Research, founded in 1937, counted among its members Judge Raymond Pace Alexander and his wife, attorney Sadie Tanner Mossel Alexander, as well as the authors Jessie and Arthur Huff Fauset. In addition, as Charles Blockson states, "Throughout this period, the local branch of the [ASNLH] mounted small exhibitions and conducted lectures in schools and other institutions throughout the city under the leadership of Judge Alexander and other dedicated Philadelphia Society members such as Philadelphia school teacher Dr. Ruth Wright, Dr. Bright and Edith Ingram." See Blockson, "The Struggle to Preserve Philadelphia's African American History: A Tricentennial Record," in Afro-American Historical and Cultural Museum, *20 Years of Reflection: 1976–1996* (Philadelphia: Afro-American Historical and Cultural Museum of Philadelphia, 1996), 8–10.

6. Smith, *Dancing in the Street,* 11.

7. Stewart and Ruffins, "A Faithful Witness," 311. Also see Amina Jill Dickerson, "The History and Institutional Development of African American Museums" (MA thesis, American University, 1988), 13–14, 22.

8. Bill Mullen, *Popular Fronts: Chicago and African American Cultural Politics, 1935–46* (Chicago: University of Illinois Press, 1999), 87.

9. Ibid., 89.

10. Ibid., 5. Penny Von Eschen's *Race against Empire: Black Americans and Anticolonialism, 1937–1957* (Ithaca, N.Y.: Cornell University Press, 1997) illustrates how activists such as Robeson and Du Bois freely engaged in an anticolonialist critique of U.S. policy at home and abroad, and forged "transnational" ties with anticolonialist movements in Africa and India during the 1930s and 1940s. With the onset of the Cold War, the U.S. government found it in their best interest to suppress domestic activists who called attention to inequality in the United States. As a result, the anticolonialist critique that African American activists nurtured during the 1930s and 1940s radically dissipated in the 1950s. Black middle- and working-class interest in Africa subsequently declined (although it resurfaced in the early 1960s, as is evident in the DuSable's exhibits).

11. Since the group did not operate an actual museum, in the traditional sense of this term, the word "Museum" in the NNMHF's title confused some of its members. Margaret Burroughs asked the chairman of the group, Bishop James Bray, why the word was in their name. He replied, "we should aim to have a museum in the future. I walked away thinking, 'Well maybe that's where I come in!'" See Margaret T. G. Burroughs, *Life with Margaret: The Official Autobiography* (Chicago: In Time Publishing and Media Group, 2003), 100. Burroughs died in 2010 at the age of 95.

12. Margaret Burroughs, "Some Aspects of the Black History Movement in Chicago since the 1940's to the Present," n.d. [c. 1978], DuSable Museum of African American History, Chicago, 2, 4. Chicago's governor also proclaimed a statewide celebration of Negro History Week during the late 1940s. By the 1930s, Negro History Week had made inroads into some white schools. Both black and white newspapers began to advertise events associated with the week. Outside of urban areas, Negro History Week reached some rural schools by the late

1940s. Woodson distributed "kits" to these schoolteachers at a cost of two dollars each. The kits contained writings, speeches, books, and photographs. Black museums adapted Woodson's technique during the 1960s by creating and distributing their own educational outreach programs and materials to schools. See Pero Gaglo Dagbovie, "Making Black History Practical and Popular: Carter G. Woodson, the Proto Black Studies Movement and the Struggle for Black Liberation," *Western Journal of Black Studies* 27, no. 4 (Winter 2003): 267.

13. In 1953, artist Charles Burroughs, whom Margaret married in 1949, wrote to Chicago Governor William G. Stratton, calling for the state of Illinois's assistance in distributing pamphlets for Negro History Week: "We will as usual appreciate your past promptness in preparing the proclamations in at least one thousand copies since we distribute them to schools, churches, organizations and institutions and calls have already begun to come in for them." Other organizations that sponsored Chicago's Negro History Week included the NAACP, the Chicago Urban League, the Federated Women's Club, and the DuSable History Club. M. T. Blanton, Chrysolia Smith, and Charles Burroughs to Governor William G. Stratton, January 11, 1953, folder "Margaret," box 1, DuSable Museum Papers, DuSable. Margaret Burroughs also initiated a letter-writing campaign in 1951 to "All Presidents and Officers of Social, Civic, Charitable and Educational Clubs of Chicago" to ask for their support in observing Negro History Week from February 11 to February 18. See William I. Flanagan to Margaret Goss Burroughs, January 29, 1951, folder "Margaret," box 1, DuSable Museum Papers, DuSable.

14. Burroughs, "Some Aspects," 3.

15. Margaret Burroughs to Governor Otto Kerner, August 25, 1961, folder "Margaret," box 1, DuSable Museum Papers, DuSable.

16. Burroughs, *Life with Margaret*, 97.

17. Jon Anderson, "Margaret Burroughs Is Still Skating Through Life," *Chicago Tribune*, May 20, 2004. See also Mullen's discussion of poet Gwendolyn Brooks's reactions to Burroughs's salons, 97.

18. Pero Gaglo Dagbovie, " 'Most Honorable Mention . . . Belongs to Washington, DC': The Carter G. Woodson Home and the Early Black History Movement in the Nation's Capital," *Journal of African American History* 96, no. 3 (Summer 2011): 310, 312.

19. See Burroughs's discussion regarding her admiration of Paul Robeson in *Life with Margaret*, 59–65. IAM founder Charles Wright was also deeply interested in Robeson's work and activism. In 1975, Wright published *Robeson, Labor's Forgotten Champion* (Detroit: Balamp Publishing Company, 1975). Several IAM exhibits and outreach programs during the early mid-1970s also focused on "uncovering the real story" of Robeson. For example, the IAM produced a two-hour televised profile of him in conjunction with the Canadian Broadcasting Company. Other projects included the production of two albums, "An Evening with Paul Robeson," and "Paul Robeson at the Peace Arch Park, 1973." The IAM also created greeting cards featuring Robeson. In 1978, the IAM, in conjunction with the Board of Education and Wayne State University, produced an eight-day eightieth birthday salute for Robeson. See Newsletter, "The Voice of the Century," October 1970, folder 13, box 7, WSU Teacher's Corporation, WPR, 3; Margaret B. Jones, "Significant Lectures," box MAAH Publications, 1969–1990, Charles H. Wright Museum of African American History (hereafter MAAH), Detroit; greeting cards: see Board Minutes, December 19, 1971, folder MS/MAAH: Board Meetings-Reports, 1964–1971, MAAH; birthday salute: see "Joint Ventures between the Museum and outside Agencies," folder IAM Founding 1965, box 3, CHWMAAH Historical Records, MAAH.

20. Burroughs, *Life with Margaret*, 72–73.

21. Ibid., 99–100.

22. Dickerson, "The History and Institutional Development of African American Museums," 97, 108. For more information on what is today known as the "Griffiths-Burroughs House," see Landmark Designation Report, Griffiths-Burroughs House 3806 S. Michigan Avenue, Department of Zoning and Land Use Planning, 2009, www.cityofchicago.org/dam/city/depts/zlup/Historic_Preservation/Publications/Griffiths_Burroughs_House.pdf.

23. Lillian Walker, "A History of the Du Sable Museum of African American History and Art" (MA thesis, Governor's State University, University Park, Ill., 1978), 15, citing from Du Sable Museum of History, Minutes of the Steering Committee, January 20, 1961.

24. Stewart and Ruffins, "A Faithful Witness," 329.

25. "Black History on Display," *Muhammad Speaks*, May 21, 1965.

26. Walker, "A History of the Du Sable Museum of African American History and Art," Appendix A.

27. Fabio Rojas, *From Black Power to Black Studies: How a Radical Social Movement Became an Academic Discipline* (Baltimore: Johns Hopkins University Press, 2007), 41–42.

28. Burroughs, *Life with Margaret*, 102. Eugene Feldman, who also worked at the DuSable, traveled with Margaret Burroughs as she made presentations to potential donors. As she asserted, "the fact that I had this gentleman with me of the *other persuasion* gave them more confidence in what I was trying to do and what I said I was going to do. Because they figured that at least he'd be watching the money." Burroughs's sly emphasis is intentional, as Feldman was white, and Jewish. Fleming and Burroughs, "Dr. Margaret T. Burroughs," 44.

29. Walker, "A History of the Du Sable Museum of African American History and Art," Appendix F.

30. Margaret Burroughs, "Annual Report for 1966," n.d., DuSable.

31. The Atlanta University Library and the Harmon Foundation also contributed materials. DuSable Museum Calendar of Events, 1966, box 4, DuSable.

32. Advertisement, "Make Negro History Live!" *Chicago Daily Defender*, August 26–September 1, 1967, DuSable.

33. Smithsonian Institution Archives, Oral Histories, RU 9558, Louise Daniel Hutchinson Interviews, 1987. Prior to her work with the ANM, Hutchinson was a researcher at the Smithsonian's National Portrait Gallery from 1971 to 1973. She also implemented the ANM's oral history program and helped form the Anacostia Historical Society. Hutchinson retired from the ANM in 1986.

34. Amanda Seligman, *Block by Block: Neighborhoods and Public Policy on Chicago's West Side* (Chicago: University of Chicago Press, 2005), 31.

35. Ibid., 69, 72.

36. Margaret Burroughs to Lemuel Bentley, August 8, 1964, cited by Walker, "A History of the Du Sable Museum of African American History and Art," Appendix D. Today, the neighborhood surrounding the site of the original DuSable Museum consists of a mix of vacant lots, deteriorated housing, and commercial stock, as well as a small resurgence of condominiums and renovated buildings. Burroughs, who had originally envisioned this site as only a temporary museum, continued to lobby for museum expansion during the 1960s. She was particularly interested in obtaining a building connected to Chicago's African American heritage. In a letter to the Second Ward's alderman in 1969, Burroughs appealed for assistance in securing a former Armory building at 35th and Giles Avenue for the DuSable Museum. The Armory had a special connection to Chicago's African American community: prior to

World War I, black members of the "Fighting Eighth" military regiment in Chicago had no place to practice their drills. A donation campaign led by Chicago's black residents enabled the Armory, which is now designated a Chicago landmark, to be constructed. Thus, as Burroughs wrote, "What can we do to get that site back for the black people of Chicago to serve all of the people?" Although the Armory procurement did not materialize, Burroughs later secured an abandoned Chicago Parks and Recreation building for the new DuSable Museum; see Margaret Burroughs to Second Ward Alderman, April 14, 1969, included in Walker, "A History of the Du Sable Museum of African American History and Art," Appendix E. For information on the Armory, see City of Chicago Department of Planning and Development, Landmarks Division, "Chicago Landmarks, Eighth Regiment Armory," www.ci.chi.il.us/Landmarks/E/EighthRegiment.html.

37. Some scholars argue that the public housing philosophy of the 1960s, which produced such behemoths as the now demolished Cabrini Green complex, changed from the earlier notion that public housing was a "temporary way station on the path to economic integration." Instead, public housing had become a place to "contain groups characterized by long-term poverty and social problems." See Carolyn Adams et al., *Philadelphia: Neighborhoods, Division, and Conflict in a Postindustrial City* (Philadelphia: Temple University Press, 1991), 109–10.

38. Lillian Calhoun, "Negro Dignity Is Aim of Museum," *Chicago Sun-Times,* February 13, 1966.

39. David Sibley, "Outsiders in Society and Space," in *Inventing Places: Studies in Cultural Geography,* ed. Kay Anderson and Gay Gale (Melbourne: Longman Cheshire, 1992), 112.

40. The extensive body of literature on Detroit in the postwar era includes, for example, Thomas Sugrue's *The Origins of the Urban Crisis: Race and Inequality in Postwar Detroit* (Princeton, N.J.: Princeton University Press, 1996); Heather Thompson, *Whose Detroit? Politics, Labor, and Race in a Modern American City* (Ithaca, N.Y.: Cornell University Press, 2001); Suzanne Smith, *Dancing in the Street: Motown and the Cultural Politics of Detroit* (Cambridge, Mass.: Harvard University Press, 1999).

41. Detroit was hit hard by the practice of "redlining" from the 1950s to 1980s. Redlining occurs when banks identify neighborhoods where mortgage loans are to be discouraged or prohibited. The basis for this discrimination often rests on the racial makeup of the neighborhood. John Jakle and David Wilson stated, "as blacks were closely associated with poverty and blight, the color of people could trigger 'defensive' bank actions helping to set up the very conditions feared." In New York City, for example, census tracts with predominantly white residents received "seven times as many mortgages as predominantly nonwhite areas in 1985 and 1986." See Jakle and Wilson, *Derelict Landscapes: The Wasting of America's Built Environment* (Savage, Md.: Rowman and Littlefield, 1992), 159–60.

42. The riot began with a rumor that spread among Detroit's black community: a white man had supposedly thrown a black woman and her baby off a bridge at Belle Isle, a large recreational park. An angry crowd subsequently gathered on Woodward Avenue—Detroit's main thoroughfare—and began breaking windows and looting stores. Another rumor spread among a group of whites in a white residential neighborhood west of Woodward that blacks had raped and murdered a white woman, also at the Belle Isle Bridge. For a comprehensive analysis of the 1943 riot, see Dominic J. Capeci, Jr., and Martha Wilkerson, *Layered Violence: The Detroit Rioters of 1943* (Jackson: University of Mississippi Press, 1991).

43. Chrysler, Ford, and GM built twenty-five new plants in suburban Detroit from 1947 to 1958. Most of the new plants, however, were built in cities in Ohio and Indiana, and especially California. Sugrue, *The Origins of the Urban Crisis,* 128.

44. The last major freeway completed in Detroit was the Walter P. Reuther (I-696) in 1989—thirty-three years after it was first envisioned. The major cause for the project's delay was the opposition of Pleasant Ridge, an upper-middle-class community. For more information on the history of Detroit's expressways, see Michigan Highways, "Highways 250 through 696," michiganhighways.org/listings/MichHwys250-696.html.

45. Sugrue, *The Origins of the Urban Crisis*, 47.

46. Detroit lost 134,000 manufacturing jobs between 1947 and 1963, and entry-level manufacturing positions became particularly scarce, which overwhelmingly affected black workers. Ibid., 126, 128, 147.

47. Thompson, *Whose Detroit?* 18. After World War II the total number of white inhabitants in Detroit dropped, while the number of black residents increased to more than one-third of Detroit's population. The pattern continued during the following decade: from 1970 to 1980, 310,000 whites fled Detroit for the suburbs, while the percentage of African Americans who lived in Detroit rose from 53.7 to 67.1 percent. See Heather Thompson, "Rethinking the Politics of White Flight in the Postwar City, Detroit 1945–1980," *Journal of Urban History* 25, no. 2 (January 1999): 164.

48. Robert Self, *American Babylon: Race and the Struggle for Postwar Oakland* (Princeton, N.J.: Princeton University Press, 2003), 16.

49. Thompson, "Rethinking the Politics of White Flight in the Postwar City," 183.

50. Smith, *Dancing in the Street*, 10–11. Smith also cites the emergence of the International Afro-American Museum as evidence of a space carved out by Detroit's black community that helped contribute to Motown's success. Smith, who incorrectly terms the IAM as the "first" African American history museum in the country, references the lyrics of "Dancing in the Street" by the Motown group Martha and the Vandellas as evidence of the close connection between African American cultural production and politics in Detroit. The seemingly lighthearted lyrics of the song, which debuted in 1964, in fact spoke to a more pressing issue: in Detroit—as in other cities all around the United States during the 1950s and 1960s—the streets were the sites of marches, protests, and rebellions led by African Americans.

51. Anderson, "Margaret Burroughs Is Still Skating Through Life." For the founding of the AAMA, see Lorraine Kee, "Plan to Build Black History Museum Here Will Take Lots of Cash, Patience," *St. Louis Post-Dispatch*, April 24, 2000.

52. Wright served as an assistant clinical professor of ob-gyn at Wayne State University Medical School in Detroit from 1969 to 1983 and practiced medicine until his retirement in 1986.

53. Charles Wright, interview, April 15, 1997, box 2, Interviews Series, Kellogg African American Health Care Project Records, 1997–1998, Bentley Historical Library, University of Michigan, Ann Arbor. See also Dorothy E. Roberts, *Killing the Black Body: Race, Reproduction, and the Meaning of Liberty* (New York: Pantheon Books, 1997). Roberts explores how black women's ability to control their reproductive decisions has historically been tempered by an ideology that has marked their bodies as targets of physical violence, a disproportionate amount of government and medical interference, and public neglect.

54. Wright, interview, 13–14.

55. Minutes of Project "I AM" Meeting, March 10, 1965, folder IAM Founding, 1965, box 3, CHWMAAH Historical Records, MAAH, 3.

56. Quoted in Joseph Rhea, *Race Pride and the American Identity* (Cambridge, Mass.: Harvard University Press, 1997), 100.

57. Minutes of Project "I AM" Meeting, March 10, 1965, folder IAM Founding, 1965, box 3, CHWMAAH Historical Records, MAAH, 3.

58. Ibid.

59. Pamphlet, "A Ten Year Report of a Decade of Service," 1975, loose papers, box MAAH Publications, 1969–1990, MAAH, 3.

60. Minutes of Project "I AM" Meeting, March 10, 1965, 1–2.

61. Ibid., 3. Emphasis added by author.

62. Steve Estes, *I Am A Man! Race, Manhood, and the Civil Rights Movement* (Chapel Hill: University of North Carolina Press, 2005), 140–41.

63. Verona Morton, "A Man's Reach Should Exceed His Grasp, Else What's a Heaven For?" IAM 10th Anniversary Issue Newsletter, 1975, loose papers, box MAAH Publications, 1969–1990, MAAH.

64. Minutes of the International Afro-American Museum Committee, June 16, 1965, folder IAM founding 1965, box 1, Joan Hallier Series I, MAAH, 1. The "Proposal for the Creation of an International Afro-American Museum, June 16 1965" is included in these minutes.

65. "Proposal for the Creation of an International Afro-American Museum, June 16, 1965."

66. Ibid.

67. Ibid.

68. Minutes of the International Afro-American Museum Committee, June 16, 1965, 1.

69. Minutes of Project "I AM" Meeting, March 10, 1965, 1–2; "Proposal for the Creation of an International Afro-American Museum, June 16, 1965."

70. Minutes of the International Afro-American Museum Committee, September 29, 1965, folder IAM Founding 1965, box 1, Joan Hallier Series I, MAAH.

71. "International Afro-American Museum (A Tentative Statement of Purpose)," 1.

72. Minutes of Project "I AM" Meeting, March 10, 1965, 4.

73. IAM Brochure, n.d., folder MS/MAAH Board Letters, 1968–1971, box 3, CHWMAAH Historical Records, MAAH.

74. Robert Peck, "Central Vision: The City as a Living and Civil Model," in *Capital Visions: Reflections on a Decade of Urban Design Charrettes and a Look Ahead, Symposium Sponsored by Library of Congress Geography and Map Division and the Washington Area Architectural Group, March 31 1995*, ed. Iris Miller and Ronald E. Grim (Washington, D.C.: Geography and Map Division, Library of Congress, 1995), 32.

75. Mr. and Mrs. John W. Southall, interview by J. B. Southall, August 12, 1969, vertical file no. 2, Anacostia Community Museum (hereafter ACM), Washington, D.C., 168.

76. Percy Battle, interview by Telford Anderson, August 29, 1989, D.C. Historic Preservation Division, Neighborhood Oral History Transcripts, Anacostia-Barry Farms, City Museum of Washington, D.C., 2, 7. Battle's citation of Martin Luther King Avenue (formerly Nichols Avenue) reinforces geographer Derek Alderman's study of the politics of naming streets after Martin Luther King. Most of these are in predominantly African American (and economically depressed) areas. See Alderman, "Street Names and the Scaling of Memory: The Politics of Commemorating Martin Luther King, Jr. within the African American Community," *Area* 35, no. 2 (2003): 163–73.

77. Mr. and Mrs. John W. Southall, interview by J. B. Southall, 169. On assignment from the Farm Security Administration and the Office of War Information, Gordon Parks took a series of photographs of Anacostia and the "Douglass Heights" Housing Project during the 1940s.

78. Percy Battle remembered, "there was a bus that went from Barney Circle, 17th and Pennsylvania, S.E., across the Pennsylvania Avenue Bridge, and it terminated at Nichols Avenue at U streets . . . and that bus never had over two or three people on it. But that bus . . . always had white people on it." Battle, interview by Telford Anderson, 8–9.

79. Ibid., 17–18.

80. Erma Katherine Simon (Anderson), interview by Robert Simon, n.d., D.C. Historic Preservation Division, Neighborhood Oral History Transcripts, Anacostia-Barry Farms, City

Museum of Washington, D.C., 10. Also see Alana Samuels, "I remember when . . . 'It Took a Village' in Old Anacostia," *East of the River* (April 2003): 32. These schools were also active in the early black history movement. See Dagbovie, "'Most Honorable Mention . . . Belongs to Washington, DC,'" 306.

81. Erma Katherine Simon (Anderson), interview by Robert Simon, 8.

82. Ibid., 33–34.

83. Although local planning agencies in Chicago set the precedent for private (rather than federal) implementation of urban renewal programs, Congress's establishment of urban renewal policies in the District of Columbia during the postwar era situated Washington, D.C., as "the true test of future policy." Howard Gillette argues that policymakers failed this test on a devastating scale: urban renewal as envisioned and executed by the federal government continually ignored the needs of those who actually lived and worked in Washington, D.C. Howard Gillette, *Between Justice and Beauty: Race, Planning, and the Failure of Urban Policy in Washington, D.C.* (Baltimore: Johns Hopkins University Press, 1995), x, 150, 155–156. Local organizations such as the Southwest Displaced Persons' Grievance Committee and the Citizen's Rights Council agreed, concluding that "if, as we have been told, urban renewal in Washington is to serve as a pilot project for the rest of the country, it is a horrible example of what not to do in that field." Bryton Barron and Ella Barron, *The Inhumanity of Urban Renewal: A Documentation* (Springfield, Va.: Crestwood Books, 1965), 19. In 1966, residents filed the "Anacostia Suit," a class-action lawsuit that called for stronger land-use regulation, better housing programs, and a city-wide effort to "provide citizens living east of the river with the same adequate and essential services enjoyed by residents in the other three quadrants of the city." Joan Kramer, "The Anacostia Tree: How a Neighborhood Museum Has Become a Source of Pride to 'the other' Washingtonians," *Washington Sunday Star*, May 13, 1973.

84. Insufficient, overcrowded housing was coupled with other problems typical of poorly zoned residential and commercial spaces: no curbs or sidewalks (thus making it difficult for people to walk safely), land erosion, problems with inadequate trash collection and resultant rodent infestation, and congested schools. *Washington's Far Southeast 70: A Report to the Honorable Walter E. Washington, District of Columbia* (Washington, D.C.: D.C. Office of Community Renewal Programs, 1970), 32.

85. Tanya Edward Beauchamp, "The Anacostia Historic District," (Washington, D.C.: D.C. Historic Preservation Office, 2001), 14. The subject of mass transit in Washington, D.C., generated a significant amount of controversy when a group of citizens named the Emergency Committee on the Transportation Crisis (ECTC) protested the construction of the North Central Freeway through Washington, D.C. (and the confiscation of homes and property to build the freeway). Ultimately, the North Central Freeway proposal was defeated; however, the Anacostia Freeway took its place. During the 1970s–1980s, ANM director John Kinard took up the fight to bring the metrorail to Anacostia and improve mass transit for its residents. See Records of the Emergency Committee on the Transportation Crisis (ECTC), 1960–1978, Washingtonia Collection, Martin Luther King Jr. Memorial Library, Washington, D.C. For John Kinard's involvement in Anacostia's transportation issues, see Zora Martin-Felton and Gail S. Lowe, *A Different Drummer: John Kinard and the Anacostia Museum, 1967–1989* (Washington, D.C.: Anacostia Museum, Smithsonian Institution, 1993), 40–41.

86. Richard Severo, "This Is Anacostia," *Washington Post*, May 8, 1966. Likewise, a 1984 *Washington Post* article compared the blighted Anacostia River, which separates Anacostia from the rest of Washington, D.C., with an industrial marker that typically divides other American cities and towns—the railroad: "In many cities, the railroad drives a wedge between people

whose income, education and occupation—on paper—are different. In Washington, it is the river that divides—not the Potomac, but the Anacostia. . . . To live east of the river is to be exiled from the business, government and commercial centers of Washington. . . . Most people do not arrive by choice." Pat Press, "The Changing Face of Washington 4: 'East of the River,'" *Washington Post*, June 27, 1984.

87. Hutchinson, Oral Histories interview, 46.

88. Anacostia Neighborhood Museum, *Anacostia Neighborhood Museum, Smithsonian Institution, September 15, 1972* (Washington, D.C.: Smithsonian, 1972), 6. Ripley served as secretary of the Smithsonian Institution from 1964 to 1984. The ANM received financial gifts from the Carnegie Corporation of New York, the Eugene and Agnes E. Meyer Foundation of Washington, and the Anne S. Richardson Fund of Connecticut to renovate the Carver Theater.

89. Zora Martin-Felton and Gail S. Lowe, *A Different Drummer*, xi, cited from Kenneth Hudson, *Museums of Influence* (Cambridge: Cambridge University Press, 1987), 181. While Hudson's mention of the ANM as a pioneer in the museum field is certainly valid, the IAM's earlier achievements are overlooked in the study of the black museum movement.

90. Smithsonian Institution, "Smithsonian Head Forms Committee to Plan Washington 'Drop-In' Museum." November 2, 1966, folder ANM misc. brochures/memos, box 2, Smithsonian Institution Archives, RU 390, Anacostia Museum, Education Department, Records, 1–2. Also see Caryl Marsh, "Dedication and Opening of the Anacostia Neighborhood Museum," September 15, 1967, ACM. Although the records indicate that the Smithsonian—led by Ripley—first broached the idea of establishing a neighborhood museum in Washington, D.C., that would cater to a "nontraditional" audience, the sources conflict about the extent of the Smithsonian's initiative in proposing the museum. One pamphlet produced by the ANM corroborates Ripley's leadership, reporting that in January 1967, Anacostia community leaders "enthusiastically offered to cooperate in creating an experimental neighborhood museum in Southeast Washington." Other documents, however, maintain that Anacostia community organizations first demanded the museum, and the Smithsonian followed suit. Rewriting the creation story of the ANM in this fashion grants agency entirely to Anacostia's African American residents—a trend we again see with debates regarding the origins of other African American museums emerging during this period.

91. "A Proposal to Establish an Experimental Neighborhood Museum," n.d., unnamed folder, box 3, Series I, Assistant Secretary for Public Service and Related Records, 1961–1972, Smithsonian Institution Archives, RU 145, Smithsonian Institution.

92. Ibid.

93. S. Dillon Ripley, *The Sacred Grove: Essays on Museums* (New York: Simon and Schuster, 1969), 105.

94. Despite Ripley's paternalistic pronouncements regarding the relationship between the Smithsonian and the ANM, Kinard professed respect for Ripley's intentions. According to Kinard, Ripley "made no pretense of saying, 'You're free,' and then putting a chain around your leg . . . his words were, 'If the people won't come to the museum, let's take the museum to the people and see how they want to handle it.' He knew blacks weren't coming to the museum." Smithsonian Institution Archives, Oral Histories, RU 9538, John R. Kinard Interview, 1987, 12.

95. Ibid., 12–13.

96. Michele Gates Moresi, "Exhibiting Race, Creating Nation: Representations of Black History and Culture at the Smithsonian Institution, 1895–1976" (PhD diss., George Washington University, 2003), 2.

97. Kinard, Oral Histories interview, 8–9. The Greater Anacostia Peoples Corporation, as

well as the PTA, the Public Health Nursing Service, the National Capitol Housing Authority, and neighborhood churches, were among the organizations that successfully lobbied for Anacostia as the site of the new museum, and chose Kinard to be its director. Other sites considered for the museum included the Carolina Theatre Building in the Capitol Hill Area; in northwestern D.C., an empty restaurant at 2015 14th St. Northwest, and an empty grocery store at 17th and Corcoran. See Charles Blitzer, Helen Bronheim, "Possible Locations for Neighborhood Museum," March 3, 1967, folder ANM; Concept, Suggestions and Commentaries, box 3, Series I, Assistant Secretary for Public Service and Related Records, 1961–1972, Smithsonian Institution Archives, RU 145, Smithsonian Institution.

98. Kinard, Oral Histories interview, 32–33.

99. *Anacostia Neighborhood Museum, Smithsonian Institution, September 15, 1972,* 4.

100. Ibid., 1–2.

101. Kinard and Nighbert, "The Anacostia Neighborhood Museum," 103.

102. Kinard, Oral Histories interview, introduction.

2. *"Not in My Backyard": The Contested Origins of the African American Museum of Philadelphia*

1. Jeanne Theoharis, "Introduction," in *Freedom North: Black Freedom Struggles Outside the South: 1940–1980,* ed. Komozi Woodard, Jeanne Theoharis, and Matthew Countryman (New York: Palgrave, 2003), 2.

2. Matthew Countryman, *Up South: Civil Rights and Black Power in Philadelphia* (Philadelphia: University of Pennsylvania Press, 2005), 1–2.

3. Ibid, 6.

4. Ibid., 290–92.

5. Ibid., 286–89. Also see William L. Van Deburg, *New Day in Babylon: The Black Power Movement and American Culture, 1965–1975* (Chicago: University of Chicago Press, 1992), 302.

6. Countryman, "'From Protest to Politics': Community Control and Black Independent Politics in Philadelphia, 1965–1984," *Journal of Urban History* 32, no. 6 (September 2006): 835–36. Carolyn Adams notes that, although black voter registration in Philadelphia declined from 1950 to 1960, by the 1980s, 98 percent of Philadelphia's eligible black voters had registered. In 1983, black voter turnout "exceeded the city-wide average for the first time in Philadelphia's history," resulting in the election of the city's first black mayor, W. Wilson Goode. See Carolyn Adams et al., *Philadelphia: Neighborhoods, Division, and Conflict in a Postindustrial City* (Philadelphia: Temple University Press, 1991), 133; Howard Gillette, *Between Justice and Beauty: Race, Planning, and the Failure of Urban Policy in Washington, D.C.* (Baltimore: Johns Hopkins University Press, 1995), 155.

7. In 1966, Public Act 93-179 established the American Revolution Bicentennial Commission. The commission, which Congress dismantled and replaced with the American Revolution Bicentennial Administration (ARBA) in 1973, coordinated satellite Bicentennial planning agencies in cities around the United States. ARBA also distributed federal grants to the states, as well as grants to selected cities. Constance M. Greiff, *Independence: The Creation of a National Park* (Philadelphia: University of Pennsylvania Press, 1987), 235.

8. "Detroit Bicentennial: Catalyst for Progress," n.d., folder 1966, box CHWMAAH Historical Records, 1965–1987, MAAH. Also see Michele Gates Moresi, "Exhibiting Race, Creating Nation: Representations of Black History and Culture at the Smithsonian Institution, 1895–1976" (PhD diss., George Washington University, 2003), 177.

9. Greiff, *Independence,* 233. The sources also list the "Philadelphia Bicentennial Corporation" as the "Philadelphia Bicentennial Commission."

10. The Philadelphia 1976 Bicentennial Commission, *Toward a Meaningful Bicentennial*, (Philadelphia: The Corporation, 1969), Urban Archives (hereafter UA), Temple University, Philadelphia, 7.

11. Jane Jacobs, *The Death and Life of Great American Cities* (New York: Random House, 1961).

12. Adams, *Philadelphia*, 107.

13. Andrew Feffer, "Show Down in Center City: Staging Redevelopment and Citizenship in Bicentennial Philadelphia, 1974–1977," *Journal of Urban History* 30, no. 6 (September 2004): 791.

14. "Detroit Bicentennial: Catalyst for Progress," 9. The Bicentennial celebration corresponded with another civic milestone for Detroit: the 275th "birthday" of the city.

15. Ibid., 4. Woodward Avenue is one of the main thoroughfares of the city.

16. Ibid., 2–4.

17. The Philadelphia 1976 Bicentennial Commission, *Toward a Meaningful Bicentennial*, 44.

18. Ibid., 12.

19. Ibid., 44.

20. "Scattered Anniversary," *Time*, June 12, 1972. Also see Nixon's official explanation for the withdrawal of the international exposition from Philadelphia, in The American Presidency Project, "Message to the Congress Withdrawing Philadelphia as the Site of an International Exposition during American Revolution Bicentennial Celebrations," May 22, 1972, www.presidency.ucsb.edu/ws/index.php?pid=3426.

21. Stefano Luconi, "Frank L. Rizzo and the Whitening of Italian Americans in Philadelphia," in *Are Italians White? How Race Is Made in America*, ed. Jennifer Guglielmo and Salvatore Salerno (New York: Routledge, 2003), 180–81. According to Luconi, blacks made up one-third of Philadelphia's population in 1970. Also see Feffer, "Show Down in Center City," 795.

22. Theodore Cam, "Feasibility Study, Museum: Black History Exhibition, for Philadelphia '76 Inc.," December 1974, box 1, William Rafsky papers, Philadelphia '76, Philadelphia City Archives (hereafter PCA), Philadelphia, 2.

23. Ibid., 3.

24. Brian C. Feldman, "Bicen Officials Expect Word Friday on Expo," *Evening Bulletin*, April 18, 1972. The *Evening Bulletin* was also referred to as the *Philadelphia Bulletin*, or simply, *The Bulletin*. I use the standard *Philadelphia Bulletin* unless the source indicates otherwise.

25. Gerard P. William to Hon. Judge Raymond Pace Alexander, May 3, 1974, folder Black History Museum, box 1, William Rafsky papers, PCA. William provided a list of potential board members from both the white and the black communities. Among the black community leaders William signaled out were clerical leaders (such as the Reverend Henry Nicols from the Jones Methodist Church), educators (Dr. Ruth Hayre, school superintendent), legal and political representatives (Mrs. Anna J. W. James, Commission on Human Relations), and leaders of black cultural institutions (Mrs. Edith Ingram, Association for Study of Afro-American Life and History).

26. Memo, Jerry Grundfest [Coordinator for Historical Programs, Philadelphia '76] to William Rafsky, March 14, 1974, folder Black History Museum, box 1, William Rafsky papers, PCA. Grundfest is the author of "George Clymer, Philadelphia Revolutionary, 1739–1813" (PhD diss., Columbia University, 1973).

27. Ibid., 2.

28. Caroline Golab to William Rafsky, March 15, 1974, folder Black History Museum, box 1, William Rafsky papers, PCA. Golab also wrote *Immigrant Destinations* (Philadelphia: Temple University Press, 1977), which examines immigration in Philadelphia during the late nineteenth and early twentieth centuries.

29. Caroline Golab to William Rafsky, March 15, 1974.

30. Ibid.

31. Len Lear, "Black Bicen Plans Run Into Roadblocks," *Philadelphia Tribune*, October 5, 1974.

32. White organizers of the 1893 Columbian Exposition in Chicago played upon similar perceptions of disagreement within the black community regarding participation and exhibition in the event. See Ida B. Wells-Barnett and Robert W. Rydell, *The Reason Why the Colored American Is Not in the World's Columbian Exposition* (Urbana: University of Illinois Press, 1893, 1999).

33. Paul Garabedian to John Saunders, October 8, 1974, box 1, Ethnic/Nationalities Programs, Philadelphia '76 Inc., PCA.

34. Paul Garabedian to William Rafsky, October 4, 1974, box 1, Ethnic/Nationalities Programs, Philadelphia '76 Inc., PCA.

35. Memorandum, Jerry Grundfest to William Rafsky, March 14, 1974, folder Black History Museum, box 1, William Rafsky papers, PCA, 3.

36. Robert A. Donner to Paul Garabedian, October 3, 1974, box 1, Ethnic/Nationalities Programs, Philadelphia '76 Inc., PCA.

37. Created in September 1974 and overseen by Philadelphia '76, the AHCC served as the main planning organ for the proposed African American museum. Reddick (1910–95) authored numerous works on African American history and politics, including *Worth Fighting For: A History of the Negro in the United States during the Civil War and Reconstruction* (Garden City, N.Y.: Doubleday, 1965), and *Blacks and U.S. Wars* (New York: National Urban League, 1976). See August Meier's and Elliott Rudwick's discussion of Reddick in *Black History and the Historical Profession, 1915–1980* (Chicago: University of Illinois Press, 1986), 103–4. Other African American community leaders who chaired the AHCC were Judge Raymond Pace Alexander, Reverend Gus Roman, and Ralph Jones. See Theodore Cam, "Some Notes on Zoning and Urban Renewal Plan Considerations with Respect to the Proposed Black History Museum Located at 6th and Pine–6th and Lombard Streets, Philadelphia, PA), n.d., box 1, William Rafsky papers, Philadelphia '76, PCA, 7–8.

38. Lawrence Reddick, "Will the Bicentennial Celebration Be an Accurate Picture of American Life and History and Be Fair to All of the American People?" May 1974, folder 1, box 1, William Rafsky papers, PCA. The number of African American organizations that submitted proposals for the Bicentennial is unknown. A few of the more prominent organizations included, of course, Mother Bethel AME Church, which proposed the creation of a "national museum dedicated to the history of the Black in America." The museum—as distinct from the exhibit or museum proposed by AAMP advocates—would contain Mother Bethel Church's collection of artifacts. Another group called "Cobbs Creek" proposed an exhibit titled "200 Years of Black Progress in the U.S.A." Cobbs Creek was a predominantly African American neighborhood in Philadelphia. A group called "Portfolio Associates" proposed the creation of a "one volume history documenting the evolution of the Black theater in the Delaware Valley." Philadelphia '76 ultimately rejected their proposal. As Portfolio Associates later assisted Mother Bethel AME Church in creating their mobile exhibit, it is likely that the group was African American. See Len Alexander to Beverly Harper [President, Portfolio Associates Inc.], March 13, 1975, folder Black History Museum, box 1, William Rafsky Papers, PCA.

39. Veronika von Nostitz to Gerard William, July 24, 1974, folder Black History Museum, box 1, William Rafsky papers, PCA.

40. Reddick, "Will the Bicentennial Celebration Be an Accurate Picture of American Life?" 3. Reddick does not identify the author of this particular proposal.

41. Remarks of L. D. Reddick, "Black Participation in the Bicentennial: Philadelphia: A Case Study," October 24, 1974, Conference on Black Participation in Bicentennial, Ben Franklin Hotel, folder Black History Museum, box 1, William Rafsky papers, PCA.

42. Ibid., 3.

43. The Ile Ife Black Humanitarian Center, a black dance company founded in Philadelphia in 1969, represented one of the few African American groups in Philadelphia to receive Bicentennial funding by 1974. Ile-Ife received federal funding from the Model City program in 1970, and in 1972, Ile-Ife director Arthur Hull created the Ile-Ife Museum of Afro-American Culture. The company suffered when these "Great Society" programs were cut during the mid-1970s. With funding from the city's Bicentennial committees, African American cultural organizations like Ile-Ife received temporary relief, but the disintegration of the Model Cities initiatives meant that the long-term survival of these organizations was jeopardized. In addition to my discussion on Minneapolis's African American museum (also funded by the Model Cities program), see Melanye White-Dixon, "The Legacy of Black Philadelphia's Dance Institutions and the Educators Who Built the Tradition," *Dance Research Journal* 23, no. 1 (Spring 1991): 25–30; Daniel Webster, "Ghetto Dancers' Dream Is Threatened," *Philadelphia Inquirer,* May 25, 1975.

44. Ibid., 6. Reddick also asked about a rumor that had circulated among the black community: "is it true that a well-known Black scholar offered to work with the top Philadelphia '76 staff a year ago? And, that when he was interviewed and presented his credentials, which included a Phd from an outstanding American University . . . that the member of the Bicentennial staff, who did the interviewing, felt that such a scholar would outrank him; and so he broke off negotiations. . . . Is this a true story?"

45. Ibid., 7.

46. Naedele, "Black History Museum Urged." Dr. Eugene Raymond Jones founded Heritage House in 1949. It closed in the early 1970s.

47. Reddick, "Will the Bicentennial Celebration Be an Accurate Picture of American Life?" 1–2.

48. Roberta White to Dr. Jaipaul, June 21, 1973, folder Ethnic Heritage Affairs Institute, box 1, Ethnic/Nationalities Programs, Philadelphia '76 Inc., PCA. The Ethnic Heritage Affairs Institute was founded in 1972. Its president, Dr. Jaipaul, went by his surname alone.

49. Dr. Jaipaul to Frank Rizzo, June 25, 1973, folder Ethnic Heritage Affairs Institute, box 1, Ethnic/Nationalities Programs, Philadelphia '76 Inc., PCA.

50. Dr. Jaipaul to William Rafsky, October 12, 1973, folder Ethnic Heritage Affairs Institute, box 1, Ethnic/Nationalities Programs, Philadelphia '76 Inc., PCA.

51. Len Lear, "City Moves to Scrap Plans to Build 1.5$ Million Black History Museum: Al Gaudiosi Behind the Efforts to Halt Project," *Philadelphia Tribune,* December 10, 1974.

52. Samuel G. Freedman, *The Inheritance: How Three Families and the American Political Majority Moved from Left to Right* (New York: Simon and Schuster, 1996), 424.

53. Lear, "City Moves to Scrap Plans to Build 1.5$ Million Black History Museum."

54. Harry Gould, "Black History Museum Planned, Rafsky Insists," *Philadelphia Inquirer,* December 11, 1974.

55. Lear, "City Moves to Scrap Plans to Build 1.5$ Million Black History Museum."

56. Walter F. Naedele, "Black History Museum Urged," *Philadelphia Bulletin,* December 13, 1974. The "Mummers" of Philadelphia, who claim roots in the city's colonial era, dress in fanciful costumes and masks, and march (and compete) in the city's New Year's Day parade. A museum commemorating Mummer history was constructed in 1976 as part of the Bicentennial and still stands today. The Mummers Museum, "About Us," www.mummersmuseum.com/about_us .html.

57. Michael B. Coakley, "Rizzo Oks Black Museum," *Philadelphia Bulletin*, December 15, 1974.

58. Grant Agreement, October 23, 1975, folder Kulue Melee Afro-American Dance Ensemble, Afro-American Correspondence, box 1, Ethnic/Nationalities Programs, Philadelphia '76, PCA.

59. The Philadelphia Dance Company was founded in 1970. Grant Agreement, October 23, 1975, folder Kulue Melee Afro-American Dance Ensemble, Afro-American Correspondence, box 1, Ethnic/Nationalities Programs, Philadelphia '76, PCA.

60. Grant Agreement, November 15, 1975, folder Ile-Ife Black Humanitarian Center, box 1, Ethnic/Nationalities Programs, Philadelphia '76, PCA.

61. The "new conservatives" who transformed segments of the Democratic Party during the late 1960s and 1970s based their political identity, at least partially, on their hostile opposition to what Nikhil Pal Singh identifies as perceptions of "black 'special pleading' or pandering in the marketplace and black misbehavior in the public square." Nikhil Pal Singh, *Black Is a Country: Race and the Unfinished Struggle for Democracy* (Cambridge, Mass.: Harvard University Press, 2004), 9.

62. Dan Enoch, "Black Bicen Museum Voted," January 8, 1975, paper unknown, UA.

63. For additional discussion of the tensions surrounding this move, see my discussion in chapter 5, note 14.

64. Cam, "Some Notes on Zoning and Urban Renewal Plan Considerations," 125, 138.

65. Ibid., 63, 71.

66. Ibid., 146.

67. Valerie Sue Halverson, "Society Hill, Philadelphia: Historic Preservation and Urban Renewal in Washington Square East" (PhD diss., University of Minnesota, 1976), 91.

68. Halverson, "Society Hill, Philadelphia," 135.

69. Feffer, "Show Down in Center City," 808.

70. Countryman, "'From Protest to Politics,'" 820.

71. Adams studied Philadelphia's Eastwick neighborhood, which is located in a mostly industrial area in far southwest Philadelphia, near the Philadelphia International Airport and the Delaware border. In the late 1940s, the Philadelphia Redevelopment Authority proposed relocating African Americans from Philadelphia's northern and western neighborhoods to Eastwick and redeveloping Eastwick to accommodate this displacement. The proposal sparked intense opposition from Eastwick residents, both black and white, over the next several decades. Adams, *Philadelphia*, 120.

72. Joanne Dentworth to Society Hill Residents, "Notice to Residents of Blocks from 5th to 7th and Spruce to Lombard," May 23, 1972, box 7, Society Hill Civic Association Records (hereafter SHCA), UA. The Society Hill Area Residents' Association, together with the Home Owners Residents Association, merged in 1965 to become the Society Hill Civic Association. See Halverson, "Society Hill, Philadelphia," 140.

73. Walter F. Naedele and Carol Rich, "Dr. Allen Opposes Black Museum Site," *Evening Bulletin*, January 10, 1975.

74. Dolores Hayden, *The Power of Place: Urban Landscapes as Public History* (Cambridge, Mass.: MIT Press, 1995), 41, citing from Henri Lefebvre, *The Production of Space* (Oxford: Blackwell, 1991), 286.

75. Hayden, *The Power of Place*, 16.

76. John Francis Smith III (President, SHCA) to William Rafsky, February 13, 1975, folder Afro-American Historical and Cultural Museum, box 1, William Rafsky papers, PCA.

77. Cited by Feffer, "Show Down in Center City," 802.

78. Ibid.

79. John Francis Smith III to William Rafsky, February 13, 1975, folder Afro-American Historical and Cultural Museum, box 1, William Rafsky papers, PCA.

80. John Francis Smith III to Honorable George X. Schwartz, January 14, 1975, folder Black History Museum, box 4, SHCA, UA.

81. Ibid.

82. "Petition to Philadelphia '76, Inc. Zoning Board of Review, and Philadelphia City Council," folder Black History Museum, box 4, SHCA, UA.

83. John Francis Smith III to Honorable George X. Schwartz (President City Council), January 14, 1975.

84. "Petition to Philadelphia '76, Inc. Zoning Board of Review, and Philadelphia City Council."

85. Ibid.

86. Ibid.

87. Eugene Newman to John Smith III, January 30, 1975, folder Black History Museum, box 4, SHCA, UA.

88. Augustine A. Salvitti to John Francis Smith III, January 16, 1975, folder Black History Museum, box 4, SHCA, UA.

89. George B. MEBUS, Inc., Consulting Engineers, "Traffic Impact Analysis for the Black History Exhibition Museum Prepared for Phila. 76 Incorporated," February 1975, box 1, William Rafsky papers, Philadelphia '76, PCA, 10.

90. "2 Society Hill Units Battle Black Museum Site," *Evening Bulletin,* February 21, 1975. In a later event, Gerard William informed William Rafsky about a letter written by Dr. Robert Steiner to the *Philadelphia Inquirer* on March 28, 1975, regarding the Zoning Board of Adjustment's approval of the museum site at 6th and Pine. Steiner argued that their approval of the site was "disgraceful." Gerard William took offense at Steiner's characterization, arguing that "there were a number of expert witnesses who testified . . . that the effect of the Museum in their best technical judgment, would have a minimum negative impact on the Society Hill Community, and further substantiated its predominantly residential character would in no way be impaired." William viewed Steiner's article as "just another example of the subterfuge used by many opponents to this worthwhile project to justify from a public point of view, their opposition" to the museum. See Gerard P. William to William L. Rafsky, May 9, 1975, folder 2, box 1, William Rafsky papers, PCA, 2–3.

91. Acel Moore, "New Site Likely for Museum," *Philadelphia Inquirer,* March 26, 1975.

92. Interestingly, Triplett opposed building the museum in Society Hill, arguing that its construction would "desecrate" the historic value of Mother Bethel A.M.E. Church, which by 1976 was listed as a state historic site: "No building is worth the price of desecrating the A.M.E. Church and Mother Bethel simply to exhibit Black history. If this is so important, and it is very important, then it will stand equally somewhere else of its own merit. Everything of significance to Blacks did not occur at Sixth and Pine Streets." Triplett advised the AME Church to inform its congregation and leaders of the danger an African American museum in Society Hill would pose to the church. Some Society Hill residents also offered financial assistance to Mother Bethel AME Church in order to help them build an archive and a park instead of a permanent museum. Reverend Joiner, pastor at the AME Church, indicated that they were "considering the proposal."

Perry Triplett to William L. Rafsky, March 27, 1975, folder Black History Museum, box

4, SHCA, UA; Tyree Johnson, "Museum Finds Home Near Mall," *Daily News*, April 1, 1975, folder Black History Museum, box 4, UA.

93. For example, the committees protested the expansion of an A&P grocery store when the store's owners wanted to build an 8,100-square-foot addition to their existing store on 5th Street, located between Spruce and Pine Streets. Neighborhood organizations also fought to protect rapidly disappearing green space. In 1977, the president of the Washington Square East Condo No. 1 Council, Gladys Grossman Wieder, objected to the "piecemeal development of the tract south of Locust Walk, with resultant destruction of the beauty and the open spaces we were assured in the development plan approved by the Redevelopment Authority and the Society Hill Civic Association." Gladys Grossman Wieder to Society Hill Club, November 26, 1977, folder Society Hill Club, box 4, SHCA, UA.

94. Sub-Committee on the Afro-American Historical and Cultural Museum, "Progress Report," February 28, 1975, AAMP. Also see Acel Moore, "New Site Likely for Museum," *Philadelphia Inquirer*, March 26, 1975.

95. "Proposed Resolution of Membership of Society Hill Civic Assoc regarding Proposed Museum at 6th and Pine Streets," n.d., SHCA, UA.

96. While presenting their objections to the museum as representative of a unified group, the SHCA itself suffered from internal divisions. For instance, in a January 23, 1975, letter from Society Hill resident Richard Nelson to SHCA president "Mrs. R. Speck," Nelson wrote: "As to the purposes of the SHCA, I am hardly qualified to speak. I don't go to meetings, because I have heard too often that the meetings tend to be dominated by people whose mouths are too big for their thoughts and who indulge in crude personal attacks on others." Richard M. Nelson to Mrs. R. Speck, January 23, 1975, folder SHCA Misc. Correspondence 1/3/75–4/29/75, box 5, SHCA, UA.

97. "Black Museum Is Still Zoning Issue," *Welcomemat*, March 5, 1975, folder Black History Museum, box 4, UA.

98. Theodore Cam, "Some Notes on Zoning and Urban Renewal Plan Considerations with Respect to the Proposed Black History Museum Located at 6th and Pine–6th and Lombard Streets, Philadelphia, PA), n.d., box 1, William Rafsky papers, Philadelphia '76, PCA, 9–10.

99. Minutes, Philadelphia '76 Inc., February 10, 1975, box 1, African American Museum of Philadelphia (hereafter AAMP), Philadelphia, Pa., 2.

100. John Francis Smith III to Natale F. Carabello, Jr., and Honorable George X. Schwartz, January 14, 1975, folder Black History Museum, box 1, William Rafsky papers, PCA. Also see Sub-Committee on the Afro-American Historical and Cultural Museum, "Progress Report," February 24, 1975, AAMP.

101. "Museum Controversy Buried in Society Hill," *Daily News*, April 4, 1975, folder Black History Museum, box 4, UA.

102. "Model of Museum to Be a Symbol," *Philadelphia Daily News*, April 2, 1975, folder Black History Museum, box 4, UA. The SHCA scored a victory for their neighborhood, but not without cost. In an April 16, 1975, letter addressed to residents of Society Hill, Joseph B. Centifanti admitted that "success did not come cheaply. Legal costs (including counsel fees, expert witness fees, filing costs, duplicate costs, etc.) exceeded $5,000.00." If the recipient of the letter was "opposed to the building of what was to be a 'popular' Museum in our residential neighborhood," then they should donate money to the cause. Joseph Centifanti to Society Hill residents, April 16, 1975, folder SHCA Misc. Correspondence, 1/3/75–4/29/75, box 5, SHCA, UA.

103. Afro-American Historical and Cultural Museum, *20 Years of Reflection: 1976–1996* (Philadelphia: Afro-American Historical and Cultural Museum of Philadelphia, 1996), 12.

3. Confronting the "Tyranny of Relevance": Exhibits and the Politics of Representation

1. Joan Kramer, "The Anacostia Tree: How a Neighborhood Museum Has Become a Source of Pride to 'the other' Washingtonians," *Washington Sunday Star*, May 13, 1973.

2. Herman Schaden, "A Happy Birthday in Anacostia: New Museum Takes History to the Neighborhood," *Washington Sunday Star*, September 15, 1968.

3. Lillian Walker, "A History of the Du Sable Museum of African American History and Art" (MA thesis, Governor's State University, University Park, Ill., 1978), 11, citing from DuSable Museum, Minutes of Board Meeting, October 1962.

4. "Ebony Museum Plans Water Color Exhibit," *Chicago Daily Tribune*, October 29, 1961, S2. Also see Walker, "A History of the Du Sable Museum of African American History and Art," 8.

5. Thomas J. Davis, "'They, Too, Were Here': The Afro-American Experience and History Museums," *American Quarterly* 41, no. 2 (June 1989): 328–40.

6. Juliet E. K. Walker, *Free Frank: A Black Pioneer on the Antebellum Frontier* (Lexington: University Press of Kentucky, 1983).

7. Walker, "A History of the Du Sable Museum of African American History and Art," Appendix C.

8. Newsletter, "DuSable Museum of African American History," n.d., DuSable.

9. Jones's dioramas also portrayed African American women, such as Phyllis Wheatley, as well as Africa's contributions to science and industry. As the diorama on "African Contributions" explained, "Africa gave the science of smelting iron to the world. It also showed others how to construct buildings. Here is a diorama showing iron smelting in Africa and another showing the famous pyramids of Egypt." Ibid.

10. W. Fitzhugh Brundage, "Meta Warrick's 1907 'Negro Tableaux' and (Re) Presenting African American Historical Memory," in *Museums and Difference*, ed. Daniel J. Sherman (Bloomington: Indiana University Press, 2008), 205–49.

11. "Black History on Display," *Muhammad Speaks*, May 21, 1965.

12. Newsletter, "DuSable Museum of African American History," n.d., DuSable.

13. Margaret T. G. Burroughs, *Life with Margaret: The Official Autobiography* (Chicago: In Time Publishing and Media Group, 2003), 102.

14. Walker, "A History of the Du Sable Museum of African American History and Art," Table 1, 9–10. Not all children came with their schools; some belonged to clubs and organizations, such as the fifteen members of the "Modern Teens Club" of Rogers Park who visited on February 12, or the ten members of the "Boys Brotherhood Republic" who visited on February 22, 1962. During August 1962, 241 children visited the museum—the second highest total of children. The number of adult visitors was highest in July, with 339 visiting the museum. Adult visitors declined during the rest of the year, with an average of 102 adults visiting the museum each month. Walker's table is drawn from "Ebony Museum of History and Art Attendance Figures for October 21, 1961 to September 30, 1962," DuSable Museum Minutes, Steering Committee, November 1962. These original sources were unavailable during my research. Based on Walker's table, it is unclear how many children (and adults) came attached to school groups, as opposed to simply coming with their families or by themselves.

15. Ibid., 8–9. By 1966, Margaret Burroughs noted that an average of 150 people visited the DuSable Museum each week. Approximately 20,000 had toured the museum since its

opening in 1961. See Lillian Calhoun, "Negro Dignity Is Aim of Museum," *Chicago Sun-Times,* February 13, 1966.

16. "Negro History Museum Opens Essay Competition," *Chicago Daily Tribune,* January 21, 1962.

17. Burroughs, "Annual Report for 1966."

18. Eugene Feldman, "Negro History Educational Materials Bulletin," n.d., box 4, DuSable.

19. Doris Giller, "Chicago Couple Establish Museum of Negro History," *Montreal Star,* August 25, 1965.

20. Newsletter, DuSable Museum of African American History and Culture, December 1970, DuSable.

21. DuSable Museum of African American History and Culture, Annual Report, 1978–1979, folder Margaret, box 1, DuSable Museum Papers, DuSable. The DuSable also featured a weekly radio program on black history, as well as a program for schoolchildren called "After School—Off the Street Negro History School," which placed "special emphasis . . . on the lives of Negro Americans who have achieved success against great odds, as a means of inspiring today's Negro youth." See "Black History on Display," *Muhammad Speaks,* May 21, 1965.

22. Newsletter, DuSable Museum of African American History and Culture, n.d. (c. 1968), DuSable.

23. The Museum of Negro History and Art Inc., "Source List of Materials on the Negro in History for Educational Use," n.d. (pre 1964), DuSable.

24. The calendar drew attention to the museum's own activities: in 1974, for instance, the calendar featured information and images of the DuSable's planned move to a new building in nearby Washington Park, and the museum's $1.5 million fund-raising campaign. "Name Change Announced by Ebony Museum," *Chicago Tribune,* November 17, 1963.

25. Burroughs, "Annual Report for 1966," 2.

26. Newsletter, DuSable Museum of African American History and Culture, December 1970, DuSable.

27. Ibid.

28. The DuSable Museum of African American History, "Educators' Committee Second Annual Luncheon-Colloquium," February 16, 1974, box 1, DuSable Museum Papers, DuSable.

29. Ibid.

30. Lary Davis, "The Afro-American Museum—The First Decade,"1975, loose files, box MAAH Publications, 1969–1990, MAAH, 3.

31. The IAM produced "You Can Be a Doctor" in conjunction with the Detroit Medical Society. The film was distributed by McGraw Hill and premiered at the National Medical Society convention in 1968. "The Bank is Open to You" was produced in 1969 with the National Bank of Detroit and distributed by the American Bankers Association. See loose files, box MAAH Publications, 1969–1990, MAAH. Marvin R. Dunn, Associate Dean of Woman's Medical College of Pennsylvania, wrote Charles Wright on November 11, 1968, and requested copies of "So You Want to Be a Doctor" so that medical schools in Philadelphia could use it as a recruitment tool. See Marvin R. Dunn to Charles Wright, November 11, 1968, folder 1968, box 3, CHWMAAH Historical Records, 1965–1987, MAAH.

32. IAM brochure, n.d., folder MS/MAAH Board letters, 1968–1971, CHWMAAH Historical Records, 1965–1987, MAAH.

33. Untitled document, n.d., folder 1968, CHWMAAH Historical Records, 1965–1987, MAAH. Also see Minutes of the Oral History Committee, 1966, folder Oral History Committee, box 8, Joan Hallier Series IV, MAAH.

34. IAM brochure, n.d., "Help us to put . . . History on Wheels with the New International Afro-American Museum History Mobile," CHWMAAH Historical Records, 1965–1987, MAAH. The idea for the IAM mobile exhibit van probably stemmed from the success of the "bookmobile." Bookmobiles, which act as mobile extensions of libraries, began in Maryland in 1905 and soon spread throughout the United States.

35. Lary Davis, "The Afro-American Museum—The First Decade," 1975, loose files, box MAAH Publications, 1969–1990, MAAH, 3.

36. IAM brochure, "Help! Abolish Racism . . . ," n.d., folder 1973, CHWMAAH Historical Records, 1965–1987. Although this brochure is undated and placed in the 1973 folder, its actual date is probably just prior to the mobile exhibit's debut in 1967.

37. Ibid.

38. "IAM Mobile Unit to Project 'Image,'" *Michigan Chronicle*, May 20, 1967.

39. The early history period examined the "origin of man in East Africa," with specific attention paid to African civilizations. The medieval history period featured subjects such as the "golden trade of the moors, Old Mali and the story of Mansa Musa's pilgrimage," as well as achievements in art, science, and technology in African kingdoms. Finally, the modern era explored colonialism in Africa, trade, and the establishment of modern nations. "Proposal for the Establishment of Mobile Units Dealing with the History and Cultures of African and Negro American Peoples," folder 1968, box CHWMAAH Historical Records, 1965–1987, MAAH, I.

40. Ibid.

41. "Black Arts Convention," June 29, 1967, folder 24, box 14, Detroit Commission on Community Relations, WPR. Note this intersection between Detroit's African American religious institutions and black power organizations.

42. Program, Black Arts Convention, June 2–July 2, 1967, folder 24, box 14, Detroit Commission on Community Relations, WPR, 14.

43. Minutes of Project "I AM" Meeting, March 10, 1965, 1–2; "Proposal for the Creation of an International Afro-American Museum, June 16, 1965," MAAH.

44. United States, *Riots, Civil and Criminal Disorders. Hearings before the United States Senate Committee on Government Operations, Permanent Subcommittee on Investigations,* 90th Cong., 2nd sess., 1968, Part 5 (Washington, D.C.: U.S. Government Printing Office, 1968), 1206.

45. Heather Thompson, *Whose Detroit? Politics, Labor, and Race in a Modern American City* (Ithaca, N.Y.: Cornell University Press, 2001), 42; Also see Sidney Fine, *Violence in the Model City: The Cavanagh Administration, Race Relations, and the Detroit Riot of 1967* (Ann Arbor: University of Michigan Press, 1989), 228.

46. United States, *Riots, Civil and Criminal Disorders,* 1206. Rioting was not limited to Detroit; industrial cities with large black populations, such as Flint, Grand Rapids, and Lansing, experienced similar disturbances.

47. Jeffrey C. Stewart and Fath Davis Ruffins, "A Faithful Witness: Afro-American History in Historical Perspective, 1828–1994," in *Presenting the Past: Essays on History and the Public,* ed. Susan Porter Benson, Stephen Brier, and Roy Rosenzweig (Philadelphia: Temple University Press, 1986), 330–31. According to the authors, after the riots, public history organizations began to receive additional corporate and federal funding. Stewart and Ruffins argue that increased funding to organizations such as the IAM occurred "partially because it was easier to spend money on a cultural institution than to finance an economic reconstruction of inner city ghettos" (301).

48. IAM Board of Trustees Minutes, August 15, 1971, folder MS/MAAH Board Meetings-Reports-1964–1971, box 3, CHWMAAH Historical Records, 1965–1987, MAAH.

49. Neomi Hill to Charles Wright, n.d., folder Mobile Unit Information, box Miscellaneous Correspondence and Publications, 1965–1969, MAAH.

50. C. Elrie Chrite to "Friend," September 23, 1967, folder 1967, box 3, CHWMAAH Historical Records, 1965–1987, MAAH.

51. In 1968, for example, the museum received numerous requests for the mobile unit. A February 15, 1968, letter to Charles Wright from A. A. Banks, Jr., pastor of the Second Baptist Church of Detroit, commented: "We were more than pleased to have the museum at Second Baptist Church on February 4, 1968. We hope that you can arrange to come again on April 7, 1968, as we discussed when you were here." A. A. Banks, Jr., to Charles Wright, February 15, 1968, folder 1968, box 3, CHWMAAH Historical Records 1965–1987, MAAH. The mobile van also visited Detroit's Second Baptist Church, Scott Methodist Church, The Church of the Madonna, New Light Baptist Church, and Bethel A.M.E. Church. The van visited a total of eighteen churches during 1968. See "International Afro-American Museum Churches Mobile History Van Has Visited, 1968," n.d., folder Mobile Unit Information, box Miscellaneous Correspondence and Publications, 1965–1969, MAAH.

52. Doris DeDeckere to Miss Brown, February 19, 1968, folder 1968, box 3, CHWMAAH Historical Records 1965–1987, MAAH.

53. Neomi Hill, "Report on Mackenzie High School," n.d., folder Mobile Unit Information, box Miscellaneous Correspondence and Publications, 1965–1969, MAAH.

54. Norman Mark, "Where the Negro Can Find His Image," *Chicago Daily News,* July 15, 1967.

55. Cited by Jeffrey Abt, *A Museum on the Verge: A Socioeconomic History of the Detroit Institute of Arts, 1882–2000* (Detroit: Wayne State University Press, 2001), 174.

56. Joy Hakanson Colby, "Detroit's Longest-Serving Art Critic Looks Back," *Detroit Metro Times,* June 21, 2006. See also Willis F. Woods, "African Art in the Collections of the Detroit Institute of Arts," *African Arts* 4, no. 4 (Summer 1971): 16–23.

57. Abt, *A Museum on the Verge,* 177.

58. "IAMARAMA," 1972, folder 1972, box MAAH Publications, 1969–1990, MAAH.

59. Brochure, "Black Awareness, New Directions. A Conference to celebrate the occasion of its Fourth Anniversary, Saturday, March 22, 1969," folder Black Historical Museums Conference, 1969, box 3A, Joan Hallier Series III, MAAH.

60. IAM Letter, March 12, 1969, folder Black Historical Museums Conference 1969, box 3A, Joan Hallier Series III, MAAH.

61. Judith Wragg Chase to Charles Wright, September 22, 1969, folder Black Historical Museums Conference 1969, box 3A, Joan Hallier Series III, MAAH. Chase, who worked at the Old Slave Mart Museum, said that while she could not attend the conference, Wright might be interested in contacting the Frederick Douglass Institute in Washington and The Negro History Associates in New York; he should also ask Margaret Burroughs about other possible museums. Chase and Louise Alston Grave (both white) founded the Old Slave Mart Museum in 1937. The museum's collection "provided a leading outlet for researchers on slavery and slave arts and crafts." Amina Jill Dickerson, "The History and Institutional Development of African American Museums" (MA thesis, American University, 1988), 33.

62. Records from these conference proceedings are, to date, unavailable. Program, "National Black Museums Conference, Saturday, September 27, 1969," folder Black Historical Museums Conference 1969, box 3A, Joan Hallier Series III, MAAH. This conference marked the first of several black museum conferences in Detroit. The Second National Black Museums Conference was held May 30–31, 1975; its theme was "Black History Museums: A Mirror of

the African Heritage." The IAM also hosted the fourth National Black Museums Conference October 8–9, 1976.

63. "Income and Expenditure Jan–June 1969," folder MS/MAAH Board Meetings-Reports-1964–1971, box 3, MAAH.

64. Charles Wright to Longworth Quinn, *Michigan Chronicle*, July 31, 1968, folder 1968, box Miscellaneous Correspondence and Publications, 1965–1969, MAAH. Wright sent a copy of the IAM's July 31, 1968 news release to Quinn, writing "in desperation I am sending this statement . . . directly to you. So far, nothing that we have done has been very fruitful in getting publicity in the *Chronicle.*"

65. IAM News Release, July 31, 1968, folder 1968, box Miscellaneous Correspondence and Publications, 1965–1969, MAAH. The IAM Board of Trustees also mailed personal funding pleas to specific members of Detroit's African American community. For example, a 1969 letter from board member Dr. Charles Vincent to an unnamed Detroit doctor stated, "The success or failure, (the latter we cannot let happen) of our museum is dependent entirely on the support of the Black community . . . a contribution (tax deductible) from you will let our community know of your support of our (your) museum." See Charles C. Vincent, M.D., to unnamed doctor, December 10, 1969, folder MS/MAAH: Letters to Doctors, 1969, box 3, CHWMAAH Historical Records, MAAH.

66. "Dear Fellow Board Members," August 8, 1968, folder 1968, box Miscellaneous Correspondence and Publications, 1965–1969, MAAH.

67. Michele Wallace, *Black Macho and the Myth of the Superwoman* (New York: Verso, 1991), 73. See also Peniel Joseph's discussion of Eldridge Cleaver's *Soul on Ice* in *Waiting 'til the Midnight Hour: A Narrative History of Black Power in America* (New York: Henry Holt, 2006), 212–14. Cynthia Griggs Fleming explains that black cultural nationalists emphasized "black male strength, which was defined in the context of an idealized image of a submissive black woman." Fleming, "Black Women and Black Power: The Case of Ruby Doris Smith Robinson and the Student Nonviolent Coordinating Committee," in *Sisters in the Struggle: African American Women in the Civil Rights-Black Power Movement*, ed. Bettye Collier-Thomas and V. P. Franklin (New York: New York University Press, 2001), 208.

68. Steve Estes, *I Am A Man! Race, Manhood, and the Civil Rights Movement* (Chapel Hill: University of North Carolina Press, 2005), 140–41.

69. Morton, "A Man's Reach Should Exceed His Grasp, Else What's a Heaven For?"

70. Ibid.

71. See Elaine Tyler May's discussion of "momism"—the idea that frustrated women smother their children, making men weak and passive—in *Homeward Bound: American Families in the Cold War Era* (New York: Basic Books, 1999), 74.

72. Lisa Ann Meyerowitz, "Exhibiting Equality: Black-Run Museums and Galleries in 1970s New York" (PhD diss., University of Chicago, June 2001), 167.

73. Studio Museum in Harlem, *Harlem Artists 69: [Exhibition] The Studio Museum in Harlem, New York, July 22–September 7, 1969* (New York: The Museum, 1969).

74. Romare Bearden et al., "The Black Artist in America: A Symposium," *Metropolitan Museum of Art Bulletin* 27, no. 5 (January 1969): 246–47.

75. Oral history interview with Cliff Joseph, 1972, Archives of American Art, Smithsonian Institution.

76. Lawrence Reddick, "Will the Bicentennial Celebration Be an Accurate Picture of American Life and History and Be Fair to All of the American People?" May 1974, 4–6, folder 1, box 1, William Rafsky Papers, Philadelphia City Archives.

77. Smithsonian Institution Archives, Oral Histories, RU 9558, Louise Daniel Hutchinson Interviews. vii, 31–32.

78. Kenneth Hudson, *Museums of Influence* (Cambridge: Cambridge University Press, 1987), 22. In 1966, Smithsonian staffer Sam Suratt wrote to Charles Blitzer with a few caustic suggestions about what to display at the new museum: "A stuffed horse equipped with a saddle and a long bull whip, facing a panorama of cotton fields with happy white field hands just a pickin away. . . . An electric cattle prod with a life size model of Bull Conner. . . . A cell block containing wax replicas of the Chief of Police, head of the Washington Board of Trade, and Senator Robert Byrd (W. Va.)." Sam Surratt to Charles Blitzer, October 26, 1966, folder I ANM, Planning of Exhibits, box 2, Series I, 1961–1971, Assistant Secretary for Public Service and Related Records, 1961–1972, Smithsonian Institution Archives, RU 145, Smithsonian Institution.

79. Caryl Marsh, "Dedication and Opening of the Anacostia Neighborhood Museum," September 15, 1967, ACM.

80. Michele Gates Moresi, "Exhibiting Race, Creating Nation: Representations of Black History and Culture at the Smithsonian Institution, 1895–1976" (PhD diss., George Washington University, 2003), 153.

81. Wilcomb E. Washburn to Charles Blitzer, January 18, 1968, folder I ANM, Planning of Exhibits, box 2, Series I, 1961–1971, Assistant Secretary for Public Service and Related Records, 1961–1972, Smithsonian Institution Archives, RU 145, Smithsonian Institution.

82. According to Portia James, the Smithsonian did not allow the ANM to create a permanent collection until the early 1990s. See James, "Building a Community-Based Identity at Anacostia Museum," in *Heritage, Museums, and Galleries: An Introductory Reader,* ed. Gerard Corsane (London: Routledge, 2005), 346.

83. S. Dillon Ripley to Silvio Bendini and Richard Cowan, June 11, 1968, folder I ANM, Planning of Exhibits, box 2, Series I, 1961–1971, Assistant Secretary for Public Service and Related Records, 1961–1972, Smithsonian Institution Archives, RU 145, Smithsonian Institution.

84. Silvio Bendini to S. Dillon Ripley, June 17, 1968, folder I ANM, Planning of Exhibits, box 2, Series I, 1961–1971, Assistant Secretary for Public Service and Related Records, 1961–1972, Smithsonian Institution Archives, RU 145, Smithsonian Institution.

85. In a 1968 letter to Mrs. Carolyn B. Pogue, Kinard requested funding for three specific areas—education, the hiring of research assistants from colleges or high schools, and public relations—in order for the ANM to successfully make the shift from serving as general community museum to a museum of African American history and culture. See John Kinard to Mrs. Carolyn B. Pogue, August 20, 1968, folder ANM Archives, prior to '72–'73, box 2, Smithsonian Institution Archives, RU 265, Anacostia Neighborhood Museum, Office of the Director, Records.

86. Hutchinson, Oral Histories interview, vii, 31–32.

87. Anacostia Neighborhood Museum, *Anacostia Neighborhood Museum, Smithsonian Institution, September 15, 1972* (Washington D.C., Smithsonian, 1972), 17–18.

88. Ibid., 14–15.

89. John R. Kinard and Esther Nighbert, "The Anacostia Neighborhood Museum," *Museum* 24, no. 2 (1972): 105–6.

90. Zora B. Martin, "Anatomy of an Inner City Museum," *Alma Mater,* Moravian College (Bethlehem, Pa.: 1970), 8–12.

91. Anacostia Neighborhood Museum, "Calendar of Events, November 16, 1969–January 25, 1970," folder "The Rat: Man's Invited Affliction," box 11, Smithsonian Institution Archives, RU 390, Anacostia Museum, Education Department, Records.

92. Smithsonian Institution Archives, Oral Histories, RU 9538, John R. Kinard Interview, 24.

93. Ibid.

94. Emily Dennis Harvey and Bernard Friedberg, eds., *A Museum for the People: A Report of Proceedings at the Seminar on Neighborhood Museums, held November 20, 21, and 22, 1969, at MUSE, the Bedford Lincoln Neighborhood Museum in Brooklyn, New York* (New York: Arno Press, 1971), 28–29.

95. Kinard, Oral Histories interview, 24.

96. "Anacostia Neighborhood Museum Celebrates Fifth Anniversary," *Washington, D.C. Federal Times,* October 4, 1972, vertical file no. 2 (Anacostia Community), box 130C, ACM.

97. Hutchinson, Oral Histories interview, 64–65.

98. Ibid., 65.

99. Audrey S. Gomes, "The Anacostia Story: 1608–1930," *Oral History Review* 5 (1977): 75–76.

100. Louise Daniel Hutchinson, *The Anacostia Story, 1608–1930* (Washington, D.C.: Smithsonian Institution Press, 1977), ix.

101. Ibid., x, 139.

102. *Anacostia Neighborhood Museum, Smithsonian Institution, September 15, 1972,* 52.

103. Troy R. Spencer to John Kinard, n.d., folder Visitors prior to 1973, box 9, Smithsonian Institution Archives, RU 265, Anacostia Neighborhood Museum, Office of the Director, Records.

104. American Association of Museums, *America's Museums: The Belmont Report. A Report to the Federal Council on the Arts and Humanities* (Washington, D.C., 1969). In 1967, President Lyndon Johnson requested that the Federal Council on Arts and Humanities study the status of American museums. The AAM's *Belmont Report* presented these findings. The report cites the efforts of a few museums, such as the Chicago Field Museum and the New York Botanical Gardens, which started outreach programs for disadvantaged schoolchildren. The Field Museum provided jobs for "college students from the Negro Sections of Chicago" through a work-study project begun by the Economic Opportunity Act of 1964. The Museum of Arts and Sciences in Rochester, New York, was also noted for its outreach efforts; however, John Kinard later strongly criticized museums (including the Rochester museum) that decentralized without first implementing change within their own administration. The report also mentions the ANM's work, but contends that "the problem of financing the Anacostia branch museum has yet to be solved." See *America's Museums: The Belmont Report,* 13–16, 20.

105. Elisabeth Stevens, "Neighborhood Mini-Museums: 'Art Is the Tool for Social Change,'" *Washington Post,* June 25, 1972. In the article, Martin Friedman, director of the Walker Art Center in Minneapolis, reflected on the concept of museum "decentralization." Friedman defined decentralization as the method by which museums distributed exhibits formerly housed in one building to various community organizations. For Friedman, decentralization was a difficult process: "The easy way to decentralize is to rent a few storefronts and put some objects in them. . . . But the thing is not simply to fracture yourself into smaller pieces—you have to begin with ideas not objects. And it's a mistake to think a museum has a single audience. It has many. You have to go out and find them."

106. S. Dillon Ripley to John Hope Franklin, May 3, 1968, folder Negro History, box 14, Series I, Smithsonian Institution Archives, RU 145, Smithsonian Institution, Assistant Secretary for Public Service, Subject Files.

107. S. Dillon Ripley, "MHT has 'Moral Responsibility,'" *The Smithsonian Torch* (February 1969).

108. Moresi, 172–73, citing from Memo, John E. Anglim, Chief, Office of Exhibits, to Mr. Frank A. Taylor, Director, MHT, August 19, 1968, box 2, Public Service, Smithsonian.

109. Ibid.

110. Memo, Frank A. Taylor to all Smithsonian museums, "Summary of Exhibits of Negro History and a Course of Action," July 24, 1968, folder Negro History, box 14, Series I, Smithsonian Institution Archives, RU 145, Smithsonian Institution, Assistant Secretary for Public Service, Subject Files.

111. Ann Margaret Webb, "Incorporating African Americans into the Public Identity of the South via Museum Exhibits" (MA thesis, University of North Carolina at Wilmington, 1997), 118.

112. Jerry M. Flint, "Museums Responding to New Needs," *New York Times, July 4, 1969,* 10.

113. John Canaday, "Happy Birthday—Are You Relevant?" *New York Times,* October 12, 1969.

114. Elaine Woo, "J. S. Holliday, 82; Wrote Classic History of the Gold Rush Era," *Los Angeles Times,* September 10, 2006; Carle Nolte, "J. S. Holliday: 1924–2006," *San Francisco Chronicle,* September 2, 2006. Records on J. S. Holliday's firing are held by the California Historical Society, and are restricted to the public.

115. Evan H. Turner, "Introductory Comments for AAM Conference, 1972, Mexico City," folder Mexico, A.A.M. 1972 Address, box 8, Smithsonian Institution Archives, RU 265, Anacostia Neighborhood Museum, Office of the Director, Records. See Kinard's handwritten notes next to Turner's speech.

116. Ibid.

117. Grace Glueck, "1930's Show at Whitney Picketed by Negro Artists Who Call It Incomplete," *New York Times,* November 18, 1968.

118. Besides Ghent, protesters at the Whitney exhibition included African American artist Tom Lloyd, whose exhibit on light sculptures was featured at the SMH's opening, and sculptor William Williams, who directed the artist-in-residence program at the SMH. See Meyerowitz, "Exhibiting Equality," 17. Also see Benny Andrews, "The BECC: Black Emergency Cultural Coalition," *Arts Magazine* (Summer 1970): 18–19; Glueck, "1930's Show at Whitney Picketed by Negro Artists Who Call It Incomplete."

119. In 1971, the Whitney faced a similar controversy, again led by the BECC, when fifteen black artists (out of a total of 75) withdrew from an exhibition titled Contemporary Black Artists in America. Although the BECC initially planned the show in conjunction with the Whitney, the group charged that the Whitney failed to follow through on two aspects of their agreement: "that the exhibition would be selected with the assistance of black art specialists, and that it would be presented 'during the most prestigious period of the 1970–71 art season.'" Whitney director John Baur, who argued that the BECC "stands for a kind of separatism I don't believe in," countered these charges. See Grace Glueck, "15 of 75 Black Artists Leave as Whitney Exhibition Opens," *New York Times,* April 6, 1971.

120. Hilton Kramer, "Differences in Quality," *New York Times,* November 24, 1968. While critical of Invisible Americans, Kramer was also not overly praiseworthy of the Whitney's The 1930s, characterizing the exhibit as "varied and unwieldy."

121. Henri Ghent, "White Is Not Superior," *New York Times,* December 8, 1968.

122. Ibid.

123. Steven Dubin, *Displays of Power: Controversy in the American Museum from the Enola Gay to Sensation* (New York: New York University Press, 2001), 18–63.

124. Bearden et al., "The Black Artist in America," 244. Curators divided Harlem on My Mind into themed decades. For example, 1900–1919 ("From White to Black Harlem") discussed the changing demographics of the Harlem neighborhood, while the 1950s explored Harlem's "Frustration and Ambivalence." Accompanying newspaper articles from Harlem's

black newspaper, *Amsterdam News,* as well as the *New York Times* contextualized the images and objects for each decade. In a significant—and prescient—departure from traditional exhibition design, Schoener relied heavily on various forms of media, such as slide shows, audio recordings, photographs, and films of community leaders, to chronicle Harlem's social and cultural history. See *Harlem on My Mind: Cultural Capital of Black America, 1900–1968,* ed. Allon Schoener (New York: Random House, 1968; New York: The New Press, 1995).

125. "Harlem Cultural Council Drops Support for Metropolitan Show," *New York Times,* November 23, 1968.

126. African American artists Benny Andrews and Cliff Joseph also cochaired the BECC.

127. "Museum Pickets Assail Hoving over Coming Harlem Exhibition," *New York Times,* January 15, 1969. Some prominent members of the black community publicly supported Harlem on My Mind, and for this they drew extensive criticism. See Allon Schoener, ed., "Introduction to the New Edition," *Harlem On My Mind: Cultural Capital of Black America, 1900–1968* (New York: Random House, 1968; New York: The New Press, 1995); Rudy Johnson, "2 Harlem Pastors Disagree on Exhibit," *New York Times,* January 20, 1969.

128. Bearden et al., "The Black Artist in America," 246.

129. Martin Arnold, "Hoving Accepts Onus for Furor," *New York Times,* January 22, 1969. Much to the dismay of museum officials, another apparent response to Harlem on My Mind was the defacement of several masterpieces at the Met. Some paintings, including a Rembrandt, were scratched with a small "H." The papers speculated that this "H" perhaps stood for "Harlem," or for "Hoving," though this was not proven and no suspects were caught. See Martin Arnold, "Paintings Defaced at Metropolitan; One a Rembrandt," *New York Times,* January 17, 1969.

130. Hoving left the Met in 1970. Peter Kihss, "Museum Withdraws Catalogue Attacked as a Slur on Jews," *New York Times,* January 31, 1969.

4. *"To Satisfy a Deadline but Little Else": The Public Debut of the African American Museum of Philadelphia*

1. Oakley N. Holmes, Jr., *The Complete Annotated Resource Guide to Black American Art* (Spring Valley, N.Y.: Black Artists in America, 1978), 115.

2. See Meyerowitz's discussion of these protests, led by groups such as the BECC, the Guerrilla Art Action Group, and the Ad Hoc Women Artists Committee. Lisa Ann Meyerowitz, "Exhibiting Equality: Black-Run Museums and Galleries in 1970s New York" (PhD diss., University of Chicago, 2001), 70–73.

3. "Anacostia Neighborhood Museum Bicentennial Exhibits, Materials and Programs for Classroom Use," n.d., folder Anacostia Neighborhood Museum, box 6, Joan Hallier Series IV, MAAH.

4. John Kifner, "Black Injured at Boston Rally Plan Action against Officials," *New York Times,* April 8, 1976.

5. "The Bicentennial Blues," *Ebony* 31 (June 1976): 152–53. Also see the Bicentennial-themed articles published by the ASALH in *Negro History Bulletin* 39, no. 1 (January 1976); *Negro History Bulletin* 39, no. 3 (March 1976): 539; *Negro History Bulletin* 39, no. 4 (April 1976): 560.

6. "The Bicentennial Blues," 152.

7. J. Rupert Picott, "Editorial Comment: America: The Third Century," *Negro History Bulletin* 39, no. 1 (January 1976): 495.

8. The ASALH followed in the footsteps of the National Park Service's own efforts to recognize historic African American sites. In 1971, the NPS hired the Afro-American

Bicentennial Corporation to supervise this project. Headed by Robert and Vincent DeForrest, and including other black advisers (such as Shirley Chisholm and Benjamin Quarles), the organization received $540,000 in funding to identify black historic landmarks. By 1977, there were sixty-one black historic landmarks (including the Carter G. Woodson home) that had been approved for National Historic Landmark status by the National Park Service. Pero Gaglo Dagbovie, "'Most Honorable Mention . . . Belongs to Washington, DC': The Carter G. Woodson Home and the Early Black History Movement in the Nation's Capital," *Journal of African American History* 96, no. 3 (Summer 2011): 316.

9. Picott, "Editorial Comment," 495.

10. *Slavery and Freedom in the Age of the American Revolution,* ed. Ira Berlin and Ronald Hoffman (Charlottesville: University Press of Virginia, 1983).

11. John Bodnar, *Remaking America: Public Memory, Commemoration, and Patriotism in the Twentieth Century* (Princeton, N.J.: Princeton University Press, 1992), 231.

12. "People's Bicentennial," *New York Times,* July 5, 1976.

13. Bodnar, *Remaking America,* 232–36.

14. "Uncovering Chicago's Revolutionary History," reprinted from *The Chicago Patriot,* November 1975, folder: Margaret, box 1, DuSable Museum Papers, DuSable.

15. Richard Phillips, "Marquette Pk. Parade OKd for Black Group," *Chicago Tribune,* July 10, 1976.

16. Ibid.

17. Bodnar, *Remaking America,* 243.

18. The phrase "hypocrisy and a sham" is from Minutes, People's '76–Board of Directors, n.d., folder People's '76–Board of Directors—Meeting Minutes, box 5, Philadelphia Council of Neighborhood Organizations, UA.

19. "People's '76 Calls all Concerned Citizens to Demonstrate at our Own Liberty Pole," n.d., folder: People's '76–Board of Directors—Meeting Minutes, box 5, Philadelphia Council of Neighborhood Organizations, UA.

20. People's '76 also rallied around issues such as the "denial of full health care to all who need it; the illegal surveillance of individuals and political groups; the lack of equal treatment under law." Ibid.

21. Pamphlet, People's '76, box 5, Philadelphia Council of Neighborhood Organizations, UA.

22. Andrew Feffer, "Show Down in Center City: Staging Redevelopment and Citizenship in Bicentennial Philadelphia, 1974–1977," *Journal of Urban History* 30, no. 6 (September 2004): 792.

23. Ibid., 818.

24. News Release, March 8, 1976, folder Project List, October 2, 1973, box 4, US Bicentennial Collection, The University Archives and Records Center, University of Pennsylvania, Philadelphia, Pa.

25. Ibid. See also Charles Blockson, *Pennsylvania's Black History* (Philadelphia: Portfolio Associates, 1975). For information on the Mother Bethel A.M.E. exhibit, see Press Release, Portfolio Associates Inc., "Pennsylvania's Black History is Displayed in Mobile Exhibit," August 2, 1976, folder 2, box 1, William Rafsky papers, PCA.

26. Harold J. Haskins, "A Proposal to Produce a Black International, National and Local Art Exhibition in Philadelphia," n.d., folder "Black International, National and Local Art Exhibition: Proposal," box 4, US Bicentennial Collection, University Archives and Record Center, University of Pennsylvania, Philadelphia. It is unclear whether or not this particular exhibition ever saw the light of day.

27. Bodnar, *Remaking America,* 230.

28. "Bicentennial Museum Grants," *New York Times,* August 26, 1975.

29. Untitled pamphlet, n.d., folder 1975, box MAAH Publications, 1969–1990, MAAH. For other Bicentennial events in Detroit, see Detroit Bicentennial Commission, *Spirit of '76: A City Celebrates* (Detroit, Mich.: The Commission, 1977). Ida Roberta Bell (1902–92) was elected to the National Institute of American Doll Artists in 1970—the first African American to receive the honor. In addition to the IAM, Bell's dolls are displayed at The Philadelphia Doll Museum, among other locations.

30. With regard to this popular exhibit, Michele Moresi explains that "African American experiences of forced removal and enslavement melded with the migration of Europeans to delineate a 'shared experience.' The distinction of those experiences and their impact on American culture and social life were rendered mute." Michele Gates Moresi, "Exhibiting Race, Creating Nation: Representations of Black History and Culture at the Smithsonian Institution, 1895–1976" (PhD diss., George Washington University, 2003), 196. Also see Peter C. Marzio, *A Nation of Nations: The People Who Came to America as Seen through the Objects and Documents Exhibited at the Smithsonian Institution* (New York: Harper and Row, 1976).

31. "From the Suggestion Box: Blacks in West," September 1975–January 1976, folder: Speeches, Awards, Bios for Zora Feldon, box 5, Smithsonian Institution Archives, Record Unit 390, Anacostia Museum, Education Department, Records. See also Anacostia Neighborhood Museum, *Blacks in the Westward Movement* (Washington, D.C.: Smithsonian Institution Press, 1975).

32. A few negative comments focused specifically on the exhibit design. For example, one commentator wrote: "I came to be impressed. Unfortunately I'm not. This just isn't my idea of a museum. Where are the Black exhibits? Except for Flipper's blanket and some photos there aren't any. What kind of a rip-off is this?" See "From the Suggestion Box: Blacks in West."

33. Ibid.

34. Feffer, "Show Down in Center City," 801.

35. Ibid.

36. Pamphlet, "Afro American Historical and Cultural Museum," n.d., AAMP.

37. Nessa Forman, "Top Director Quits Post at Black Culture Museum," *Philadelphia Bulletin,* January 25, 1977. Outgoing director Gerard William reported that the AAMP was negotiating with the city in an effort to eliminate this deficit. He estimated that the museum needed $500,000 per year in operating expenses, $300,000 of which could be raised through admissions and contributions.

38. Cam, "Feasibility Study, Museum: Black History Exhibition, for Philadelphia '76 Inc.," 12–13.

39. Ibid., 51–52.

40. "At Black Museum," *Philadelphia Bulletin,* November 3, 1977. The exhibit ran through November 20, 1977.

41. According to the museum's one-year plan for 1978, four major exhibits were scheduled, including The Work of Alan Crite, an artist known for his religious graphics and paintings. The AAMP described this exhibit as the "largest, most extensive and expensive exhibit the Museum has ever undertaken. The estimated cost is $25,000.00." See AAMP Board Minutes, May 10, 1978, AAMP.

42. Winnie Owens and Winston Kennedy, *Genetic Memories* (Philadelphia: The Museum, 1978), 5.

43. H. Alonzo Jennings to the Honorable James Barber, Chairman, State Legislative Black Caucus, April 11, 1978, box 1, AAMP.

44. AAMP Board Minutes, May 10, 1978, AAMP.

45. H. Alonzo Jennings to the Honorable James Barber.

46. Ibid.

47. Ibid.

48. As Joy Ford Austin notes in the 2003 *National Survey of African American Museums,* school groups remain the dominant audience for most African American museums. For example, of the 47 percent of museums that responded to the survey, "school groups account for 26 percent—50 percent of total visitors. For 30 percent of the museums, school groups account for more than 50 percent of total visitors. Joy Ford Austin, *National Survey of African American Museums: Prepared for the National Museum of African American History and Culture Plan for Action Presidential Commission* (Washington, D.C.: National Museum of African American History and Culture Plan for Action Presidential Commission, 2003), x.

49. Editorial, "Now, What Kind of Museum?" n.d., folder Afro-American Historical and Cultural Center, box 1, William Rafsky papers, PCA. The clipping does not include the name of the newspaper.

50. Nessa Forman, "One Man's Collection," *Philadelphia Bulletin,* December 18, 1977.

51. Nessa Forman, "Exhibit Spotlights Black Inventors," *Philadelphia Bulletin,* March 4, 1977.

52. Nessa Forman, "Of Politics and Power at Black Museum: Why Two Quit Their Posts," *Philadelphia Bulletin,* October 23, 1977.

53. Afro-American Historical and Cultural Museum, *20 Years of Reflection: 1976–1996* (Philadelphia: Afro-American Historical and Cultural Museum of Philadelphia, 1996), 19.

54. The Afro-American Historical and Cultural Museum, *Of Color, Humanitas, and Statehood: The Black Experience in Pennsylvania over Three Centuries 1681–1981* (Philadelphia: The Afro-American Historical and Cultural Museum, 1981), 111. Lawrence Reddick, an early advocate of the AAMP, wrote the introduction to the exhibit.

55. Cam, "Feasibility Study, Museum: Black History Exhibition, for Philadelphia '76 Inc," 19.

56. Ibid.

57. Editorial, "Now, What Kind of Museum?"

58. Perry Triplett to William L. Rafsky, March 27, 1975, folder Black History Museum, box 4, SHCA, UA.

59. Editorial, "Now, What Kind of Museum?"

60. Pamphlet, Afro American Historical and Cultural Museum, n.d., AAMP, 5.

61. AAMP Board Minutes, May 10, 1978, AAMP, 4.

62. Newsletter, DuSable Museum of African American History and Culture, December 1970, DuSable.

63. David Ashenfelter, "Museum Is Accused of Letting Pages of History Fade," *Detroit Free Press,* November 11, 2006.

64. Amina Jill Dickerson, "The History and Institutional Development of African American Museums" (MA thesis, American University, 1988), 58.

65. Forman, "Of Politics and Power at Black Museum." In this same quote, Forman inaccurately stated that the museum was the "first center in America built expressly to deal with the black experience."

66. David Sibley, "Outsiders in Society and Space," in *Inventing Places: Studies in Cultural Geography,* ed. Kay Anderson and Gay Gale (Melbourne: Longman Cheshire, 1992), 112–13.

67. American Studies Association, Conference Proceedings, "Groundwork: Space and Place in American Cultures," November 3–6, 2005, Washington, D.C.

68. Michael A. diNunzio, General Counsel, to Mayor Frank Rizzo, n.d., folder Black History Museum, box Frank Rizzo Correspondence, 1976, PCA. Gerard William's questionnaire is included in this file.

69. Forman, "Of Politics and Power at Black Museum."

70. Dickerson, "The History and Institutional Development of African American Museums," 87 (emphasis added). Doke was appointed in 1982.

71. Nessa Forman, "Top Director Quits Post at Black Culture Museum," *Philadelphia Bulletin*, January 25, 1977.

72. Ibid.

73. Nessa Forman, "Director Quits Afro Museum," *Philadelphia Bulletin*, October 17, 1977.

74. Edgar Williams, "Head of Black Museum Resigns," *Philadelphia Inquirer*, October 18, 1977.

75. Ibid.

76. Matthew Countryman, *Up South: Civil Rights and Black Power in Philadelphia* (Philadelphia: University of Pennsylvania Press, 2005), 262.

77. Laura Murray, "Director's Exit Underscores Museum's Woes," *Philadelphia Daily News*, October 17, 1977.

78. Forman, "Of Politics and Power at Black Museum."

79. Ibid.

80. Murray, "Director's Exit Underscores Museum's Woes."

81. In addition to outreach programs such as "Evenings at the Afro," Jennings pursued more active fund-raising strategies, including seeking corporate and philanthropic grants; selling memberships at a cost ranging from five dollars (students) to one hundred dollars (for patrons) and increasing membership from 800 to 10,000 people. See Thomas M. Burton, "Jazz Concerts Proposed to Keep Museum 'Alive,'" *Evening Bulletin*, April 4, 1978.

5. Rocky Transitions: Black Museums Approach a New Era

1. The AAMA had ninety-nine institutional members in 1988; this number does not include African American museums that were not yet members of the AAMA. African American Museums Association, *Profile of Black Museums* (Washington, D.C.: African American Museums Association; Nashville, Tenn.: American Association for State and Local History, 1988), xiii.

2. Lorraine Kee, "Plan to Build Black History Museum Here Will Take Lots of Cash, Patience," *St. Louis Post-Dispatch*, April 24, 2000. Margaret Burroughs and Charles Wright initiated the formation of The Association of African American Museums in the late 1960s. The organization did not formally begin until 1978. For additional information, see African American Museums Association, *Profile of Black Museums*, 4.

3. Cheryl V. Jackson, "DuSable Plans Expansion as Others Falter; African-American History Museum Bucks National Trend of Closings and Cutbacks," *Chicago Sun-Times*, February 1, 2005.

4. Joel Rose, "Difficulties African American Museums Are Facing to Raise Funds and Attract a Broader Audience," transcript, *Morning Edition*, National Public Radio (NPR), June 23, 2004. Also see Naeemah Khabir, "Black Museums Face Funding Crisis," *Philadelphia Tribune*, September 23, 2004; Julekha Dash, "Selling the Past: Struggles in Other Cities Serve as Lesson for Lewis Museum as It Readies for June Opening," *Baltimore Business Journal*, December 17, 2004. The National Afro-American Museum and Cultural Center in Wilberforce, Ohio, which depended on funding from the Ohio Historical Society (OHS), struggled because the state slashed the

OHS's budget. Likewise, the African American Museum in Cleveland closed its doors for several months because it could not pay its utility bills. Once again, volunteers managed the museum, rather than paid staff. Wilberforce director Vernon Courtney speculated that the September 11, 2001, attacks affected museum attendance at both his museum and the Cleveland museum. According to Courtney, attendance declined to about 20,000 visitors a year after 2001, compared with 50,000 prior to 2001. See Kelly Lecker, "Hard Times Hit Black-History Museums," *Columbus Dispatch*, August 22, 2004.

5. The "culture wars" of the early-mid 1990s swirled around the Smithsonian, which scrambled to repair the extensive public relations damage that stemmed from their 1994 exhibit proposal, The Crossroads: The End of World War II, the Atomic Bomb and the Cold War. As part of the exhibit, the Smithsonian displayed the *Enola Gay*, the airplane that dropped the atomic bomb on Hiroshima. The Smithsonian's battle over how to display and interpret the *Enola Gay* underscores the politics of memory at work in museums and other sites of public history. For an extensive analysis of the backlash against the NEA, the NEH, and the Smithsonian Institution during the early 1990s, see *History Wars: The Enola Gay and Other Battles for the American Past*, ed. Edward T. Linenthal and Tom Engelhardt (New York: Metropolitan Books, 1996).

6. Katherine Lewis, *The Changing Face of Public History: The Chicago Historical Society and the Transformation of an American Museum* (DeKalb: Northern Illinois University Press, 2005), 81.

7. Ellen Futterman, "African American Museums Succeed in Other Cities: In Chicago, The DuSable Wins Fans, But Not Always Funds," *St. Louis Post Dispatch*, June 6, 1999.

8. Jackson, "DuSable Plans Expansion as Others Falter."

9. Paul D. Williams, *A Crisis in Culture: A Report and Analysis on the African American Museum of Art and History, Minneapolis, Minnesota* (Council on Black Minnesotans: July, 1986). Williams bases his report primarily on oral interviews of staff members. The AAMAH's location in Minneapolis presents an interesting comparison to the other museums in this study, as Minneapolis and its "twin" city of St. Paul had substantially smaller black populations, with fewer African Americans who had attained political office than, for example, Detroit. The 1970 census recorded just over 19,000 African Americans living in Minneapolis out of a total population of 434,000 (all races). The black population of Detroit in 1970 numbered over 660,000 out of a total population of 1,511,482 (all races). Still, the trials of African Americans in the Twin Cities during the 1950s and 1960s echoed those of people who lived in cities that were beginning to be identified as "black." Urban renewal programs destroyed African American neighborhoods in the Twin Cities such as the enclave known as the Rondo neighborhood in St. Paul in the 1960s. Interstate 94 replaced this once tight-knit community. See Evelyn Fairbanks, *The Days of Rondo* (St. Paul: Minnesota Historical Society Press, 1990). For census figures, see U.S. Bureau of the Census, *1970 Census of Population: Characteristics of the Population* I, part 25: Minnesota (U.S. Dept. of Commerce, 1973); U.S. Bureau of the Census, *1970 Census of Population: Characteristics of the Population*, vol. 1, pt. 24, Michigan (Washington, D.C.: U.S. Government Printing Office, 1973).

10. Williams, *A Crisis in Culture*, 7, 9, 17. Federal and state funding cutbacks to programs such as the Community Development Block Grants (CDBG) and the Housing and Urban Development Department hit the museum during the early 1980s. In 1982, CDBG funds were eliminated, and the AAMAH was forced to limit their activities. The AAMAH had no contingency plans or other sources of funding apart from these government allocations, and efforts to attract corporate and foundation support faltered. Interestingly, a new African American museum—this time located in a historic mansion listed on the National Register of Historic Places—was (tentatively)

scheduled to open in Minneapolis around 2015; as of 2012, however, the museum has been unable to secure the one million in state grant money needed to open. CBS Minnesota, "Black History Museum Faces Major Setback," September 19, 2012, minnesota.cbslocal.com/2012/09/19/black-history-museum-faces-major-setback.

11. Hank Burchard, "Anacostia's Forgotten Museums," *Washington Post*, March 9, 1979.

12. Anacostia Neighborhood Museum, *Anacostia Neighborhood Museum, Smithsonian Institution, September 1966/1977* (Washington, D.C.: The Museum, 1977), 2.

13. Michele Gates Moresi, "Exhibiting Race, Creating Nation: Representations of Black History and Culture at the Smithsonian Institution, 1895–1976" (PhD diss., George Washington University, 2003), 174.

14. The Studio Museum of Harlem in New York City faced similar challenges during the mid-1970s, when its board began to explore the possibility of relocating the museum to a more suitable facility. Since its founding in 1968, the Studio Museum had been housed in a small apartment building at 2033 Fifth Avenue and 125th Street in Harlem, close to other ordinary neighborhood businesses, such as a supermarket and a liquor store. One possible site for the Studio Museum's relocation was a building in an area in East Harlem, also known as Spanish Harlem. This building was also within walking distance of institutions such as the Metropolitan Museum of Art, the Whitney Museum of American Art, and the Guggenheim. According to Meyerowitz, without the stigma of "black" Harlem attached to the museum, the board believed it would attract more economically and racially diverse audiences. Not surprisingly, this news inflamed community members, who argued that the board's objectives subverted the Studio Museum's original intent to serve as a grassroots, African American museum. Critics alleged that board members were more concerned about pleasing their "aspiring bourgeois constituents" than reaching out to the black working class—a charge that enveloped the museum even on its opening day on September 26, 1968. In a further attempt to shift the identity of the Studio Museum, the board also voted to institute a name change. Instead of the "Studio Museum in Harlem," it proposed that the museum be renamed the "Museum of African American Art." Thus, while the Studio Museum would still be physically tied to Harlem by dint of its location (albeit in an area of Harlem not historically tied to African Americans), changing the name to the more expansive "Museum of African American Art" demonstrated the board's desire to appeal to audiences beyond the local. Ultimately, however, the Studio Museum remained in "black" Harlem, and the name change never materialized. The New York Bank for Savings donated a five-story office building on 144 West 125th Street to the museum, and the Studio Museum opened in this new location, less than a half mile from its original site, in 1981. See Lisa Ann Meyerowitz, "Exhibiting Equality: Black-Run Museums and Galleries in 1970s New York" (PhD diss., University of Chicago, 2001), 180–186; Michael Brenson, "New Home and Life for Studio Museum in Harlem," *New York Times*, June 17, 1982; C. Gerald Fraser, "Harlem Museum a Center for Literati," *New York Times*, May 23, 1972; C. Gerald Fraser, "Studio Museum Finds a Harlem Home," *New York Times*, November 10, 1979; Romare Bearden et al., "The Black Artist in America: A Symposium," *Metropolitan Museum of Art Bulletin* 27, no. 5 (January 1969): 252.

15. The Chicago Police Department had been located in the Park District building, but then vacated it. Margaret Burroughs recalls that some of her high school students noticed that the building was empty, at which point she and her students began a letter-writing campaign to acquire it: "Luckily election year was coming up, and I guess the mayor figured it might look . . . good to see his picture in the paper presenting me with the keys to this building, for the black folks to see this. So the word was given to let us have the building. And we got the building, and I found out later that all of the museums that are located on state land, this is

state land, are entitled by law to support from the tax levy. The Art Institute museums all get a certain amount of the operational money from the tax levy which is administered by the Chicago Park District. So you see, it was very important that we got in here, because if I had to find someplace . . . to build it, we wouldn't even be in existence." Burroughs thus clearly understood how to play the political game in order to benefit the DuSable. John E. Fleming and Margaret T. Burroughs, "Dr. Margaret T. Burroughs: Artist, Teacher, Administrator, Writer, Political Activist, and Museum Founder," *Public Historian* 21, no. 1 (Winter 1999): 41.

16. *Profile of Black Museums,* 4.

17. María-José Moreno, "Art Museums and Socioeconomic Forces: The Case of a Community Museum," *Review of Radical Political Economics* 36, no. 4 (Fall 2004): 507. See also Arlene Davila, "El Barrio's 'We Are Watching You' Campaign: On the Politics of Inclusion in a Latinized Museum," *Aztlan* 30, no. 1 (Spring 2005): 153.

18. Ramon Price interview, February 18, 1988, box Correspondence, 1978–1993 (curatorial), DuSable. Although the interviewer's identity is not indicated, it is likely that the study was initiated internally.

19. "The Future of Du Sable Museum is a Matter of Concern," n.d., DuSable, 2–3.

20. Davila, "El Barrio's 'We Are Watching You' Campaign," 169.

21. Pamphlet, "The Committee to Save the DuSable Museum," October 7, 1994, DuSable.

22. Adrienne Drell, "Group Wants Reform at DuSable Museum," *Chicago Sun-Times,* October 31, 1994.

23. Lori Rotenberk, "Activists Demand Rehiring of DuSable Museum Chief," *Chicago Sun-Times,* August 4, 1994.

24. Ibid.

25. Pamphlet, "Committee to Save the DuSable Museum," August 1994, box 1, DuSable Museum Papers, DuSable. Emphasis in original.

26. Drell, "Group Wants Reform at DuSable Museum."

27. Ibid.

28. Oscar Brown, Jr., "The Road to Cultural Revolution," n.d., DuSable.

29. Pamphlet, "The Committee to Save the DuSable Museum," August 1994.

30. Della De LaFuente, "Experienced Hand Takes Helm of DuSable Museum," *Chicago Sun-Times,* September 28, 1997.

31. Drell, "Group Wants Reform at DuSable Museum."

32. One year after the DuSable's 1993 expansion, many cultural institutions in Chicago suffered financial distress. In 1994, the Chicago Park District Board turned down a one-million-dollar operating budget request from Chicago museums, including the DuSable. See Futterman, "African American Museums Succeed in Other Cities"; Miriam Di Nunzio, "DuSable Museum Adds New Harold Washington Wing," *Chicago Sun-Times,* February 5, 1993.

33. Veronica Anderson, "Museum Exhibits Growing Pains: Management Turmoil Hurts DuSable Fund Drive," *Crains Chicago Business* 17, no. 33 (August 15, 1994).

34. Futterman, "African American Museums Succeed in Other Cities."

35. Eric Gable has analyzed the problems surrounding the "mainstreaming" of black history into formerly "white" public history sites, such as Colonial Williamsburg (CW). Mainstreaming African American life into the interpretative programs at CW meant that the site's guides must discuss, not only the lives of white landowners, but also those of the slaves who worked and lived on these lands. Most of the site's white guides, however, avoided discussing miscegenation, despite the fact that it was a reality for African American slaves and white landowners. In avoiding this issue, white guides thought they were being objective, presenting only the truths of history.

African American guides who spoke about miscegenation, on the other hand, were criticized by white guides for their overly "passionate" and "nonobjective" reactions to this history. See Gable, "Maintaining Boundaries, or 'Mainstreaming' Black History in a White Museum," in *Theorizing Museums: Representing Identity and Diversity in a Changing World*, ed. Sharon Macdonald and Gordon Fyfe (Cambridge: Blackwell Publishers, 1996), 181.

36. Emily Dennis Harvey and Bernard Friedberg, eds., *A Museum for the People: A Report of Proceedings at the Seminar on Neighborhood Museums, held November 20, 21, and 22, 1969, at MUSE, the Bedford Lincoln Neighborhood Museum in Brooklyn, New York* (New York: Arno Press, 1971), 35, 38–39.

37. *Anacostia Neighborhood Museum, Smithsonian Institution, September 15, 1972,* (Washington, D.C.: Smithsonian Institution, 1972), 13–14.

38. Kinard reiterated this point in 1972, when he served as a consultant for the Rochester Museum and Science Center in Rochester, New York. Expressing dismay over the few minorities on the museum's staff, Kinard argued that developing a separate neighborhood museum should not be equated with delaying the Science Center's own responsibility in internally transforming their own institution. If the Science Center could diversify its programs "based on the predetermined needs of the great Rochester community," Kinard suggested that the center might then be able to function as a neighborhood museum in its own right. John Kinard, "Report on the Meeting with the Ad Hoc Committee of the Rochester Museum and Science Center," March 9, 1972, folder: Museum Correspondence, 1972–1974, box 8, Smithsonian Institution Archives, Record Unit 265, Anacostia Neighborhood Museum, Office of the Director, Records.

39. Harvey and Friedberg, *A Museum for the People,* 35.

40. Ibid., 28.

41. Smithsonian Institution Archives, Oral Histories, RU 9538, John R. Kinard Interview, 14. Emphasis in original.

42. Adam Gopnik, "The Mindful Museum," *Museum News* 86, no. 6 (November/December 2007): 37–41.

43. Spencer R. Crew, *Field to Factory: Afro-American Migration 1915–1940* (Washington, D.C.: National Museum of American History, Smithsonian Institution, 1987). Crew became director of the NMAH in 1994 and CEO of the Cincinnati National Underground Railroad Freedom Center in 2001.

44. Smithsonian Institution Archives, Oral Histories, RU 9558, Louise Daniel Hutchinson Interviews, 56–58. Also see Von Hardesty and Dominick Pisano, *Black Wings: The American Black in Aviation* (Washington, D.C.: National Air and Space Museum, Smithsonian Institution), 1983.

45. "A Question of Cultural Apartheid," *Chicago Tribune,* September 26, 1994, 16. See also Thomas J. Jablonsky's review of *Neighborhoods: Keepers of the Culture* in *The Public Historian* 19, no. 4 (Autumn 1997): 94–97.

46. Lewis, *The Changing Face of Public History,* 112.

47. "A Question of Cultural Apartheid," *Chicago Tribune,* September 26, 1994.

48. Ibid.

49. *Museums and Communities: The Politics of Public Culture,* ed. Ivan Karp, Christine Mullen Kreamer, and Steven D. Lavine (Washington, D.C.: Smithsonian Institution Press, 1992), 7.

50. Bill Cunniff, "Douglas/Grand Boulevard Exhibit Opens Sunday," *Chicago Sun-Times,* April 28, 1995.

51. Lewis, *The Changing Face of Public History,* 112.

52. James Oliver Horton, "Slavery in American History: An Uncomfortable National Dialogue," in *Slavery and Public History: The Tough Stuff of American Memory,* ed. James Oliver Horton and Lois E. Horton (New York: New Press, 2006), 49–53. For a bracing analysis of the

meaning and practice of "edutainment" in public history, see Mike Wallace, *Mickey Mouse History and Other Essays on American Memory* (Philadelphia: Temple University Press, 1996).

53. Sandhya Somashekhar, "Black History Becoming A Star Tourist Attraction," *Washington Post*, August 15, 2005.

54. The debates that took place from 2002 to 2004 regarding the National Park Service's plans to house the Liberty Bell in a new visitor's pavilion in Philadelphia also reflect this tension. Community members, the NPS, and the Independence Hall Historical Planners (INHP) debated whether they should interpret the Liberty Bell as the symbol of white colonists fighting against Britain, or whether they should also insert commentary about the ironic juxtaposition of their revolutionary fight with the institution of slavery. Even the physical location of the pavilion planned to house the Liberty Bell contained a heritage shadowed by the disconnect between freedom and enslavement. The pavilion was set to be constructed upon the footprint of a mansion first built in the 1750s by Philadelphia's mayor and largest slaveholder, William Masters; the mansion was later occupied by George and Martha Washington, who owned around thirty indentured servants and slaves along with free employees.

INHP planners believed that expanding the interpretation of the Liberty Bell and the President's House site to include such facts would be disastrous. Instead, they attempted to railroad through a celebratory narrative without consulting historians or Philadelphia's African American community. Public protests from Gary Nash, AAMP advocate Charles Blockson, and like-minded scholars and community activists who opposed the plans to eliminate the Liberty Bell's controversial history ensued. Extensive media coverage, most of it favorable toward the protestors' efforts, finally pressured the NPS to reconsider its "disremembering of history." In September 2003, the Liberty Bell Center opened to the public, featuring exhibits that reminded visitors of the uneasy coexistence of freedom and slavery. Throughout 2003 and 2004, groups such as the Ad Hoc Historians, the Independence Hall Association, and the Avenging the Ancestors Coalition, an African American organization formed specifically to protest the Park Service's plans, continued to pressure for the reinterpretation of the President's House site. Gary B. Nash, "For Whom Will the Liberty Bell Toll? From Controversy to Cooperation," in *Slavery and Public History: The Tough Stuff of American Memory*, ed. James Oliver Horton and Lois E. Horton (New York: New Press, 2006), 77–78, 100–101.

55. Jeffrey Abt, *A Museum on the Verge: A Socioeconomic History of the Detroit Institute of Arts, 1882–2000* (Detroit: Wayne State University Press, 2001); 174, 244–45.

56. Keith Bradsher, "A Rich Museum in Detroit and Its Poor Cousin," *New York Times*, May 28, 1997.

57. Abt, *A Museum on the Verge*, 186–87.

58. Ibid., 244–45.

59. The city allowed the MAAH to hire nonunion security guards and maintenance workers, whereas the DIA was required to employ unionized workers, who typically received higher pay. See Suzette Hackney and Joy Hakanson Colby, "DIA Awaits Cash Lifeline from Archer," *Detroit Free Press*, April 13, 1997.

60. Regina Gersch to Editor, *Detroit Free Press*, April 14, 1997.

61. "Biggest Black History Museum: Thousands Visit New Detroit Institution," *Ebony* 53, no. 4 (February 1998): 58–62; David Lyman, "Glittering Debut," *Detroit News and Free Press*, April 12, 1997.

62. Hackney and Hakanson Colby, "DIA Awaits Cash Lifeline from Archer."

63. Bradsher, "A Rich Museum and Its Poor Cousin."

64. On February 1, 1998, the DIA Founder's Society took control of the DIA under an

agreement between the City of Detroit and the Founder's City. See Irvin Corley, Jr., Fiscal Analyst, to Graham Beal, Director DIA Arts Department, April 30, 2003, www.ci.detroit .mi.us/legislative/CouncilDivisions/FiscalAnalysis/doc/AGDailies/Arts03-04.doc (no longer available). Even after this transfer, however, the financial discrepancy between the DIA and the MAAH persisted. For example, in 2004, reports indicated that the MAAH received $1.5 million annually from the city of Detroit, whereas the DIA received just $400,000 annually. The DIA's operating budget was approximately $30 million, compared to the MAAH's $6.8 million. See Frank Provenzano, "Fighting for Survival: The Charles H. Wright Museum Faces Declining Attendance and Revenue," *Detroit Free Press,* February 8, 2004.

65. Karen Miller, "Whose History, Whose Culture? The Museum of African American History, The Detroit Institute of Arts, and Urban Politics at the End of the Twentieth Century," *Michigan Quarterly Review* 41, no. 1 (Winter 2002): 4.

66. Abt, *A Museum on the Verge,* 245.

67. By contrast, the Detroit Institute of Arts, with its European-oriented collections and seemingly outdated architectural classicism, represented the "metaphorical embodiment of white, suburban, middle-class culture and (supposed) white political powerlessness in the city." Miller, "Whose History, Whose Culture?" 5.

68. Bradsher, "A Rich Museum and Its Poor Cousin."

69. Christopher Clarke-Hazlett, "Exhibition Review: Of the People," *American Quarterly* 51, no. 2 (1999): 426–28. See also Charles Pete Banner-Haley, "The Necessity of Remembrance: A Review of the Museum of African American History," *American Quarterly* 51, no. 2 (1999): 423.

70. Alison Landsberg, *Prosthetic Memory: The Transformation of American Remembrance in the Age of Mass Culture* (New York: Columbia University Press, 2004), 2.

71. Ibid., 82.

72. Provenzano, "Fighting for Survival."

73. Ibid.

74. "Museum Needs Our Support," *Michigan Chronicle,* April 13, 2004. Also see David Josar, "African American Museum Spends More on Administration than Exhibits," *Detroit News,* May 18, 1998.

75. "Charting a New Course; Museum CEO Reflects on Some of the Mistakes and Looks Ahead to Brighter Days," *Michigan Chronicle,* April 20, 2004.

76. Provenzano, "Fighting for Survival." Provenzano pointed out that recent statistics showed that despite their poverty Detroit residents ranked high on charitable giving. They donated most of their money, however, to religious organizations.

77. Coleman became CEO when Kimberly Camp resigned in 1999. "Charting a New Course," *Michigan Chronicle.*

78. Minutes of Project "I AM" Meeting, March 10, 1965, folder IAM Founding, 1965, box 3, CHWMAAH Historical Records, MAAH, 4.

79. Frank Provenzano, "Charles H. Wright: Hero of History," *Detroit Free Press,* February 12, 2002.

80. Memo, Dr. Charles Wright to Dr. Marian Moore, October 22, 1989, folder Dr. Wright, box 2, Dr. Marian Moore collection, MAAH. Moore, on the other hand, felt that Wright often overstepped his duties as chairperson of the board of directors, which threatened Moore's own position and authority. In one case, Moore reprimanded both Wright and his daughter, Stephanie Wright Griggs (who became the MAAH's development officer in 1986), for their role in developing museum programs without Moore's approval. Dr. Marian Moore to Dr. Charles Wright, April 25, 1989, folder Dr. Wright, box 2, Dr. Marian Moore collection, MAAH.

81. Joy Hakanson Colby, "Wright Museum Celebrates 40 Years," *Detroit News*, April 21, 2005.

82. Dr. Charles Wright, Daily Log, December 2, 1990, folder 1990, box 1, Charles Wright Papers, MSS121, MAAH. Wright eventually publicly supported the third version of the MAAH; in 1998, the museum changed its name to the Charles H. Wright Museum of African American History.

83. "Charting a New Course," *Michigan Chronicle.*

84. Ibid.

85. Young's distinction between having the "best" black museum versus making do with a "ghetto on the block" institution paralleled the conflict that took place at New York's El Museo del Barrio in 2002, as community activists clashed over El Museo's exclusion of Puerto Rican art and heritage in favor of a broader focus on Latino identity. As Arlene Davila comments, "the local press was quick to frame the issue in terms of facile dichotomies of 'Puerto Ricans versus Latinos,' or purported divisions between those who wanted to keep El Museo as a 'ghetto or barrio museum' and those who sought its development into a 'world-class museum.' " See Davila, "El Barrio's 'We Are Watching You' Campaign," 158.

86. "Saving Our History; CEO Discusses Status and Efforts to Sustain Museum," *Michigan Chronicle*, April 13, 2004.

87. Institute of Museum and Library Services, "African American History and Culture in Museums: Strategic Crossroads and New Opportunities," July 16, 2004 (Washington, D.C.: IMLS, April 2005), 10. Emphasis added.

88. Rose, "Difficulties African American Museums are Facing."

89. Ibid.

90. Jackson, "DuSable Plans Expansion as Others Falter."

91. The National Underground Railroad Freedom Center, which is formally affiliated with the Smithsonian Institution, officially opened in 2004, though the organization held traveling exhibits as early as 1997. See Lecker, "Hard Times Hit Black-History Museums." Rita Organ noted that, while most African American museums were located in areas populated by blacks, in the 1980s "there was a growing realization that it was as important 'to educate non-African-Americans about us' as it was to educate African-Americans about themselves." See Kee, "Plan to Build Black History Museum Here Will Take Lots of Cash, Patience."

92. Rose, "Difficulties African American Museums Are Facing."

93. Ibid. Pijeaux's statistics mesh with the results of the survey of African American museums conducted by the National Museum of African American History and Culture Plan for Action Presidential Commission in 2003. At 30 percent of the museums surveyed, non-African American audiences comprised between 26 to 50 percent of the museum's total audience—the range that Pijeaux mentioned in the interview. At 18.2 percent of the African American museums surveyed, non-African American visitors comprised an even higher range—between 51 and 75 percent of the total visitors. Finally, just over 13 percent of the surveyed museums reported that their audience was over 75 percent non-African American. Still, most (38 percent) of the museums in the survey reported that non-African American visitors comprised just 25 percent or less of total visitors. For statistics, see Joy Ford Austin, *National Survey of African American Museums: Prepared for the National Museum of African American History and Culture Plan for Action Presidential Commission* (Washington, D.C.: National Museum of African American History and Culture Plan for Action Presidential Commission, 2003).

94. Rick Moss, interview by author, May 20, 2011, African American Museum and Library at Oakland, California.

6. A Museum for the Future: The National Museum of
African and American History and Culture

1. James Tyner, *The Geography of Malcolm X: Black Radicalism and the Remaking of American Space* (New York: Routledge, 2006), 39.

2. Keith Mayes, e-mail message to author, January 29, 2008.

3. Peniel Joseph, *Waiting 'til the Midnight Hour: A Narrative History of Black Power in America* (New York: Henry Holt, 2006), 297.

4. Funded in part by the Department of Housing and Urban Development, The American Association of Museums (AAM) created a committee on urban museums and social responsibility in the early 1970s. James Oliver Horton and Spencer R. Crew, "Afro-Americans and Museums: Towards a Policy of Inclusion," in *History Museums in the United States: A Critical Assessment,* ed. Warren Leon and Roy Rosenzweig (Chicago: Board of Trustees of the University of Illinois, 1989), 221.

5. Carter G. Woodson recognized the intangible quality of securing a "national" identity when he relocated the Association for the Study of Negro Life and History (ASNLH) from Chicago to Washington, D.C. The ASNLH benefited not only from Washington's status but also the city's regional placement. Essentially located halfway between the North and the South, the city bridged the customs of both. Local black leaders became, in effect, national leaders by virtue of their very presence in Washington. Pero Gaglo Dagbovie, "'Most Honorable Mention . . . Belongs to Washington, DC': The Carter G. Woodson Home and the Early Black History Movement in the Nation's Capital," *Journal of African American History* 96, no. 3 (Summer 2011): 299.

6. In 2012, the National Underground Railroad Freedom Center merged with the Cincinnati Museum Center in an effort to stabilize its finances and open up audience access. Sharon Coolidge and Mark Curnutte, "Money Woes Lead to Underground Railroad Museum Merge," *USA Today,* February 14, 2012. The fate of the United States National Slavery Museum in Fredericksburg, Virginia, offers a different perspective on what it means to declare an institution to be "national." L. Douglas Wilder, the first African American governor of Virginia, proposed the museum in 2001. The museum was intended to be 300,000 square feet, located on 38 acres; Bill Cosby donated a significant amount to the fundraising campaign. Yet since the proposal, nothing has been done: the land set aside for the museum is now up for auction by the city; the museum owes $215,000 in property taxes; and anger on the part of donors regarding the unknown whereabouts of their artifacts has cast profound doubts on the future of this museum. See Kate Taylor, "Tax Bills Imperil Slavery Museum," *New York Times,* July 20, 2011.

7. Alison Landsberg, *Prosthetic Memory: The Transformation of American Remembrance in the Age of Mass Culture* (New York: Columbia University Press, 2004), 109.

8. Kate Taylor, "The Thorny Path to a National Black Museum," *New York Times,* January 22, 2011.

9. Smithsonian National Museum of African American History and Culture, "Overview History of Museum," nmaahc.si.edu/section/about_us.

10. Minutes of the International Afro-American Museum Committee, September 29, 1965, 2.

11. Minutes of Project "I AM" Meeting, March 10, 1965, folder IAM Founding, 1965, box 3, CHWMAAH Historical Reocrds, MAAH, 2. Also see Minutes of the International Afro-American Museum Committee, September 29, 1965, folder IAM Founding 1965, box 1, Joan Hallier Series 1, MAAH, 2.

12. Minutes of Project "I AM" Meeting, 4.

13. Charles Wright to Carl Rowan, March 7, 1966, folder Charles H. Wright—correspondence, 1965, box CHWMAAH Historical Records, 1965–87, MAAH.

14. James Scheuer to Colleague, February 5, 1968, folder Conference 1968, box Miscellaneous Correspondence and Publications, 1965–69, MAAH. Around the same time that Scheuer introduced this legislation into the House of Representatives, Senator Hugh Scott (R-PA) also introduced into the Senate a proposal to create a Commission on Negro History and Culture, which he stated would "conduct a study of proposals to research, document, compile, preserve and disseminate data on the role of the Negro in history." See Advance Press Release, February 16, 1968, folder 1968, box Miscellaneous Correspondence and Publications, 1965–69, MAAH.

15. James Scheuer to Colleague, February 5, 1968. The conference program was included in Scheuer's letter to his congressional colleagues, February 5, 1968. Numerous African American leaders, as well as some noted white scholars, attended the conference, including Sterling Tucker, executive director of the Washington Urban League; author Ralph Ellison; and Yale historian C. Vann Woodward, author of *The Strange Career of Jim Crow*. Dr. Charles H. Wesley, executive director of the ASNLH, chaired the panel.

16. Oretta M. Todd to Editor, *Christian Science Monitor*, June 7, 1968.

17. Charles Wright to Select Sub-Committee on Education, March 12, 1968, folder MS/MAAH-Congressional—Scheuer Bill—1968–69, box 3, CHWMAAH Historical Records, 1–2. Also see "Time Is Running Out," n.d., folder Study of Urban Blacks, box 8, Joan Hallier Series IV, MAAH.

18. Charles Wright to Select Sub-Committee on Education, March 12, 1968, 2.

19. Ibid., 3. Here Wright refers to the DuSable and the Museum of African American History in Boston, founded in 1963. In addition to Wright, other witnesses at the hearing in New York City included writer James Baldwin; Roy Innis, associate national director of CORE; Jackie Robinson (acting as "special assistant to Governor Rockefeller"); and Charles Wesley, executive director for the ASNLH.

20. Ibid., 2.

21. Charles Wright to Bill Hall (SNCC, D.C.), June 24, 1968, folder Congressional Scheuer Bill, 1968–69, box 3, CHWMAAH Historical Records, MAAH. Also see Newsletter, "The Gallery," *American Association of Museums* 13, no. 1 (September 1979), folder 1979, box MAAH Publications, 1969–90, MAAH.

22. Charles Wright to Bill Hall (SNCC, D.C.), 3.

23. Charles Wright to Whitney Young, Kenneth Clark, and Roy Wilkins, June 17, 1968, folder MS/MAAH-Congressional—Scheuer Bill—1968–69, box 3, CHWMAAH Historical Records, MAAH.

24. Charles Wright to Henry Lee Moon, March 28, 1969, folder MS/MAAH-Congressional—Scheuer Bill—1968–69, box 3, CHWMAAH Historical Records, MAAH.

25. Clarence J. Brown, Jr., Seventh Ohio District, to Colleague, April 4, 1968, folder Congressional Scheuer Bill, 1968–69, box 3, CHWMAAH Historical Records, MAAH. According to Brown's bill, the Secretary of Interior would establish the museum, acquire the land, and cooperate with universities and historical societies in the development of the museum. See News Release, Office of Congressman Clarence J. Brown, Jr., Seventh Ohio District, April 8, 1968, folder Congressional Scheuer Bill, 1968–69, box 3, CHWMAAH Historical Records, MAAH.

26. Clarence J. Brown, Jr., Seventh Ohio District, to Colleague, April 4, 1968.

27. John Conyers, Jr., to Charles Wright, September 17, 1968, folder Congressional Scheuer Bill, 1968–69, box 3, CHWMAAH Historical Records, MAAH. See also *Commission on Negro History and Culture: Hearings before the United States Senate Committee on Labor and Public Welfare*, Special Subcommittee on Arts and Humanities, 90th Cong., 2nd sess., July 23, 1968 (Washington, D.C.: U.S. Government Printing Office, 1968).

28. Ohio Historical Society, "OHS Places–National Afro-American Museum and Cultural Center," ohsweb.ohiohistory.org/places/sw13.

29. Kinard's objections to the museum marked a shift in attitude, because he had previously allied himself with Tom Mack, African American president of Tourmobile, Inc., an organization that transports tourists along the National Mall. Mack proposed the federal museum idea in 1984 and collaborated with Congressman Mickey Leland (D-TX) to author a nonbinding House resolution that "affirmed in principle the idea of an African American museum on the mall." The resolution passed in 1986. Mack, however, opposed Smithsonian Institution control over an African American museum, arguing that the museum must be privately financed and directed. Fath Davis Ruffins, "Culture Wars Won and Lost, Part II: The National African-American Museum Project," *Radical History Review* 70 (Winter 1998): 81–82, 89.

30. Ibid., 91.

31. Pat Press, "The Changing Face of Washington 4: 'East of the River,'" *Washington Post*, June 27, 1984.

32. Portia James, "Building a Community-Based Identity at Anacostia Museum," in *Heritage, Museums, and Galleries: An Introductory Reader*, ed. Gerard Corsane (London: Routledge, 2005), 349.

33. Michele Gates Moresi, "Exhibiting Race, Creating Nation: Representations of Black History and Culture at the Smithsonian Institution, 1895–1976" (PhD diss., George Washington University, 2003), 115, 93.

34. Ruffins, "Culture Wars Won and Lost, Part II," 88.

35. Response of the African American Museums Association to the Report of the African American Institutional Study, 113, in "Recommendations of the African American Institutional Study Advisory Committee," April 3, 1991, Smithsonian Institution Archives, Accession 07-172, National Museum of African American History and Culture, Planning Records.

36. Ruffins, "Culture Wars Won and Lost, Part II," 96.

37. Taylor, "The Thorny Path to a National Black Museum."

38. Some proposals, such as Congressman John Lewis's introduction of H.R. 1570, presented a combination of both ideas. See Brad Mims, "History of the Project and the Committee Process," in "Recommendations of the African American Institutional Study Advisory Committee," 3; and Ruffins, "Culture Wars Won and Lost, Part II," 95.

39. Final Report of the National Museum of African American History and Culture Plan for Action Presidential Commission, 2003, Smithsonian Institution Archives, Accession 07-172, National Museum of African American History and Culture, Planning Records.

40. Ilan Kayatsky, "Smithsonian Chooses Site for African American Museum," *Architectural Record* 194, no. 3 (March 1, 2006): 49. See also Jacqueline Trescott, "Smithsonian Shares Its Treasures and Tackles the Questions of a Latino Museum," *Washington Post*, May 12, 2011.

41. Bree Hocking, "An African American Museum Will Rise. But Where?" *Roll Call*, March 15, 2005, www.rollcall.com/issues/50_87/-8511-1.html.

42. Ibid.

43. Edward Gunts, "Rich Culture, Site's Symbolism Should Suit Each Other: African American Museum Gains Prominence on Mall," *Baltimore Sun*, February 5, 2006.

44. National Museum of African American History and Culture, "Exhibitions and Programs," nmaahc.si.edu/section/programs/view/47.

45. National Museum of African American History and Culture, "Programs: Memory Book," nmaahc.si.edu/Programs/Memorybook.

46. For discussion on how museums may further encourage interactivity between and

among audiences and the museum, see Nina Simon, *The Participatory Museum* (Santa Cruz, Calif.: Museum, 2010). The Library of Congress's practice of having virtual audiences "tag" Library of Congress photographs and other archival items on Flickr also presents an excellent model for the NMAAHC. See Flickr, "The Library of Congress's Photostream," www.flickr.com/photos/library_of_congress/.

47. *Letting Go? Sharing Historical Authority in a User-Generated World,* ed. Bill Adair, Benjamin Filene, and Laura Koloski (Philadelphia: The Pew Center for Arts and Heritage, 2011).

48. Alex Pappas, "Smithsonian Revises Design for Black History Museum," *Washington Examiner,* April 7, 2011.

49. Taylor, "The Thorny Path to a National Black Museum."

50. Jacqueline Trescott, "African American Museum's Revised Design Gets Favorable Reviews by NCPC," *Washington Post,* September 3, 2010.

51. Taylor, "The Thorny Path to a National Black Museum."

52. Tiffany Jenkins, "Turning Museums into Cultural Ghettos," June 22, 2011, www.spiked-online.com/index.php/site/article/10621/.

53. Amanda Cobb, "The National Museum of the American Indian as Cultural Sovereignty," *American Quarterly* 57, no. 2 (June 2005): 485–506. See also Jim Adams, "National Museum of the American Indian Reviews: Ceremonies Were Nice but Critics Pan Content," *Indian Country Today,* October 8, 2004, indiancountrytodaymedianetwork.com/ictarchives/2004/10/13/ceremonies-were-nice-but-critics-pan-content-94073.

54. Taylor, "The Thorny Path to a National Black Museum."

55. Ibid.

56. Jacqueline Trescott, "Personal History: The African American Museum's Lonnie Bunch Looks Forward by Looking Back," *Washington Post,* October 17, 2005. Bunch expressed his frustration over the lack of minority leaders in the museum profession. Bunch, "Flies in the Buttermilk: Museums, Diversity, and the Will to Change," *Museum News* 79 (July/August 2000): 32–35; see also his article "In Black and White: Interpreting African American Culture in Contemporary Museums," *History News* 50 (Autumn 1995): 5–9. Also see Gunts, "Rich Culture, Site's Symbolism Should Suit Each Other."

57. Joy Ford Austin, National Survey of African American Museums: Prepared for the National Museum of African American History and Culture Plan for Action Presidential Commission (Washington, D.C.: National Museum of African American History and Culture Plan for Action Presidential Commission, 2003), xiv, 35–37.

58. Corey Dade, "Civil-Rights Gains Test New Memorials' Relevance," *Wall Street Journal,* May 7, 2009.

59. Rick Moss, interview by author, May 20, 2011, African American Museum and Library at Oakland, CA.

60. Ibid.

61. Taylor, "The Thorny Path to a National Black Museum."

62. Ibid. Artist Fred Wilson's Mining the Museum exhibit at the Maryland Historical Society provided a model for how curators could reinterpret a museum's existing artifacts to tell a fuller story of African American history. See Fred Wilson, *Mining the Museum: An Installation,* ed. Lisa G. Corrin (Baltimore: Contemporary; New York: New Press, 1994.)

63. Committee on House Administration, *To Establish the National Museum of the American Latino: Hearings on H.R. 4863,* 108th Cong., 2nd sess., July 22, 2004, purl.access.gpo.gov/GPO/LPS62576. Also see National Museum of the American Latino, "News," americanlatinomuseum.org/news/news.html.

64. Tey Marianna Nunn, "¿Un Museo Nacional?" American Association of Museums, 2007, www.aam-us.org/pubs/mn/museo.cfm.

65. Trescott, "Smithsonian Shares Its Treasures and Tackles the Questions of a Latino Museum."

66. Paul Bedard, "Dem Congressman: Ethnic Museums on Mall are Un-American," May 12, 2011, www.usnews.com/news/blogs/washington-whispers/2011/05/12/dem congressman ethnic -museums-on-national-mall-are-un-american. Natalie Hopkinson, "The Root: Segregated Museums Mirror History," National Public Radio, May 24, 2011, www.npr.org/2011/05/24/136605926 /the-root-segregated-museums-mirror-history.

67. Jenkins, "Turning Museums into Cultural Ghettos."

Conclusion

1. John Kinard, "To Meet the Needs of Today's Audience," *Museum News* 50, no. 9 (May 1972): 15–16.

2. Frank Provenzano, "Fighting for Survival: The Charles H. Wright Museum Faces Declining Attendance and Revenue," *Detroit Free Press,* February 8, 2004.

3. Lisa Ann Meyerowitz, "Exhibiting Equality: Black-Run Museums and Galleries in 1970s New York" (PhD diss., University of Chicago, June 2001), 182.

4. El Museo del Barrio moved multiple times—from public schools to storefronts— before settling in its current location in Spanish Harlem. David Deitcher, "Alternate Realities," *ARTFORUM,* June 7, 2010, artforum.com/inprint/id=25762.

5. "El Museo del Barrio, "El Museo's Transformation," www.elmuseo.org/en/explore-online /timeline/1990s#1996.

6. Arlene Davila, "El Barrio's 'We Are Watching You' Campaign: On the Politics of Inclusion in a Latinized Museum," *Aztlan* 30, no. 1 (Spring 2005): 153–78.

7. Ibid., 168.

8. As of 2012, this mission statement still stood. Also see Yasmin Ramirez, "Passing on Latinidad: An Analysis of Critical Responses to El Museo del Barrio's Pan-Latino Mission Statements," latino.si.edu/researchandmuseums/presentations/ramirez_papers.html.

9. Davila, "El Barrio's 'We Are Watching You' Campaign," 154.

10. Ibid., 160. According to Davila, We Are Watching You's definition of "community" was "usually used as a synonym for all that is Puerto Rican, diasporic, or working-class. In other words, the 'community' was never simply tantamount to the geographically bounded space of El Barrio/East Harlem."

11. Kevin Moore, *Museums and Popular Culture* (London: Leicester University Press, 1997), 18.

12. Davila, "El Barrio's 'We Are Watching You' Campaign," 156.

13. Gaynor Kavanagh, *Dream Spaces: Memory and the Museum* (London: Leicester University Press, 2000), 5–6.

14. Richard Sandell, *Museums, Society, Inequality* (New York: Routledge, 2002), 8.

15. Ibid., 4; emphasis in original.

16. Dolores Hayden suggests that scholars often neglect the social and political importance of the urban "vernacular landscape," which may include buildings such as saloons, apartments, and union halls. In the case of the black museum movement, the vernacular landscape also encompasses the original sites of black neighborhood museums. Dolores Hayden, *The Power of Place: Urban Landscapes as Public History* (Cambridge, Mass.: MIT Press, 1995), 41, citing from Henri Lefebvre, *The Production of Space* (Oxford: Blackwell, 1991), 11.

17. Sandhya Somashekhar, "Black History Becoming a Star Tourist Attraction," *Washington Post,* August 15, 2005. Gary Haber, "Blacks in Wax Museum Plans a $75M Expansion in East

Baltimore," *Baltimore Business Journal,* March 10, 2011. See also National Great Blacks in Wax Museum, "Expansion Plans," www.greatblacksinwax.org/expansion_plans3.htm.

18. The original mobile van burned down in 1987, and museum staff subsequently dismantled it. Chairman's Statement, August 6, 1987, folder Board of Directors, box 9, Dr. Marian Moore collection, MAAH.

19. The exhibit, which features artifacts spanning subjects from slavery to hip-hop, travels not only through Detroit but throughout the country; it has attracted donations from prominent black musicians and activists. David Sands, "Black History 101 Mobile Museum Takes History out into the World," February 1, 2012, www.huffingtonpost.com/2012/02/01/black-history-101-mobile-museum_n_1243956.html. Also see Black History 101 Mobile Museum, www.blackhistory101mobilemuseum.com.

20. The DuSable Museum of African American History, "Taking It to the Streets! The DuSable Mobile Museum," www.dusablemuseum.org/news/taking-it-to-the-streets-the-dusable-mobile-museum.

21. The IMLS report further stated that the collections of African American museums "are often composed of artifacts donated by ordinary individuals rather than private collectors or curators. Many collections are incomplete, and additional works must be acquired to tell the story adequately. Few museums, however, have sufficient funds to identify and purchase or borrow the requisite works." Institute of Museum and Library Services, "African American History and Culture in Museums: Strategic Crossroads and New Opportunities," July 16, 2004 (Washington, D.C.: IMLS, April 2005), 8.

22. "The Spirit, Fortitude and History of African Americans is the Foundation of New Exhibition 'And Still We Rise,' Opening at the Charles H. Wright Museum of African American History," *PR Newswire US,* November 23, 2004, www.lexisnexis.com/hottopics/lnacademic. For Kresge grant information, see Norman Sinclair, "Museum Gets $2.5 Million Payday: Charles H. Wright Museum Earns Grant for Boosting Its Attendance and Membership," *Detroit News,* September 15, 2006.

23. "Crisis at Charles H. Wright Museum of African American History; Black Business Leaders to Donate $1 Million to Save Museum," *Michigan Chronicle,* April 6, 2004.

24. Michelle Boorstein, "Museum Builds on Original Foundation; Anacostia Center Returns to Its Focus on Local Community," *Washington Post,* September 17, 2006.

25. For information on current and past exhibitions at the ACM, see Anacostia Community Museum, "Exhibitions," anacostia.si.edu/exhibits/current_exhibitions.htm.

26. Congress established this historic highway, site of the 1965 Voting Rights March, as a National Historic Trail in 1996. See National Park Service, "Selma to Montgomery," www.nps.gov/semo/index.htm.

27. Mike Wallace, *Mickey Mouse History and Other Essays on American Memory* (Philadelphia: Temple University Press, 1996).

28. Bernard John Armada, "'The Fierce Urgency of Now': Public Memory and Civic Transformation at the National Civil Rights Museum" (PhD diss., Pennsylvania State University, 1999), 197–98. Interestingly, Mahatma Gandhi's grandson bluntly objected to the conversion of the Lorraine Motel: "I think my grandfather and Martin Luther King had the same dream. And they don't want people to erect statues and museums in their memory. It's a waste of money." See Michael Eric Dyson, *I May Not Get There with You: The True Martin Luther King, Jr.* (New York: The Free Press, 2000), ix–x, 249–50.

29. Lonnie Bunch, "Embracing Controversy: Museum Exhibitions and the Politics of Change," *Public Historian* 14, no. 3 (Summer 1992): 63–65.

INDEX

African American Heritage Association (AAHA), 17. *See also* National Negro Museum and Historical Foundation

African American Museum and Library at Oakland (AAMLO), 154–55, 174. *See also* Moss, Rick

African American Museum of Art and History (Minneapolis), 131–32

African American Museum of Philadelphia (AAMP), 12, 15–16, 41–71, 106–29, 129–30; archival facilities, 121–23; and the Afro-American Historical '76 Bicentennial Corporation of Philadelphia, 55, 205n37; autonomy of, 125, 127; and the Bicentennial, 43, 47–57, 59, 124 25; criticism of, 119–20; educational programming, 118; exhibits, 117–21; internal conflicts, 120, 123, 126–28 (*see also* Farmer, Clarence); layout of, 123–24; leadership of, 125–28, 152; location of, 41, 57–71, 123; negative image of, 119–25, 128; as a neighborhood museum, 71, 123–24; opposition to (*see* NOT-HERE; Society Hill Civic Association; Washington Square East Project). *See also* Bicentennial, American; Forman, Nessa; Heritage House (Philadelphia); Independence National Historic Park (Philadelphia); Philadelphia 1976 Bicentennial Corporation; Rizzo, Frank; *and specific exhibits*

African American Museums Association (Association of African American Museums), 9, 27, 129, 130, 133, 222n2; and the national African American museum debate, 166, 168

African diaspora, 5, 10, 74, 92, 178, 193n36

Afro-American Historical and Cultural Museum in Philadelphia, 117

Afro-American Historical '76 Bicentennial Corporation of Philadelphia (AHCC), 51, 53, 55–57, 59, 68, 218n8

Akeju, Camille Giraud, 185

All about Africa (exhibit), 74. *See also* DuSable Museum of African American History

American Art from the Collection of Mr. and Mrs. John D. Rockefeller. *See* 1930s, The: Painting and Sculpture in America (exhibit)

American Association of Museums, 97, 101, 136

American Negro Historical Society, 8

237